REBIRTH

BOOK *TWO* OF

NO PLACE LEFT

A SAGA OF DESTINY FULFILLED

Steve Smith

VENTURES

Kingwood TX

2414 Ventures
3506 Riverwood Park Dr.
Kingwood TX 77345
2414Ventures.com

Publisher's Note: This is a work of fiction. Names, characters, places, and incidents are a product of the author's imagination. Locales and public names are sometimes used for atmospheric purposes. Any resemblance to actual people, living or dead, or to businesses, companies, events, institutions, or locales is completely coincidental.

Most Scripture quotations are taken from The Holy Bible, New International Version®, NIV® Copyright © 1973, 1978, 1984, 2011 by Biblica, Inc.® Used by permission. All rights reserved worldwide.

Book Layout © 2016 BookDesignTemplates.com

Cover Design: Jason Subers — RainShineGraphics.com

Rebirth/Steve Smith — 1st ed.
ISBN: 978-0-9969652-1-7

First printing: October, 2016

Dedicated to

the alumni of North University Park Church,
who began walking this journey with us
as deeply as those in this saga...
for the sake of His glory among the nations.

They have served as the inspiration for this series.

ACKNOWLEDGMENTS

This book has been in process for over twenty years. Many have believed in the mission of this book and its prequel, *Hastening*. My wife Laura has spurred me on at each stage. The amazing members of our church plant in Los Angeles inspired me to set this book in a church similar to ours. They have had the nations in their hearts and now live among the nations.

Many have helped with the editing process. A community of missional readers plowed through the first version of this book: Jean Smith (my mother), Laurie Ann Powell, Nancy Hoke, Elaine Colvin, Fred Campbell, Brian Rodriguez, Don Visser, and Lorena Wood. Julie Gwinn lent her expertise for a final fiction edit and added confirmation to all of our prior edits. Valery Gresham did the final copy editing, and Jason Subers designed our covers.

Thank you, everyone!

The *mission* of this saga is to stir this generation to fulfill the vision of Mt. 24:14.

We value your help and collaboration in seeking God's guidance to turn this series into something He will use widely beyond the mission community!

What could be done to enable this series to have greater impact in *YOUR* sphere of influence?

If you spot a typo, have a thought about improving *Hastening* or *Rebirth*, or would like to collaborate in some way, email us at NoPlaceLeft@mailzone.com

Thanks!

PROLOGUE...what went before

In Book One of the *No Place Left* saga, pastor Christopher Owen rallies his two best friends, businessman Nic Fernandez and university professor John Steward, to join him on a quest that changes the course of their lives and world history. Together with their wives—Chara, Stacy, and Renee—they mobilize their own church and believers around the globe to the greatest task given the global Church—taking the gospel of Christ's Kingdom to every remaining unreached people group in the world.

The group aspires to be in the generation that welcomes the return of Christ (Mt 24:14) and to hasten that day (2 Pe 3:12). They know they will not be done until there is *no place left* where Christ is not proclaimed (Rom 15:23). They realize this may mean living through the tumult of Revelation.

To force themselves in faith to attempt things they never would otherwise, the group sets a 2025 date to complete their quest. This prompts them to embrace and call other believers to a spiritual wartime mentality in place of peacetime complacency.

Colonel Win Dunbar (a retired and esteemed special forces commander) joins and aids them in their mission, along with his wife, Jeanie. Win helps Christopher and his team launch the Kingdom Preparation Force (KPF). The KPF's mobile, highly committed teams enter unengaged unreached people groups and start the first multiplying churches among them, much like the Apostle Paul and his teams did. Once these teams establish a movement with new believers living out the Great Commission, these teams then move on to other unengaged groups.

Meanwhile, U.S. Senator Michael Wroth and his assistant Marlene Hayes pursue an an agenda to usher in a new age of peace and prosperity through political mechanisms. Wroth uncovers a conspiratorial group—The Ten—that has been quietly manipulating world events for centuries toward a golden age of peace—the

Rebirth. Seeing in Wroth someone who fits their agenda, The Ten recruit him to their cause while Wroth sees The Ten as a vehicle to "influence the world without being known to influence." While being mentored secretly by The Ten, Wroth seeks to gain control over them. He is aided by long-time family friend Dr. Larson Sayers, who possesses an uncanny ability to negotiate peace between opposing parties. Amidst increasing worldwide unrest and terrorist attacks on the political center of America, Wroth is catapulted into the powerful role of Director of the new International Coalition for the Preservation of World Peace (IC). Assisted by former CIA operative Jake Simmons, Wroth receives global acclaim as he leverages his secret connection with The Ten to shut down terrorist cells around the world.

All the while, he must balance using The Ten without them knowing he is doing so. Wroth's aggressive pursuit of the Rebirth puts him at odds with Number One—leader of The Ten. Others in The Ten side with Wroth, particularly Number Three, Ethan Farnsworth.

Christopher Owen leads one of the KPF's first long-term teams overseas to China, and a Kingdom movement explodes as disciples and churches begin multiplying throughout the remote mountain regions of the Tuxiang people. However, such activity is perceived by The Ten, particularly Wroth, as a direct threat to their plans for the Rebirth, and the KPF team experiences severe opposition and persecution.

Ruth Grant becomes the KPF's first martyr, and her two companions (Lance Chu and George Yang) are imprisoned and beaten along with Christopher in a remote Chinese prison. A miraculous escape enables the three to return to the U.S. There they are both received as heroes and denounced as villains. Heroes to believers around the globe inspired to imitate their faith and devotion. Villains to those who feel they are manipulating young people into folly.

Ruth's story inspires many to join the cause, and applications to the KPF and many other sending organizations skyrocket. Yet even as the NoPlaceLeft 2025 vision is galvanizing the global Church, Ruth's parents are pursuing a lawsuit against the KPF that could obliterate it entirely.

ONE

The LED monitor on the wall glowed **3,131**. Christopher Owen glanced at it again. "Not fast enough!" he muttered as he paced. "Not fast enough!" He ran his fingers through his hair for the hundredth time. *So far to go to complete the mission!*

Christopher and his Kingdom Preparation Force teams had committed to all-out mobilization, risking their health, wealth and in some cases their lives, in their pursuit of no place left where people have not heard about Jesus.

Over three thousand people groups still to reach. All in tough places—no, the toughest. And our teams bear the brunt of the harsh conditions in the remotest corners of antagonistic realms.

Christopher turned to the tracking monitor in the basement of the KPF's Los Angeles headquarters. He reached out and gently touched the green dots on the map representing each team. "Not fast enough! Not fast enough!"

"Commander? Did you hear me, sir?" Colonel Win Dunbar sat at the planning table, his legs thrust out the other side.

"I'm sorry, Win." Christopher shook his head and focused his gaze on the field leader of the KPF's spiritual troops. "Can you repeat that?"

The others exchanged concerned glances.

"Um, Christopher," Professor John Steward said, hesitating, "this fading out on us amidst strategy sessions is happening too often. And Win's come all the way back from Southeast Asia just for this pow-wow."

Christopher nodded slowly and returned to the table.

"Hey, buddy, you feeling okay?" Nic Fernandez asked. "That head wound still bothering you?"

The KPF leader touched the scar above his eyebrow. The throbbing from the wound never disappeared. Subsided at times, but never completely disappeared—especially at times like these.

Christopher's wife Chara tiptoed down the rickety staircase and set a cup of French roast coffee in front of him.

"This ought to help, baby," she whispered as she slipped him a couple of Tylenol.

John straightened in his chair.

"Sister, more than one of us in this subterranean nerve center could benefit from the invigorating effects of java."

"Ooh! John, I'm so sorry." Chara pursed her lips as she turned toward the stairs.

"Don't pay him any mind, Chara," Renee said as she jabbed her husband's ribs. "John can brew his own. We need you here."

Christopher took a deep whiff, then sipped. *That's the ticket. Gotta get my wits together. Pay attention, Christopher!* "Win, you were saying?"

The Marine straightened and placed both palms on the table. "I was asking if you want to keep expanding the number of advance teams. Pressure from local authorities continues rising, and the frequency of incidents appears to be more than coincidence; there's a pattern. My sources tell me we are in the crosshairs of someone powerful. I just don't know who."

"I hate to add to the gloom," said Nic, the entrepreneurial prodigy, "but I'm not sure our organizational structure is scalable to the acceleration of our expansion."

"In English, Nic?" Renee interjected.

"Uh, yeah. What I mean is that the number of our two-year teams is growing rapidly, but we don't have enough experienced field leaders to handle the increase. We need more leaders to maintain our capacity and long-term hubs to cultivate longevity in the regions. We may need to slow down our expansion."

Everyone nodded, except Christopher. They were all wearing more than one hat, and it didn't help that most had full-time jobs outside of their KPF role. Their margin was non-existent.

"Makes sense." Renee agreed. She consulted her phone app that tracked the countdown of bringing the good news to each remaining Unreached People Group. "We've made good progress. Almost a hundred Unreached People Groups have been engaged. We probably need to consolidate a bit."

Christopher slammed his mug on the table. Coffee splattered nearby papers. All heads jerked his direction.

"Slow down? Are you kidding me?" Christopher pushed away from the table and paced again. "You think slowing down honors the price Ruth paid, the price Jesus paid?"

A few eyes turned to the journal excerpt framed on the wall:

No place left?
Assaulting the gates of hell will cost the Church
unlike anything in history.
Paul told us, "So death works in us, but life in you."
Life in them—the lost?
No cost is too great for their salvation.
We endure all things for the sake of the elect
that they may obtain salvation (2 Timothy 2:10).

—Ruth Grant, martyr

The room fell silent but for the quiet hum of computers.

Christopher stopped pacing and threw up his hands. "Timothy, show us the progress."

"Uh ... uh ... sure, boss." The tech whiz tapped vigorously on his keyboard. "The green dots on the tracking monitor represent KPF or other international teams in the global NoPlaceLeft effort. Renee is right. About one hundred UUPGs have been engaged since we started this venture."

All eyes focused on the world map as green dots spread across a band of tough-to-work-in nations.

"Looks like we're getting pretty decent engagement for just a year's time," said John.

Christopher ignored him. "Now, Tim."

Timothy Wu pressed ENTER, and thousands of black dots covered the monitor, drowning out the green. Even the colonel gasped at this visual of the remaining darkness.

"We've barely started among the 3,227 original UUPGs!"

Christopher walked, trancelike, to the massive screen.

"Don't you see? It's not fast enough! There are still more than three thousand places left without the gospel, with people going to hell! It's not acceptable!

"Don't look at the *progress*," Christopher said, pointing to the black dots. "Look at the *gaps*! Always look at what remains!

"When we started this quest a year ago, we embraced a total wartime footing to finish Jesus' mandate by 2025. Ten years! One year is already gone, and not quite a hundred groups have been engaged. That leaves 3,131 still unengaged. It's not fast enough."

"Christopher," John said, "we're all pushing as hard as we can. Our families are at the breaking point. We can't work harder."

"Not harder. Smarter!" Win pushed back his chair and stood to his full six-foot-four. The aging soldier lowered his head to avoid a rafter, approached the monitor and pointed at the image.

"None of us can work harder—without breaking. We need a global coalition to multiply the efforts."

Nic jumped to his feet. "Exactly! We've got a model that works. We need to franchise this enterprise! No, not franchise, but give it away. No one owns this; we share everything we know—freely."

"That's right." Christopher nodded. "We've been praying for this quest to go viral. We knew from the beginning we couldn't finish the task alone, and we never intended to. NoPlaceLeft must inspire our generation to aim to be the *last* generation—the one that welcomes Jesus' return. Our 2025 deadline must move the *global* Church into total mobilization for the final assault on the gates of hell. American believers alone are insufficient for this last lap of the race. We must stir the global Church if there is to be *no place left* standing against the King's reign."

Christopher strode to the table, chugged his lukewarm coffee and set the mug down firmly. He wiped his mouth on his sleeve and winked at John.

"No, bro, we're not slowing down. Instead we must accelerate the mobilization of the global Church."

"Whatever you say, little Napoleon." The professor shook his head and a grin crossed his face. "You know I'm all in. Always have been and always will be. But I'd have a bit more vim and vigor with a cup of joe."

Chara smiled as she rose. "Give me just a couple of minutes, Dr. Steward, sir, and I'll have you taken care of."

Renee tugged at Chara's blouse. "Let the big guy wait a bit longer, honey. I need you here for our next topic.

"Have we all forgotten this little baby?" Renee plopped a folder on the table, spreading the contents across its surface. "Ruth's parents are suing us for $45 million over Ruth's death while serving with our team in China?

"I don't care what plans we concoct in the safety of this cellar. All of this—" she waved her arms around the room, "—all your precious equipment in your precious war-room, will be gone a few short weeks from now. All our KPF funds, not to mention those of Church in the City. Gone. All the funds of our team members. Re-distributed.

"In precisely three weeks this case goes to trial—and we've chosen *not* to make a defense! In legalese we call that *stupidity* and *suicide*. I just thought I'd mention that before we finish our neat little plans."

Renee turned and looked at Christopher. Her eyes brimmed with tears. "Please, Christopher, I know you said we aren't fighting this. But think about the teams! Think about the mission!"

Christopher sat next to Renee, his friend since their freshman year of college, now serving as KPF's lawyer.

"That's exactly what I'm thinking about, sis! If we start to compromise our biblical foundations now, where do we stop? I *am* thinking about our teams and the mission. Either God will protect us or He has better plans for furthering His Kingdom. Remember? Love your enemies. No compromise."

Renee's head dropped, and she let out a long sigh. "As stubborn as my husband."

The colonel walked back and leaned on the table. "I'm afraid we're innocent pawns in a much larger drama than we imagine. I've already told the commander this. The forces against us are not merely flesh and blood. They are spiritual forces of wickedness in heavenly places."

Renee looked up. "Exactly. That's my point."

The soldier silenced her with a look honed over decades of commanding men in battle. "I said innocent, little sister, not helpless. This is first and foremost a spiritual battle, so we must begin and end the battle beseeching the Lord of Heaven's

Armies. I've walked down this path before, manipulated by forces beyond my ability. At that time I walked it without seeking God's help. I won't make *that* mistake again."

"Innocent as doves, but wise as serpents," Jeanie whispered. Win's gray-haired wife took his hand and winked at the former special forces officer.

"Wisdom to navigate this quest will come only as we abide in God's Word and cry out to Him in prayer," Jeanie continued. "This time Colonel Winthrop Dunbar is leading his troops with biblical principles toward an eternal promise. Much, much mightier weapons than he ever wielded on the battlefield."

The colonel nodded and squeezed her hand.

Christopher took Chara's hand, and all eyes turned to them.

"Before I called the colonel back from Southeast Asia," said Christopher, "I asked him to read the book of Revelation several times. Let's make no mistake. If we are the last generation, we are also the Revelation generation. And, if so, the enemy is just getting started."

Christopher paused to let this sink in. "We have all read *Foxe's Book of Martyrs,* so we know how costly the advance of God's Kingdom has proven throughout history."

Christopher surveyed his teammates. Heads bowed as they recalled the horrendous yet inspiring stories of sacrifice.

"And now dear sweet Ruth has been added to that roll call of the faithful." Christopher touched the scar above his eye as he gazed at Ruth's journal entry. Eventually he turned again to the group.

"You guys, it will only get worse before it gets *eternally* better. The cost of the Great Commission is that someone must suffer. Paul said to his disciples 'So then, death is at work in us, but life is at work in you.' Until the grains of wheat fall into the ground and die, they bear no fruit."

Christopher slowly slid his chair back and stood at attention. One by one the others followed suit.

Slowly but deliberately he said, "We knew this was the cost of being the final generation. Someone must pay it. But remember, He is worthy!"

He made eye contact with each member of the faithful band. "Are you still with me?"

"Till there's *no place left*, buddy!" Nic replied quickly. "You can't scare us off."

The others nodded and Christopher smiled. "Then let's win for the Lamb who was slain the just reward of His suffering!"

The cohort clasped hands and cried out to the Ancient of Days from the hundred-year-old cellar.

"Christopher," Renee said meekly after the last amen, "how would you like me to respond to the lawsuit?"

"Well," Christopher winked at Chara, "we do have a strategy for that—sort of. We're gonna do just what the Bible says to do—no matter the results, even though we're scared to death."

Renee's face registered dismay.

Chara hugged her. "Hold on, sis! Let's see what God does."

"We have to leave the results with our heavenly Father," Christopher said. "The authorities may take all we have. They may drive us underground. But no matter the cost, we will not shrink from taking the good news to every last people group on earth. This is the final lap—a sprint to 2025."

Christopher rolled up his sleeves and sat down again. "Now, honey, what are you doing standing there hugging your friend? Her husband needs a fresh cup of joe. In fact, we all do. It's time to get to work!"

Chara threw a wadded paper at her husband.

"'Little Napoleon' is right!" she said to John, grinning.

TWO

Patricia Grant couldn't sit still. Anger, bitterness, sorrow and hurt seethed within her. Pain over her daughter Ruth's death in China continued to wrack her soul. Nothing felt right. Not even fighting to shut down this KPF cult group.

Marlene Hayes, Director Wroth's right hand, had coached her thoroughly, and the well-oiled machinations of the International Coalition for the Preservation of World Peace hummed along. Director Wroth's full resources assured that. Highly paid lawyers kept the Grants informed of every development.

In their folly of putting up no defense, the Kingdom Preparation Force had ensured the trial would come and go even more quickly than anticipated, as if that mattered. The IC's juggernaut would steamroll the tiny missions organization, regardless.

The media was having a field day crucifying KPF founder Christopher Owen. Instead of passing quietly, the story grew exponentially, with reporters and news trucks camped out in front of the Grants' home and the KPF headquarters.

Patricia and her husband occasionally ventured out to share their feelings and give the sympathetic media updates on the case. From within her virtual prison, Patricia blogged and tweeted incessantly. And at Marlene's suggestion, Patricia formed a parents' association to denounce the KPF and discuss ways to protect young people from its evil clutches.

Still, nothing felt right.

Now, exhausted from the endless crusade, Patricia sat on the couch next to the living room window.

Rays of morning sunlight diffused through the sheer curtains. The doorbell rang. "Now what?" she muttered.

She peered at the woman standing sheepishly before her, a small book in her hands.

"Mrs. Grant?"

"Yes?" Patricia thought she recognized the face. "You spoke at Ruth's memorial service. You're one of Ruth's friends."

"Yes, ma'am. I'm sorry to bother you, and I feel awfully ashamed. You remember when you asked for Ruth's journals? We sent them all to you that night, but last night I was cleaning out her room and found this one from a few years ago. I brought it to you as soon as I could."

Patricia accepted a worn blue notebook, and the woman turned and started slowly up the sidewalk as reporters craned their necks to survey the situation.

"Wait!" Something in Patricia longed for the woman to stay.

The woman turned.

"You—you knew Ruth pretty well, didn't you?"

A tear escaped the woman's eye as she smiled. "Ruth and I were good friends. We met weekly the last year of her life."

Patricia's eyes widened. "Hold on ... You're *his* wife!" Patricia slammed the door shut.

Cameras at curbside clicked furiously.

Chara Owen turned for the lonely trek up the sidewalk, but before she had reached the gate Patricia opened the front door and ran to her. She grasped Chara's arm gently. As cameras snapped, she called out loudly through a forced smile, "I'm so glad you're here. Please come in for a moment, honey."

As she escorted Chara back toward the house, Patricia leaned close and whispered in her ear, "The media circus out there will roast you mercilessly, especially once they realize who you are. Maybe it's better if you stay for a bit. Would you come in for a cup of tea or coffee and—and—tell me about my Ruth's last few months?"

They walked swiftly to Patricia's door as reporters shouted questions from the street. One rose above the din: "Mrs. Grant! Does this visit from the wife of the cult you're suing indicate an out-of-court settlement is being negotiated?"

Patricia wavered as they reached the house.

"Mrs. Grant, you do know who I am, right? Are you sure you want me to come in?" Chara asked gently.

Tears began streaming down Patricia's cheeks from her bloodshot eyes. She reached up and smeared her running mascara. "N—no, I'm not. But j—just come in, please. I need to know more about my daughter's last few months."

Patricia stood erect and closed the front door behind them, shutting out the distractions of the reporters.

Minutes later, Patricia set a steaming teapot on the table and filled their porcelain cups. Hers sat undisturbed as she peppered her foe's wife with questions from a mother's heart.

Chara's gentle manner dismantled Patricia's defenses. *How does this woman—who should be my enemy—put my heart at ease?* Patricia went through half a box of tissues as Chara shared about Ruth's devotion to the Lord and, as much as she knew, of Ruth's activities in her last few months and days.

Patricia's body shook with sobs as Chara described Ruth's love for her parents and her earnest desire that they draw closer to God and understand why Ruth was so surrendered to Him.

Two hours later, when Chara had to leave, Patricia said, "Thank you for coming. I would never have expected to let you in, but thank you. It sounds like you genuinely loved my Ruth."

Patricia stiffened as Chara hugged her, but as the embrace continued, her body relaxed.

Patricia reluctantly showed Chara to the back door. "Slip out the alley, honey, and circle around to your car. Perhaps the media won't see you that way."

As Chara stepped through the garden trellis into the alley, Patricia shook her head. *Such simple love, faith, and peace. Here I am on the side of good. Why is it that my enemy's wife is the first truly decent person I have met, through this whole process?*

Clutching Ruth's notebook in her trembling hand, Patricia went inside and ascended the stairs to Ruth's bedroom. Seeing Ruth's mementos, Patricia cast herself prostrate on the bed and sobbed again, "Why? Why? Why?"

As her body stopped convulsing, it struck her that she had visited with Ruth's friend but never thought of visiting with Ruth *herself* through her journals.

Ruth's journals had felt sacrosanct, but now Patricia realized they held the key to understanding her daughter's heart.

"Ruth, if you can see or hear me, please forgive me."

Patricia picked up a stack of six journals, sank into a massive papasan chair in Ruth's room and began a journey through the last years of her daughter's life.

One entry in particular struck her:

How can I keep up the facade any longer?
I know so much about God. I've been to church all my life,
and my bishop talks about living a good life.
Is this all there is to religion?
When I read the Bible, it seems the people in it actually knew God!
They spoke with Him, lived with Him, and lived for Him.
It was a lifestyle and more,
a marriage that affected everything around them.
It was a new birth into a living relationship,
not a physical birth into a dead religion.
A relationship—not a list of do's and don'ts.
As much as I love my family and my church, I need new life, O God.
I need forgiveness of my sin. I need to come back to my Creator.
I want to be married to You, Jesus.

On and on Patricia read, of Ruth's new birth and how she was discipled by Christ-followers in school, of Ruth's desire to live wholeheartedly for the One Who died for her, of how she became involved in the KPF and of her hopes for the Tuxiang people in China.

Patricia read for hours. *I've never felt so confused in my life. Is this idea of being "born again" really true?*

From time to time Patricia paused her reading and managed, with great difficulty, to look up Bible verses Ruth had referenced. It appeared to her that the Bible supported Ruth's experience.

Anger began welling up inside Patricia. *Why hasn't our bishop told us anything about needing to be born again?*

Her next thought was just the opposite. *If neither our current bishop nor any of our previous bishops have told us about this new birth, maybe Ruth was the one who was mistaken.*

As Patricia wavered between these conflicting views, she couldn't shake the impression that the Bible supported Ruth's perspective. Finally she blurted toward the ceiling, "God, if there really is more to the Christian life, show me!"

I must call my bishop. He can unravel this for me.

When the bishop's secretary answered, Patricia asked for an appointment to see him the next day.

"I'm sorry, the bishop is tied up all day tomorrow. I can give you an appointment—" Patricia heard appointment book pages rustling "—let's see. How's Thursday, a week from tomorrow? Say, 2:00 in the afternoon?"

After weeks of dealing with relentless lawyers, I know there's a quicker way in.

"Now you listen to me. I have been a member of First Church all my life. My grandparents were among the founding members. My husband and I support the church quite substantially. If you want to shield the bishop from friction with the church board, and you don't want any interruption in our offerings, I suggest you make time for me on the bishop's calendar—*tomorrow.*"

"Oh, I—I—I didn't realize it was *urgent*, Mrs. Grant. You know many people just want to monopolize the bishop. But he always has time for really urgent needs of important members. Would 2:30 tomorrow be okay?"

Patricia agreed, hung up, and returned to Ruth's room. She picked up the next journal and read through the night.

* * *

At 2:30 the following day Patricia sat across from the bishop, pouring out her concerns about what she had read.

"You see, Bishop Evans, I am really uncertain about my own salvation and that of my husband. Have we been Christians in name only? What does it *feel like* to be a Christian? Shouldn't I have some sort of emotions in this whole affair?"

"Dear Mrs. Grant," the good-natured bishop chuckled, "you can't go by your feelings. I must say all this 'born again' stuff has upset quite a few of our parishioners. I'll ask you the same things I ask each of them.

"Were you baptized as an infant?"

Patricia nodded.

"Did you go through confirmation as a child?"

She nodded again.

"And have you adhered to the teachings of the church, given a portion of your wealth to the needy, and served the church in various ways?"

"Yes."

"Then you're a Christian, Mrs. Grant. Your grandparents and parents were born to this life, and so were you. You're a good Christian and have shown the fruit of it. Don't let some hot-blooded fanatic make you feel guilty about this sin stuff. You're forgiven and you're a child of God. When Jesus died on the cross, He forgave all of us. We are all children of God."

"But I don't feel forgiven. I feel guilty."

"Ah—ah—ah!" The bishop shook his finger. "There you go with feelings again. This is something you must take by faith."

"Yes, I understand that, but don't you think I should have *felt* forgiven at some point in my life?"

"My dear woman, I have no doubt you *have* felt forgiven at times. It's just that in your present emotional state, you don't remember those times. You've experienced a lot of grief and been under a lot of pressure the last several weeks. What you need now is to put this behind you and get some rest. You'll feel better when the distress is over. May I suggest a vacation?

"Now, let me pray for you. I'm afraid my next appointment is in a few minutes."

After praying for Patricia as a father would with a child, the bishop took her by the hand and led her into the reception area. She left the office numbly. *The bishop knows even less about the Christian life than I do. I at least know that I know nothing! If he doesn't have answers, who might?*

Chara? That's it, I'll call Chara Owen.

As Patricia walked toward her car, she realized she didn't know how to reach Chara. As much as she loathed the idea, she decided to call the KPF office to get Chara's phone number.

She looked up the KPF headquarters on her smart phone. With trembling hands, digit by digit, she keyed in the number.

"KPF, this is Christopher, may I help you?"

Patricia's heart pounded. *Christopher Owen? What is he doing answering the phone?*

"Hello?" Christopher repeated.

"This—this is Patricia Grant."

The line went silent.

"Listen, Mr. Owen," Patricia blurted. "I'm confused. I need to talk to Chara as soon as possible."

Patricia heard a muffled shout, then Chara's voice.

"Patricia?"

"I've just read all of Ruth's journals, and I've got questions about my salvation. My bishop doesn't have the answers, and I was—was—was wondering—well, I think you're the only person I know who can answer my questions. I know your husband must hate me, but would you be able to come over tonight? I just need to get some answers."

"Mrs. Grant! I'd be happy to come. Will your husband be there? If so, c—could I bring my husband?"

"N—no. Uh, well. I'm so confused. I don't know."

Just then Patricia saw the bishop leaving the church office for his "appointment," golf bag slung over his shoulder. Patricia stared incredulously, then jumped in her car and slammed the door.

"Yes! Yes, he may come also."

* * *

That night Patricia opened her back door to the gentle knock of Christopher and Chara Owen. She eyed Christopher warily, but Chara broke the awkwardness by hugging Patricia.

Mr. Grant ushered the two couples into the den, where they traded polite remarks as Patricia served tea.

When the small talk waned, Christopher cleared his throat. "Mr. and Mrs. Grant, this is perhaps the most awkward position we've ever been in. We loved your daughter dearly, and we—"

Patricia stopped him. "She's the reason we asked you here. My heart has been burning ever since I read her journals. We don't want to discuss the lawsuit or her death. I—we just want to know what changed in Ruth—what her salvation looked like."

The Grants listened raptly as the Owens shared the simple, wonderful news of God's love for them, and their total lostness apart from Him. Christopher shared how Jesus died on a cross to pay for their sins and then rose again to prove He is the King who governs life. The Grants looked at the floor as Christopher explained the response God requires from everyone.

"'Repent and believe.' That's what Jesus said. 'Deny yourself. Take up your cross daily and follow Me.'

"These are not the words of cultural Christianity. Yet Jesus promises that His Spirit will be in us like springs of living water in response to such complete surrender.

"He is the treasure we've all been searching for," Christopher continued. "What Ruth found, Mr. and Mrs. Grant, was a living relationship with Jesus Christ—a relationship that starts with dying to your old self through repentance and receiving forgiveness and new life through faith in Him. This isn't a once-a-week or twice-a-month faith, but a 24/7 lifestyle of living life *with* Him and *for* Him—living out the purposes for which He created you."

In the quietness of their living room, the Grants surrendered to God and experienced new birth. The surprise and joy Christopher and Chara felt over this miracle was as great as anything they had experienced in China. The four wept and talked excitedly, and Chara and Patricia embraced repeatedly.

At a lull in their celebration, Christopher said, "Mr. and Mrs. Grant, we pledged to pay all the damages you have asked for, and that won't change just because you're now our new brother and sister in Christ."

"Mr. Owen," Patricia said, taking his hand in both of hers.

"Christopher," he said gently.

"Christopher," she corrected herself, "until this evening I hated you and all I thought you stood for. But what God has done in our lives changes everything. How can I require damages from you when I am the one who has been at fault? You have given us something worth more than the $45 million we were suing you for.

"It seems to me that if one is going to live for Jesus Christ, it must be all or nothing, not this empty sham we have been living to this point. I regret the damage we have done to the KPF. I hope you can forgive us for dragging your name through the mud."

"I've experienced worse," Christopher chuckled, touching the scar above his eye. "Of course we forgive you."

Mr. Grant spoke up. "I do have one favor to ask, Christopher."

"Anything."

He leaned over and whispered in Patricia's ear. She nodded.

With trembling hands, he picked up a stack of Ruth's tattered notebooks and placed them in Christopher's arms.

"Help us get Ruth's journals published. She's famous, you know. If these journals can help others know Jesus Christ and help the KPF inspire others to share this news around the world, then maybe it can make up for some of the damage we've done. What we have just received from God—well, everyone in the world should have the chance to receive this!"

* * *

Marlene had rarely heard Michael Wroth even raise his voice. Now he pounded his fist on his desk. "What do you mean they dropped the case? And they've been *converted*? Marlene, fix this!"

Wroth's office was in confusion and dismay. One short phone call from a determined woman had ended their only legal avenue for shutting down the KPF.

Marlene had tried all her subtle persuasive tactics, then her strong-arm techniques as well. But not even the Director of the International Coalition for the Preservation of World Peace himself was able to persuade Patricia Grant to change her mind. The legal flotilla that had anchored around the Grants reluctantly sailed away.

The media stayed, but now with a bigger story. News of the Grants' conversion and their call for a Christian publishing house to print Ruth's journals created an even bigger splash than their lawsuit. Within days several offers had been submitted, and the Grants accepted one that guaranteed publication in just a matter of weeks. To the Owens' surprise, the Grants assigned all the royalties to fund the NoPlaceLeft effort!

This one decisive stroke catapulted the KPF to another level. In the following months tens of thousands of books sold, and the KPF found its coffers inundated with funds. More importantly, the number of service applications soared.

The great problem now was how to prioritize and to weed out the wishful from the faithful.

And how to maintain some semblance of order in what was fast becoming an out-of-control movement.

THREE

A **NoPlaceLeft movement** was taking North America by storm. Its waves lapped upon the shores of other continents. Churches began springing up everywhere—in church buildings, offices, homes, pancake houses, coffee shops, parks—wherever God's people could find to meet and purposefully live out Acts 2:36–47. In over 27 cities, church planting movements began to emerge.

Seekers came from all over, inspired by the story of the KPF and its initial success; they represented churches, missions agencies, and denominations. Christopher was humbled that they came to find out how a small fellowship like Church in the City and its multiplying sister churches could spawn the KPF movement that was now resulting in movements overseas.

Ultimately, Christopher told all inquirers the same thing. It had nothing to do with them, but everything to do with God. The Kingdom Preparation Force was not more spiritual than other missionaries and missions agencies and definitely not more experienced or knowledgeable. In fact, the results were not nearly as large as some of the longer-running church planting movements around the world, even if the KPF movements had started quickly.

All the KPF could claim was a desire to complete the task by 2025 and inspire others around the globe to do the same, no matter how radical the commitment had to be. KPF members had decided to act as if they were waging a war, which, in the spiritual realm, they were. They chose to live with a wartime mentality in a peacetime society. Their deep desire to hasten the return of Christ motivated them to take exceptional risks.

And KPF teams were not going to stop until there was *no place left* where the good news of Jesus had not penetrated deeply. They longed to see Kingdom movements spread to every people group. Christopher was quick to remind everyone that such resolve and the ensuing success had come with a great price

—imprisonment, beatings, deportations, death. Ultimately, Church in the City and KPF members resolved to live as if they were the last generation.

In light of that, Christopher concluded that God must have had mercy on that simple desire and commitment and had granted them success. As a result, they would gladly share their training, knowledge, insights, and resources with any Christian group that asked. And they were eager to learn from others. Only a collaborative effort by the whole body of Christ globally would fulfill the mission of the King.

And so they did. They mobilized, advised, and trained when asked, often taking members of other churches and missions groups into their own KPF boot camp. In addition, they received suggestions from others who were further down the CPM path than they were, especially about the wisest way to mentor the budding church planting movements in Southeast Asia.

Thrust into the public spotlight, KPF members were honored to be so sought out and therefore, at every turn, had to guard against pride. What inspired them the most were the stories of the many other churches and organizations that began to make sacrifices in running the final lap of the Great Commission. One particular day at their staff meeting, KPF leaders shared emails and stories they had received.

"Brothers and sisters, these are my heroes—these individuals, churches, and agencies that have made sacrifices to participate in what God wants to do in this generation!" said Christopher.

"I want to share the first story with you. Nic and I were in Ohio consulting with a rather large fellowship there. They run about fifteen hundred in worship and were getting ready for a major building program. Their building holds only seven hundred, so they have three worship services right now. They know that when they move into their proposed three-thousand-seat auditorium, they'll grow to over two thousand in a couple of months."

Chuckles came from the corner. "So what were they consulting you for?" asked Phil Young, who had been a part of the first China team.

Christopher smiled. "I don't know. I guess some of the elders were hesitant about asking their people to give basically a second tithe to finance the twenty-million-dollar facility. They wanted to give more money to missions, especially when they heard our story, but didn't see how they could."

Nic slid to sit next to Christopher and winked. "Here is the really amazing part. Christopher and I shared with them about God's heart for the world. Within a few hours, the pastor and elders decided to go through with the giving program they were proposing to finance the building."

Christopher and Nic could see everyone's shoulders slump. Someone in the circle muttered sarcastically, "Another glorious building raised for the Kingdom of God!"

Christopher said, "Don't knock buildings. Churches have to meet somewhere; it's just that we often devote too much priority to the facility. If we spent on missions all the money we spend on buildings, we could have financed and finished the task a long time ago. We don't lack the resources—just the resolve!

"This church in Ohio realized that. They decided they could handle slower growth and add even more worship services, perhaps even start a few new churches elsewhere in the city to reduce the demand on the main building."

Renee stopped him. "Wait. I thought you said they decided to go through with the building program."

Nic grinned. "Wrong! We said they decided to go through with the *giving* program, only now they've decided to use all that money to finance people from their church that will go as a team to penetrate new unreached people groups. The first team will be sent to a people group they have adopted in the Middle East! Right, buddy?"

Christopher beamed. "Yes! Twenty million bucks! Plus, some of the members who weren't that excited about giving an extra tithe to finance another building got really excited about doing something as Kingdom significant as bringing the gospel to unreached people groups. I got a call yesterday from one of the staff. The initial pledges are in, and it looks like they're going to approach the twenty-one million dollar mark! They've started a campaign to call on other churches to forsake building new structures and encourage their members to give a second tithe for missions!"

Everyone applauded, some praising God out loud.

Nic, the businessman, added, "The demand for our KPF boot camp is so high that we can't handle all the teams wanting to go through. So this Ohio church is going to help us franchise the training to be duplicated around the country, starting there first. They're sending a couple here in two weeks to participate in the next boot camp."

Grace Wu, the other IT specialist, pulled up an email on her tablet. "A lot of fellowships feel they can't reach into multiple places, but they can seriously engage just one unreached people group. One group in Georgia has already been sending out several short-term teams each year but without any real strategy; they just send teams wherever they're invited or have connections or sometimes just wherever people want to go.

"Now they have decided to consolidate and send just one long-term team to an unreached group in North Africa. Well, I guess a lot of churches are starting to do that. But this church is not as big as a lot of the others that are doing that, only about 400 people.

"But they're going to send out six members, financing them in a variety of ways: car washes, offerings, auctions, bake sales— you name it.

"What I thought was exciting was that they are adopting a wartime mentality until they successfully reach this group. They have encouraged the members to give up some pleasure like a hobby, a favorite grocery item, an extra movie each month, whatever, and give that money to the mission team. Other people have taken a part-time or Saturday job and are giving all that money to the team. They expect to send out this team before the end of the year!"

Timothy, Grace's husband, added, "Another church got very creative as well. They decided that the last Sunday offering of each month will be completely given to send their UPG team. Would you believe that those last-Sunday offerings have skyrocketed?"

John added, "I heard of another church that even sold 'war bonds' like the government did during World War II. People could buy them in amounts as low as $5. These war bonds, however, will not be paid back to the purchasers. Instead, the members know they will get heavenly interest one day!"

Everyone laughed at such a creative idea.

"They're selling them in Awanas, small groups, even Sunday morning worship times!" John finished.

"Okay, dudes, my turn," said Lance Chu, another original China team member. "Like there's this megachurch in Texas that loses three staff members. It's one of those churches that's so big it needs to have a directory board for all the staff. So, the senior pastor dude is new and is going to replace these three staff, plus just got budget to add two more.

"Like, you know what he does? He tells the church what he heard about KPF, even listened to a couple of Christopher's podcasts. He tells the church he wants to add the new staff, only he wants the dudes to live overseas in another people group!

"Almost got him fired at first, but soon the church wised up. The regular members realized they could do a lot of the things those new staff members would have had done, and they agreed to send out a team of five.

"Now, because this big church was willing to give up some staff funding at home, they're sending a team to Central Asia! They're so excited about it, they're trying to find more money in the budget they can redirect to send more people to join them in the same country so they can branch out to other people groups!"

A soft, enthusiastic voice was next after the applause. "My story," said Stacy Fernandez, "is just the opposite. It's about a fellowship in Oregon with only eighty-five people. I don't know if you guys realize it, but most churches in America have fewer than a hundred regular attenders. I think that many of them feel helpless to jump in and do what we're talking about. Eighty-five people normally can't finance a whole mission team.

"But this little fellowship wasn't going to let that stop them. They've been following the KPF blog and have been stirred by the vision and the stories.

"In their small town there are five other evangelical churches, each numbering a hundred and fifty members or less. The first church approached all the others with their desire to send a team to ignite a church planting movement among an unreached people group.

"My sweet husband," she said as she squeezed Nic's hand, "and John went there to discuss with all six fellowships just how easy this plan could be to implement.

John picked up the story from there. "We're going to do all the training for them to save them money. With involvement from all six churches and some real deep digging into their pockets, they've managed to find enough money and volunteers to send three families and one single person. They'll have to live with minimal expenses, so we helped them find a high-priority people group where the cost of living is very low!

"Get ready to meet them, guys. They'll be here for training in two weeks!"

The group waited as it became obvious that Chara wanted to share but didn't quite know how to start. "You guys know how much the Fernandezes's and our thinking was changed by the CPM training we got in Singapore. It has forever changed our approach to starting Christ-communities. We received so much from the organization that sponsored it.

"Would you believe they recently wrote us that they had received something from us? Inspired by the intense focus of our two-to-four-year teams, they have begun forming apostolic teams from their own missionaries whose responsibility is to initiate among UUPGs the same type of thing we have done. And wherever they see the fires of CPMs start, they are going to take the hot coals from those people groups to nearby people groups to do the same, much like the Tuxiang are doing. I'm just humbled by this—that God would use us!"

John said, "When a fellowship in the Philippines approached us about how to send a team of three to a people group in Laos, I was a bit skeptical. Finding the finances and then building trust to collect and channel that money without any compromises was tough. But Colonel Dunbar has had a bit of experience in that regard, right?"

Win Dunbar squirmed. "Well, yes, I've had more than my share of working with local folks in various projects." He cleared his throat. "I helped them see how they could work together through a trustworthy accountability system. I then taught them how to set aside a portion of their farms' output or livestock as a faith offering. As they surrendered to Jesus as Master and decided to give a portion of their produce to sending the team, the harvests in those portions of their fields and flocks have far outstripped the rest of their harvest.

"I'm amazed. They are going to fully support this small team in a way they had not dreamed possible. What's more, my contacts tell me that a global movement is developing as churches from many nations are sending teams to unreached areas. North America cannot and should not do it alone."

The stories kept coming—of small and large churches, new and old denominations, innovative and traditional missions agencies around the world—all inspired to make sacrificial attempts to do in their generation what few had thought could be done and to think in new ways with clear priorities. The race toward 2025 was accelerating.

And in many of these "sending" countries, church planting movements were emerging as churches renewed a commitment to sharing the gospel, discipling, starting churches, raising up leaders in a simple biblical way, and expecting new disciples to do the same. In the wake of the CPMs, many unreached people group immigrants even in North America were being swept into the Kingdom of God.

NoPlaceLeft by 2025 had become a rallying point for finishing the task. The real-time *Unengaged Unreached People Group Countdown* app had become viral, as tens of thousands of disciples tracked the progress of the Kingdom of God to the last frontiers. Christopher pulled out his smartphone and glanced at the screensaver: *3,004 UUPGs* glowed in red. *Oh Lord, over two hundred UUPGs already engaged with a church planting strategy. You're doing it! We're almost under three thousand!*

He cast his eyes around the room, amazed as he listened to the stories. Nowhere did he hear jealousy or worry about others getting more results or venturing into "KPF territory." Instead, he heard excitement that God was stirring up something big, something awesome, something much bigger than the KPF. He heard a new cooperation, a new inspiration, a new commitment, a new priority. It was all about the *Kingdom of God.*

And though church planting movements were exciting, they were not the goal. They were just the starting point to get to *no place left* where the gospel was not proclaimed.

A quiet vibration on Christopher's phone drew his eyes toward it again. The numbers now glowed *3,003 UUPGs.*

Maybe it really will happen in our generation. God, don't let it stop with this handful of stories! Let us be the final generation.

Even as he unlocked his phone, an email arrived. The subject line: "KPF group preaches false doctrine." His heart sank. A heaviness tugged at the corners of his mind.

God, do I read these things or not? Please don't let us get distracted. Please don't let me get distracted.

FOUR

Michael Wroth's power grew daily. As Director of the International Coalition for the Preservation of World Peace, he held more sheer authority and raw power than did most presidents and prime ministers. In fact, as Wroth gained increasing influence and popularity even George Springer, the handpicked successor to the president of the United States, and Vice President Philip Bowen sometimes bantered with him about who had more clout.

Wroth directed a crack security force of well over a hundred thousand troops, and while that did not approach the size of many nations' armed forces, it was large enough to suit his purposes. His troops, the International Coalition (IC) forces, were used only for *securing* peace and eliminating subversive groups. The responsibility for maintaining *ongoing* peace and order rested with local governments or, when needed, with United Nations peacekeepers. With the precision of a surgeon, Wroth inserted his highly mobile, superbly trained units into key situations, struck decisively, and moved on. Terrorist cells that appeared in headline news one week were eliminated the next week. No one complained. The world was ready for order.

IC forces, wearing their black berets embroidered with a silver triangle, quickly gained a respect—or dread—rivaling that of the Army Rangers, Green Berets, or Navy SEALs. In fact, many IC soldiers had transferred from these units. Terrorist groups feared IC forces more than they feared these others, however, because IC forces did not have to wade through bureaucratic red tape before striking. Wroth's carte blanche authority was well known, and his funding for training, weapons, and deployment seemed limitless.

Around the globe, Wroth's popularity increased daily. The masses were refreshed by his decisiveness in eliminating terrorists. As a result, no country argued when IC forces showed up on its doorstep to eradicate them, especially since the IC forces didn't stay around long. They came and went unobtrusively. Governments liked that; the IC zapped their problems but stayed out of their hair.

Drug trafficking took a nosedive. Wroth and his commandos were frequently photographed next to downed drug-laden cargo planes or on location in Colombia near a seized estate or in Vietnam near a burning poppy field. Violence diminished so greatly in Mexican border towns that formerly wary American tourists began once again to venture south of the border for excursions.

Latest in Wroth's series of successes was the distribution of food to starving masses. A severe famine had struck many of the developing countries in Africa, Central Asia, and Central America. Until the IC intervened, hundreds of thousands were starving. Corrupt local officials diverted much aid into their own pockets. Donors who saw this were reluctant to contribute—that is, until IC forces began escorting the shipments and tracking distribution. Donations quadrupled as television images relayed the success of IC-escorted shipments. Within a span of months, the famine's stranglehold was loosened as aid reached the intended recipients.

* * *

Ethan Farnsworth, Number Three, sat across the coffee table from Wroth in IC's Washington office.

"I do not like it, Michael. Number One is getting suspicious. Your popularity is too widespread. He is questioning your ability to act covertly as one of The Ten. You need to make a radical turnaround, or something dreadful may happen to you!"

"I'm surprised at you, Ethan!" Wroth leaned back on a soft cushion. "We've discussed all this before. You know as well as I do that we won't usher in the Rebirth without both our secret alliance operating from within The Ten *and* my growing popularity and acceptance on the world stage.

"Danger? Danger is an ever-present constant I accept and guard against. For instance, whom can we trust in The Ten? I mean, *unequivocally* trust?"

"There is Number Nine, my Korean partner on Religion and Education. I do not think we can trust my other partner, Number

Eight, from India." Farnsworth furrowed his brow in thought and continued. "On Science and Economics the only one we can thoroughly trust is Number Seven, the Arab. Although I must say Number Six, the African, has been deeply moved by what the IC has been doing for the starving people on that continent.

"And on Politics, well, there is you," Farnsworth smiled, "though officially you are only an apprentice. We may be able to trust Number Five, the South American, though he and Number Four, the Russian, are so close to Number One that it is hard to say."

"So, besides the two of us, there are two others we are certain of," Wroth summarized. "Now, how many are absolutely opposed to me and to our work to launch the Rebirth in the near future?"

"Definitely Number One, our Prime Director," Farnsworth said quickly.

"Uh-uh-uh! Not *our* Prime Director." Wroth grinned.

Farnsworth glanced nervously around the office and shook his head. "Okay, *the* Prime Director. Who else is opposed? Definitely Number Two, the Chinese gentleman who is head of Science and Economics. Most likely Number Four, who is like Number One's right hand."

Wroth jotted down notes as they talked:

Opposed:

  ✘ Number 1, Italian, Prime Director and head of Politics

  ✘ Number 2, Chinese, head of Science & Economics

  ✘ Number 4, Russian, Politics

  ✘ Number 8, Indian, Religion & Education

Uncertain:

  ? Number 5, South American, Politics

  ? Number 6, African, Science & Economics

Supportive:

  ✓ Number 3, British (Ethan), head of Religion & Education

  ✓ Number 7, Arab, Science & Economics

  ✓ Number 9, Korean, Religion & Education

  ✓ Number 10, American (self), Politics

"Well, see there, Ethan, things are about as I expected. Not bad on the whole. I could never carry out the work of the IC so effectively without the power and resources of The Ten.

"Don't you see?" Wroth continued reassuringly, "The IC is, in reality, just an arm of The Ten. When we—and by 'we' I mean The Ten—work publicly in this limited, anonymous way, we are hugely successful. And when we decide to go public, we will meet with the same success.

"Do you believe that, Ethan?"

Farnsworth considered the question, and its repercussions.

"Yes, Michael, I believe that. More importantly, I believe in *you*. You can make it work."

"Then, Ethan," Michael leaned forward, "it's up to you to hold things together. Buy me time with members of The Ten. The IC won't work without The Ten. But I'm not going to be in a position to bring about the Rebirth for another couple of years."

"Michael, I don't know if I can buy you that much time."

"Do your best, my friend. Meanwhile, maintain my informants in the other two offices. I need unfettered access to the raw data and the office workings if I'm going to keep the IC growing. I'll talk to the Prime Director and work out something with him."

Farnsworth shook his head as he walked out the door to return to England.

Moments later, Wroth's assistant Marlene buzzed him.

"Excuse me, Senator,"—she had continued to call him 'Senator' despite his relinquishing that office—"but a very strange thing has occurred. Dr. Larson Sayers is on the line—your private line that no one has access to."

"That's quite all right, Marlene," Wroth laughed. "That's Dr. Sayers's way. Put the call through."

Wroth smiled as he picked up the phone. "Hello, Uncle Lars! So good to hear from you!"

"And you, Michael." The normally gentle voice sounded agitated. "Sorry to cut in on your private line, but it's the only one that is truly secure in your office."

"Nonsense, Uncle Larson, I have several lines that are quite secure."

"No, actually you don't. Michael, I need to speak with you privately at my Big Sur estate."

"Well, will Thursday wor—"

"Michael, this is of utmost importance. You must do exactly as I say, or you will not survive the week. Most likely not even the night."

"What? What are you talking about?"

"My jet will land at Washington Reagan in an hour. I have a trusted driver that will collect you in exactly forty-five minutes in a sedan with blackened windows at the service entrance of your building. You must disguise yourself, Michael, and slip into the sedan unnoticed. This driver will take you to the plane.

"You must make a recording of yourself and have your assistant use it as a decoy phone call an hour after you have left the building. Thirty minutes later, have her phone someone and tell him she has to cancel a dinner date. She is to say that the two of you will be working at the office all night on some urgent business."

"Uncle Larson, this is all very unsettling and rushed. I can assure you that my security is quite good here."

"Michael," Dr. Sayers said quietly, "The Ten are very close."

Wroth stammered, "Th-the Ten? What are you talking about?"

"Michael, I don't have time to explain, and I prefer that you not feign ignorance. If we've developed any trust over your lifetime, then do exactly as I have said."

The line went dead.

* * *

Forty-five minutes later, Wroth emerged incognito from the service entrance into a misty evening. Though the measures were extreme, Sayers's awareness of The Ten alone had persuaded Wroth to comply.

A dark sedan awaited him. The driver said nothing, only drove. After fifteen minutes, they pulled into a private hangar where Wroth boarded a small executive jet. The plane itself was empty except for the pilot, co-pilot, and an immaculately dressed, bearded gentleman. "Good evening, sir," he said as he took Wroth's coat and hat.

Wroth eyes immediately lit up at the sight of Dr. Sayers's aging personal steward.

"Charles? Are you still around?"

Actually, the director wanted to laugh, as he usually did, at the man who reminded him of Mr. French, the valet of *Family Affair.* "What are you doing away from Dr. Sayers's side?"

"It is most urgent, sir. Dr. Sayers thought it best if I personally accompanied you. He also thought it prudent that no one else know about your meeting."

"I agree. It must be urgent."

Four hours later, the plane touched down in Monterey, California. Another sedan drove them the final forty-five minutes to Dr. Sayers's wooded estate, *Optasia.*

If I had to be whisked off to someplace, this is the one place I would most want to come. Wroth recalled his frequent visits to *Optasia* as a child—playing among the redwoods as the fog rolled in off the Big Sur coastline, walking the paths through the several hundred acres, and catching frequent glimpses of the rocky coastline. Those had been times of unparalleled peace in Michael Wroth's life. Not just emotional peace, but deeper. *A spiritual peace, maybe? Why haven't I returned before now?*

The car turned into the drive, and they waited as an elk paid them little attention and finally meandered off the road in search of edibles.

Then Wroth spied it atop the hill. *Optasia.* Greek for "vision" or "trance" or "divine encounter." Surely if there was any place on earth those could occur, it was here. Despite the ominous conversation that had brought him here, Wroth felt a twinge of excitement at returning, along with unexplainable peace.

"It works on you, does it not, sir? *Optasia,* that is," said Charles, noticing the change in Wroth's demeanor. "Each time we return here to the manor, it's the same—deep contentment. A spiritual and emotional retreat from the world."

"Yes, Charles. I had forgotten. It's been too long."

"Yes, sir. We've missed you, the staff and I."

As the men left the sedan, Dr. Larson Sayers limped onto the front porch, supporting himself with an exquisitely carved walking cane he'd picked up in his travels. Wroth bounded up the short flight of steps into Sayers's fatherly embrace.

"For the first time in my life, I wasn't quite sure I'd get you here safely," Sayers said, hugging him longer than normal. "Come in; the air is getting a damp chill. Dinner is ready. We must eat before we talk."

Arms around each other, the men entered the embrace of Optasia together.

FIVE

The BayMist office in San Francisco and the *Optasia* manor in Big Sur were wholly different worlds—one the public and the other the private side of Larson Sayers.

The gentle but renowned peacemaker sat across from the publicly heralded and ruthless former senator in the drawing room. The two were a study in contrasts—on separate paths, using dissimilar means, yet tied together in the quietness of after-dinner coffee and cigars. The ever-faithful Charles stood nearby.

"That will be all for now, Charles. Kindly see that we are not disturbed for the next two hours," said Dr. Sayers.

"Yes, sir," Charles murmured, closing and locking the double doors behind him as he left.

Now that they were alone, Wroth had many questions.

"Uncle Larson, could you now explain to me—"

Sayers quickly silenced him with a finger raised to his lips. He gestured for the IC Director to follow him across the room; he waved his hands, causing a section of the wall to slide back into a pocket.

Sayers stepped carefully through the portal and started to hobble down a winding stair into darkness. Wroth ducked through the doorway, and both men descended into a dimly lit area.

As the wall closed behind him, Wroth was startled by what he saw before him.

A cavernous room, lit by numerous candles set on stands along the walls, awaited him. The floor appeared to be made of marble or onyx, yet its utter blackness absorbed rather than reflected the candlelight. An ancient oriental rug covered part of the floor. It had a curious design that Wroth had never seen before. The walls of deep crimson granite glowed faintly in the light. The room was bare except for a small table at one end and four wingback chairs that formed a square around the rug in the middle of the room.

Sayers turned to Wroth and beamed.

"This is the heart of *Optasia,* and you, nephew, are the only person alive in the world—outside of Charles and myself—who knows of its existence. It is from this room that *Optasia* draws its peaceful strength. It is from this abode that I gain the wisdom to advise the world."

"Yes, yes, it *feels* impressive. But why bring me here?"

"We must have absolute secrecy," Sayers said, motioning for Wroth to sit opposite him, "and we must share openly about the future."

Wroth scratched his head. "It's a long way to bring me just to talk, but I'm all ears."

"Michael, you almost died tonight. You are a proud man and a blind one. Don't you know that pride goes before a fall? The Ten almost eliminated you tonight."

"Uncle Larson, I don't know how you know about The Ten, but I can assure you that my security is up to whatever they throw at me."

Sayers shook his head. "Is that right? Do me a favor. Take off your suit jacket."

"Whatever for?"

"Just humor an old man please, Michael."

Wroth took off his coat and handed it to the good doctor, who began to rip out the lining.

Wroth attempted to snatch it back but was too late. "What are you doing? That's a seven-thousand-dollar suit!"

"Just got it back from the cleaners, didn't you?" Sayers said as he continued to tear out the lining.

"I don't know. My aides take care of—"

Wroth stopped short as he watched Sayers pull a small card—half the size of a credit card—from the lapel.

"Ah! Look closely, Michael. See the tiny circuit imbedded on the back? On this other side, notice the small vent. Now watch."

Sayers tossed the card into the far corner of the room.

"Now, Charles," he said, though the room was empty except for the two of them.

"Right, sir," came a voice from somewhere above.

The card emitted a sudden puff of barely visible smoke that ended as quickly as it started. Michael jumped to his feet and stared incredulously.

"Cyanide, Michael. Activated by a close-range transmitter, a transmitter that was stationed in a cleaning truck outside your office. As soon as you were in your limousine on the way home, a hidden assassin was going to depress a certain key, transmitting a specific frequency, opening a tiny vent on a small card in a non-suspicious lapel. A minute puff of cyanide would have been dispensed—harmless from here but fatal in the enclosed space of a vehicle."

"How dare they!" Wroth's eyes were riveted upon the card. "Number One ...," he spoke in a daze.

"If you had not followed my instructions to the letter, you would have been a dead man as soon as you shut your car door. I don't suppose your security detail ever anticipated such forms of attack?"

"I didn't know the technology even existed."

Sayers sat in one of the wingback chairs. "Tsk, tsk. Typical of The Ten, actually. Number One prefers little gadgets like that. Sit down, Michael. As you're aware, The Ten have been operating since before the fall of the Roman Empire, trying to usher in a true Rebirth, influencing and shaping without being influenced themselves.

"Brilliant, absolutely brilliant. The concept is perfect. What you do not realize is that the men who started it, whose names I can give you, were 'enlightened' men—which is actually a misnomer. Long before the 'Enlightenment,' they were the first in a series of rationalists who denied the spiritual world."

"I think you're wrong there, Uncle Larson. As you must know, one third of The Ten are devoted to influencing the religious and educational world." Wroth sat back down.

"Do *you* believe in the spiritual world, Michael?"

"No, actually. But I don't see how that affects—"

"Michael, just listen," the older man said in a measured tone. "Though you are an atheist and rationalist, you still involve yourself with the religious domain because you know it is a human factor in this world. The original Ten also did not believe in the supernatural, yet they manipulated the religious domain, knowing it was a powerful force on people's lives.

"All the activities of The Ten have operated from the presupposition that we are our own gods. Though much of mankind runs amok, this select group believes that eventually society will be utopian. They believe we can usher in the Rebirth when we rationally control ourselves, develop our potential, and implement our plans.

"Rubbish! In all these fifteen hundred plus years, why has there been no Rebirth? Because bitter old men on The Ten have lost a vision for it, as you believe? No! It is because The Ten, for all their power, do not have what is needed to control the world. Why? Because they have founded their strategy on a faulty worldview—a non-spiritual one. They have ignored the supernatural world."

Wroth finally stirred in his seat. "Uncle Larson, I have a profound respect for you, and I know you're a deeply spiritual man. But those are just your peculiar beliefs. If they help you become more effective and more at peace, then fine. But please don't expect me to buy into a supernatural world for which we have no proof. Not one shred!

"I suppose next you'll be calling for me to be born again or to commune with some inner guide. If you brought me here to—"

Wroth's words were cut off mid-sentence as a choked gurgle escaped his mouth. He clasped his hands to his throat, gasping for air, as panic swept over him.

Sayers had risen and now stood in front of him, cane raised toward Wroth, a look of pity in his eyes.

Wroth's eyes rolled as he struggled to breathe, the choking not abating. He instinctively knew that the source of his malady lay not with his throat but with the short, bald man and the cane extended toward him.

With all his effort, Wroth tried to move toward Sayers and strike the cane from his hand, but his feet felt embedded in concrete. He could not move. After a minute his face turned blue. Still Sayers held his cane outstretched.

Two minutes passed, and Wroth collapsed on the floor. His eyes pleaded with Sayers. *Why?*

Then, as if invisible hands had turned loose of his neck, Wroth resumed breathing in short gasps. He lay on the floor, beads of perspiration dripping from his forehead.

"Why?" he managed to wheeze.

"To teach you a lesson," Sayers said, helping Wroth to a chair. "You are as stiff-necked as old Pharaoh. Moses used a staff and taught him to fear the supernatural. Though I love you, Michael, you had to be shown that the supernatural is real. It is a personal force to be reckoned with."

Wroth said nothing for several moments.

"Uncle Larson, what you did was most impressive. I must admit that. B-but that still doesn't prove there is a spiritual world. I don't want to insult your beliefs, sir, but perhaps you simply have learned how to tap into the extrasensory realm, learned how to manipulate the forces around you with senses we don't normally use. There's a very good explanation for what you interpret as spiritual."

Sayers looked at Wroth and slowly shook his head.

"Michael, please don't make us prove to you that the spiritual world is real. Why not believe? Don't you realize the price Pharaoh paid for his unbelief?"

Again Sayers raised his cane.

Wroth's eyes widened, and he felt his body elevated into the air. Suspended in midair, he was whipped with a jerk against the nearby wall, where he collapsed onto the floor. Invisible hands buffeted him from all sides, at times hurling him into the air, sometimes against the walls or floor, sometimes catching him in midair. Wroth felt himself in a volleyball match where he was the ball being pummeled around the room.

Soon Sayers lowered his cane, and the game stopped.

Wroth lay on the floor in a crumpled mass, breathing spasmodically.

"The spiritual warriors were gentle with you, Michael."

Wroth pulled himself up to sitting position and whispered, "Uncle Larson, please. No more. I believe you can manipulate the environment. Just don't ask me to believe—"

A hissing noise stopped him short. Wroth's head jerked in the direction of the noise, his eyes darting back and forth. The candles flickered. The noise grew louder until it was a tumult. Out of nowhere, gale force winds rushed through the room. Candles gave up their flames, and the room was plunged into darkness.

Sayers stood up with arms raised. "He's here!" he cried in awe, midst the swirling winds.

Who's here?

The winds grew stronger. Wroth's rationality gave way to fear. He began backing himself across the slick floor into what he hoped was one corner of the room. He covered his ears with his hands.

At the far end of the room, a faint glimmer emerged and grew steadily brighter. Wroth watched, transfixed. The glimmer was actually a small pillar of smoke swirled by the winds. The ever-growing cloud was aflame and glowing brightly.

Words from his parochial school days flooded Wroth's mind. *A cloud by day and a pillar of fire by night. The presence of God among his people. Could it be?*

He dismissed the thought as soon as it came. *It couldn't be!*

Wroth struggled to his feet and edged his way toward the stairs. As if in response, a persistent force irresistibly led him back toward the pillar of fire. Before he knew it, he bowed his face to the floor in obeisance, hands forward.

The whole room trembled, and the roar of the wind was deafening.

Then above the din—the *voice*. A voice no one could manufacture, clearly heard above the rushing wind.

It wasn't the decibel level or the intensity. No, it was the *authority* of that voice. In his deepest being, Michael Wroth knew without any doubt that he had been wrong about Dr. Sayers. This voice was real.

This must be the very voice of God.

"This is my servant," said the glowing pillar of cloud. "Listen to him! When he speaks, he speaks my words. Michael, Michael, Michael! I have chosen you above all others on this earth. You will do as I say, and I will be in you. Do not resist me any longer!"

The next transition was as startling as the voice itself.

Just as Wroth was about to pose a plethora of questions to the pillar, the wind stopped, the cloud dissipated, and the candles lit. The room was as normal as when he had entered it, save that an aura could be seen on the face of Dr. Sayers who sat quietly in a chair.

Wroth raised his head. It took all of his energy to lift his sweat-soaked body and settle it into a chair next to Sayers.

"I—I—I never realized!"

"Of course you didn't, my boy. I didn't know how he would convince you, but I am glad he did. He has the most amazing ways, doesn't he? Never the same way twice!

"We don't have time to discuss everything, for I see you have hundreds of questions. More will be unveiled in the weeks to come.

"For now, let me just tell you that you have been selected to do what The Ten could never do. Oh, don't mistake me. The Ten are important. They have set up critical mechanisms we will use to usher in the true Rebirth."

"Rebirth? It—it was all just a lie for me. I—I never really believed in the Rebirth," admitted Wroth.

Sayers tapped Wroth's knee affectionately with his cane. "No, of course you didn't. You just found it a useful tool to manipulate The Ten toward your desires for greater world domination. But, my nephew, there truly *is* to be a Rebirth. A remaking of this world as it was designed to be, and *you* are to be the instrument of that transformation. And the mechanisms of The Ten will be helpful in achieving that, though they are incomplete. But with me, and with the spiritual dimension guiding us, the world will experience a complete transformation."

Sayers smiled. "Yes, *spiritual*, Michael. I see it in your eyes. How do I know so much about The Ten? Do you not see that even a secret group like The Ten cannot totally insulate itself from outside influence when they are unaware of a whole other dimension in this world? They are only immune to every dimension *of which they are aware.*"

Wroth listened, though he was sucking air as if it were in limited supply.

"While they have secretly watched and manipulated this world, I have watched and manipulated them. Whose idea do you think it was for them to choose you?" Sayers chuckled. "Mine! Oh, they would never have chosen you. You're too much of a maverick for their closed system. Too unpredictable. But they still chose you! Ha! Ha! It took quite some doing to bring Number One to that opinion."

Sayers's eyes twinkled as he reminisced about the incident.

"They do not know about me. Of course, they have heard my name and know of my public influence, but they dismiss me as an eccentric old man. Yet I see and hear what they think no one can see and hear. Do you not remember how Elisha knew the plans that the king of Aram spoke in the secrecy of his bedroom?

"And truly, no one on this physical world can break through The Ten's cover of impenetrability. But as you have seen tonight, my eyes and ears are spiritual. Nothing blocks them. I myself watched Number One gather with a few key others. I heard him give the orders for your death. Not one of the six hundred sixty plus members before you has ever been assassinated by them, but they want *you* dead. Unprecedented! I know their strategies, back-up strategies, and back-ups to their back-ups. My ears go beyond the human world. There is a divine factor!"

Still panting, Wroth leaned in close to Sayers.

"Ah! I see the longing in your eyes. You too want this power. You will have it, nephew, in time."

Wroth said, "Uncle Larson. You have all of the power and are intimate with the divine one. Why do you need me?"

Sayers stood and raised Wroth with a gentle hand. He placed both hands on Wroth's shoulders.

"Did not the high priest Aaron have his Moses? Did not the high priest Eleazar have his Joshua? Did not these priests have access to the divine? But they were men of peace. It was for another to lead, to fight battles and gain glory. They supported and empowered another. I am simply an oracle, a prophet, a priest. I am a man of peace. The work that is needed, though, is more than that. It is a work of leading, of judging, of ruling—even destroying. That is your work.

"The forces against you are great. In your own strength, you will never succeed. Michael Wroth is not sufficient. You must be filled with the divine. Only when you have been transformed and are dependent on the supernatural will you have the strength to succeed. And I will be there with you."

Wroth listened. He grasped both of Sayers's wrists. "We must crush The Ten, then, and seize control. With our new power we can transform the world!"

Sayers subtly broke his grasp.

"Not yet, Michael. For a while longer, you will continue to be the hunted, not the hunter. This will be your time of testing, your wilderness experience. You will grow weak—yes, even unto death—before you can be strong again. We will tread the dangerous line that separates life from death. Only with absolute obedience to the divine will we succeed. Annihilation is one mistake away."

Wroth began pacing. "This is ludicrous. Why can't we crush them now? We'll be above the law. No one will ever know anything about The Ten. We are already more powerful than they are."

Once again Sayers shuffled up to Wroth and put both hands on his shoulders, transfixing him with his gaze. Gently, yet with uncanny strength, he pushed Wroth to his seat. Wroth almost tripped over a corner of the rug that lay crumpled on the floor. Unveiled was a curious gold point of a star etched into the floor.

"On the contrary, Michael, we will proceed a different way." He looked off vacantly. "By the way, has anyone ever told you what your name means?"

Startled at the sudden shift in conversation, Wroth stuttered, "N-no—all I know is it was the name of the archangel."

Sayers chuckled as if he knew personally the one referred to. "Well, yes, you're right, but the name itself has a meaning in Hebrew. It means *who is like God*."

"*Who is like God*. Is that a statement or a question?"

Sayers ignored the question, veering back to the original subject of conversation. "Now here is what we must do."

SIX

In the heart of Tuxiang-land in southwest China, tribal elders gathered in the courtyard of Yijing's parents. A single incandescent bulb hung from a tree, casting the only dim light on a cloudy evening. Trusted young men stood watch around the periphery to guard the meeting from eavesdropping ears.

Zhao Hong's father rose from his stool and addressed the secret assembly. "Brothers, it was in my village that Preacher Ruth's blood was shed. It was my hands that helped lift her fallen body into the cart. I have always felt a deep burden to repay the debt we owe her. Now, our entire village believes in Jesus. We have made it our responsibility to ensure that all villages receive the good news. Brother Yi, I can proudly say that 513 villages now have churches!"

The group murmured with excitement over this news. The Tuxiang elders lived so far from each other that this meeting was a difficult feat of travel and timing.

Yijing's father waited for the murmurs to subside and then stood before the assembly.

"Brothers, we have always tried to be faithful with the gift God has given us that we might share this news with all the Tuxiang villages. You remember how we harbored the three preachers and partnered with them to bring the good tidings to many of your districts. Because our Lord may return soon, we have sent out the good news as on eagles' wings through all the Tuxiang valleys.

"As much as we rejoice in this, brothers, it is not enough. Young Li Tao, my son-in-law, tells me that there are many other tribes like ours that have yet to receive the message. We *must* tell them before the Lord returns. We waited two thousand years for this light to come to us; they, too, are still waiting. The fires burn brightly here. We must take the hot coals from here and start fires there."

Elder Yi strode toward Li Tao and raised him up from his stool. "Li Tao has just graduated from university. He and my daughter, Yijing, have been mentored by the American preachers. Listen to him."

Though Li Tao was young, the Tuxiang elders nodded in respect as he stood before the assembly. "Uncles, I remain in contact with the Americans by phone. They have helped me to identify other tribes not far away that need the light. They have given us a pattern we can follow with other tribes. We can cross the mountains into Laos into places no white person can go. *We can finish the task Jesus gave us.*"

"But where can we go?" asked a voice from the circle.

"We must first go to the Phunoi people of Laos, near Phongsaly. Brothers, there are fifty thousand of them, and they have waited years for this message we hold in our hearts. Around them are several smaller tribes."

Another person asked, "Who will go? And how will they find the way?"

All heads snapped around as a young woman jumped into the circle of light, hands on her hips. Yijing shouted, "*We* will go! My husband and I! Uncles, you know that God, in His mercy, saw fit to heal me and save me first of all of the Tuxiang. I *must* show my gratitude by going to the Phunoi and beyond. My husband and I have been offered jobs in Kunming. It is what we always had dreamed of."

Li Tao strode up to her and took her hand in his. He said, "But God has changed our dream. We have no money, and we have no means, but if you will send us, we will go instead to Laos. We will find our way across the mountains and into the valleys of the Phunoi. The Spirit will guide us!"

The council of elders listened to Li Tao and Yijing then dismissed the young couple and embarked upon a time of prayer and discussion. Near midnight they summoned the couple back into the circle.

Elder Yi stood before them. "The words that you have spoken are good ones. We will send you as the first gospel-runners from the Tuxiang to other tribes. We have little to give you but these few things. First, we will send Li Tao's older brother with you to serve as a faithful partner. Second, we send you each with a sack of rice to fill your bellies. We didn't have time to gather much, but the hour is urgent. All must hear before Jesus returns!"

Another elder then stood and walked over with a small pouch held in his trembling hands. "We have collected 947 *renminbi*. It is all we have. May God multiply it for your journey, for you leave tomorrow after we have laid hands on you. We will send more money to you as we collect it from the churches."

As he uttered this pronouncement, the full moon escaped from the sheltering clouds to shine upon the small gathering.

SEVEN

At **2:30 in the morning**, Sue Jenkins looked up from the massive binocular telescope and yawned. She blinked her eyes several times and peered out from the remote Arizona peak to regain focus. She jogged around the observatory to shake off the effects of her forty-eight-hour stint.

The previous night Sue had been routinely scouring the "Main Belt," the massive asteroid belt between Mars and Jupiter, when she had happened upon an anomaly. Twelve hours into her stint, adrenaline began coursing through her veins. Through the night she had captured a series of time-delayed photos of a tiny spot in the night sky. Her advanced computer program overlaid photo upon photo with relentless monotony—while Sue waited.

All during the daylight hours, she had continued studying the photos and double-checking calculations.

Tonight should confirm her fears—or not. She jogged back over to the $100-million eye into space. She continued her vigil of peering through the lens, taking shots, and comparing photos. The computer could do much of it, but she trusted her human eye for the final conclusions.

Sue brushed her tangled tresses from her eyes as she looked up a final time and sat down at the large table in the observation room. Absentmindedly she rolled her chair to the counter and then grabbed and downed her fourth mug of stale, burned coffee. She rolled her chair back and stared at the images spread in order across the tabletop.

Though no one else shared her vigil in the observation tower, she spoke aloud, "Come on, baby. What are you? Reveal yourself!"

A number of brighter streaks appeared against a dark background in the progression of photos, but only one beckoned to Sue.

For an hour she stared at the photos she chose to print out, looking for a pattern. For the following hour, her fingers moved into overdrive, measuring with a ruler and marking pictures with a wax pencil.

Then her activity came to halt. She froze in place and gazed out into the starlit sky.

She blinked her eyes rapidly. "It can't be."

She shoved her chair back, clanging it against the coffee counter. She reached for the phone and dialed.

A groggy male voice answered, "Yeah? Who's this?"

"Dr. Dodd? This is Sue."

"Sue? What time is it?"

"Uh, I don't know. Uh, 4:53 a.m., I guess. Anyway, Dr. Dodd, I think I've discovered a rather large NEA."

"An N-E-what?"

"You know, an NEA—a near-Earth asteroid."

Sue could hear Dodd stirring. "Yes, yes, I know what an NEA is. I just didn't know if you really meant to wake me up about an NEA. Sue Jenkins, tell me about it later today. This is my night off."

"But, Dr. Dodd, this asteroid is quite sizable. I've been tracking it for two nights and comparing it with some previously taken photos. This rock looks to be ten, maybe twenty, kilometers in diameter."

At the other end of the line, Dodd yawned. "Sue, in an asteroid belt with 500,000 rocks orbiting the sun, you know a lot of bumping takes place. Do you know how many asteroids get bumped out of their orbits and pass within a few million kilometers of earth?"

Sue grimaced. "Quite a few, with one or two each year passing closer than the moon."

"Precisely. What you're describing is a normal occurrence."

Sue picked up her photographs and once more studied her calculations. "But, professor, this NEA's trajectory is dangerously close to Earth's orbit. We're talking about a pass within a *few thousand kilometers* or less. The rock's roughly 522 days out. Actually, it could pass a lot closer, but ..."

Sue could hear Dodd heave himself out of bed. "Sue, you've been tracking it only two days?"

"Yes, sir, but—"

"And the previously taken photos weren't taken with this asteroid in mind, nor were they calibrated systematically to track it, am I right?"

"Well, no, sir, no one knew at the time."

"So, you're calling me at five in the morning on my night off to tell me about an NEA that has only a what—5% probability—of heading on the trajectory you project at the mass and speed you project? Sue, what's gotten into you?"

"But, Dr. Dodd, what if I'm right?"

"Sue, it sounds *more* like you've pulled another 48-hour shift, despite my warnings. You're gonna kill yourself that way. Get some sleep! There's no way you're gonna find something that big that NASA has missed."

Sue could tell Dodd was about to hang up on her. "Dr. Dodd! Listen to me! You know it takes a good five hundred days to institute the Icarus Project and—"

Dodd choked on the other end of the line. "The Icarus Project! You honestly expect me to call NASA and tell them they need to spend several hundred billion dollars to implement an asteroid deflection program, pulling moth-balled rockets and nuclear warheads out of storage, modifying them, and shooting them into space all at the instigation of an impetuous doctoral student's two days' worth of findings? Not to mention the mass hysteria we would create by telling people a huge rock was going to fall from heaven!

"Listen, Ms. Jenkins, act like a Ph.D. student and do some serious research here. Track that thing for two solid weeks, and then give me a written report with a thorough compilation of all your data. *Then* I'll take you a little more seriously. Good night!"

Sue heard the connection drop. *Why doesn't he understand? Administrative fool! Well, I'll track this little baby. But what am I supposed to do when it goes behind the sun in six days? I'll lose contact with it for two weeks or more. Too late! Too late!*

* * *

Six days later, a red-eyed Sue Jenkins walked into Dr. Dodd's office and tossed a report on his desk. "Here you go, professor."

Dodd looked up from his work. "What's this?"

"The report you asked for on the NEA."

"Sue, I asked for this after two weeks, minimum. What's it been—five, six days?"

"Six."

"Well, then, it's premature."

"Dr. Dodd, the rock has passed behind the sun. I won't regain contact with it for two or three weeks. As I have calculated it, the NEA is on a direct course for earth; time of impact was a little off previously. I'm projecting it at 508 days out."

Dodd snorted. "You expect me to call NASA now, knowing that we can't give them anything more concrete for at least a month? Their greatest expenses are in the first few weeks when they pull the birds out and dust them off."

Dodd propped his reading glasses on the end of his nose, picked up the report, and thumbed through it slowly. "Aha! What about Mars's gravitational pull? You didn't calculate that into your figures. That'll sweep it much farther out of Earth's solar orbit."

"No, sir, I considered that. I felt that even at its closest pass to Mars, once I calculated the mass of the asteroid and its distance from Mars, I make it a 90% likelihood to result in a negligible trajectory change."

Dodd was satisfied he had scored some points. "But you don't *know* for sure. If the rock is smaller or traveling faster than you think, it may be swung way off the projected path. And I assume most of your sightings have been taken close to dawn when you are unable to get firm readings, right?"

"Of course! But look, Dr. Dodd, This is the *most likely* scenario. If it's correct, then we need to notify NASA at once. If we are wrong, they can always cancel the project. But if we're right, they need to start now!" she exclaimed.

Sue watched a bead of sweat form on Dodd's forehead despite the blast from the air conditioner.

"But ... if you don't want to call NASA yet, I can upload my findings to the Spaceguard coalition and see if any other sky-gazers have noted anything similar. Perhaps someone has calibration photos that predate the ones we have."

Dodd stood up. "No way, young lady. You're not putting one iota about this online." He cupped a hand behind his ear and batted his eyes. "'Hi! This is Sue Jenkins. We think a twenty-kilometer rock is going to hit Earth in five hundred days. Has anybody out there found anything to confirm this?' That'd go over well. We'd end up with mass hysteria."

Sue looked down at her toes. "I could do it discreetly."

"Discretion is not found in the Internet dictionary. No, you won't put anything online."

Sue said nothing but looked at him with puppy-dog eyes. The gray-haired professor really wasn't as gruff as many made him out to be, but his tough exterior helped him manage his research students.

Dodd softened a bit. "Sue, a *lot* of our funding comes from NASA. If we put this out there and we're wrong, heads are going to roll—*my* head—and funding is going to dry up. *Your* research will be at an end."

He looked into her eyes and shook his head. "Oh, okay. I'll call Rod at NASA. *But*—I'm going to shoot straight with him and give him my opinion. Where he takes it after that is his business. Got it?"

Sue hugged the old codger. "Thank you, Dr. Dodd! I'll polish up a final draft in case you want to send it to him." She hurried out the door to the analysis room.

Sue finished the final draft that day and dropped it on Dr. Dodd's desk on her way to a much-awaited and well-deserved couple of weeks of rafting in the Grand Canyon. After all, she wouldn't be able to make any more calculations for two or three weeks.

Dr. Dodd came in at the end of the day and noticed the report on his desk. He glanced at his watch. Six p.m. *Too late to call tonight.* He wrote "Call Rod @ NASA" on his to-do list right below the reminder to order a new mirror for the back-up telescope.

As he prepared to leave the office, his phone rang. "Dodd here."

His wife was on the line. "Darryl, are you sitting down?"

"What's wrong?"

"Well, I don't know how to say this, dear. Your mother...has just passed away."

"Oh, my gosh! I-I'll be right there!"

* * *

Sue arrived back in Phoenix two days before she expected the NEA to appear in the sky again. Rafting down the Colorado River had worked wonders for her, but she was eager to hear what NASA had to say.

She ignored the elevator and walked up the four flights of stairs to the astronomy department office. An elderly secretary behind the desk brightened. "Hey, Sue, welcome back. How was your first vacation in three years of doctoral work?"

Sue plopped down in the chair next to the desk. "Invigorating! But not long enough! Hey, Carol, has Dr. Dodd mentioned if he has talked to a fella named Rod at NASA recently?"

"Dr. Dodd? Not that I know of."

"Okay, I'll go talk to him. Is he still around?"

"Around? Of course not, he's still in—oh, that's right, honey, you don't know. His mother died two weeks ago. He's been in New York for the funeral and has taken a little time off. Expect him back in a couple of days, I think."

Sue's heart began racing. "He's been gone? When did he leave?"

The secretary flipped through her calendar. "Hmm, let's see. Thursday, two weeks ago."

"That's the same day I left to go rafting. Are you sure he didn't get any calls from NASA since then?"

"No, none. I'd remember that. What's so important about this anyway?"

"Oh, nothing—at least, nothing I can talk about." The secretary raised her eyebrows and whistled. "Stop it, Carol," snapped Sue. "Where can I reach Dr. Dodd?"

"You can't. He's on vacation and didn't leave a number. And he's not answering his cell." The secretary smiled apologetically.

Sue's eyes darted back and forth for a moment. "Okay, well, could you just let me in his office for a minute? I left some critical data in there, and I need the figures to continue my research tonight."

Dodd's office confirmed the adage that a messy office is the sign of a great mind, albeit in this case, also a forgetful one. Sue began searching the piles of papers and books looking for—there it was! A yellow sticky note with a barely legible to-do list. Everything from attending an oral defense to buying groceries, with several items checked off.

Then she saw it: *Call Rod @ NASA.*

No check mark.

Did that mean Dr. Dodd had not called NASA, or did it simply mean that he forgot to mark it off his list before leaving in a hurry? And leave in a hurry he did, for his mug warmer was still turned on, burnt coffee stuck to the bottom of the mug.

Sue uneasily evaluated her options. She had already promised not to talk about the NEA or upload info onto the Internet. Maybe she should just wait until the professor got back. They had already passed the 500-day mark.

Sue made a beeline for her cubicle in the doctoral student offices. She uploaded a copy of the complete report to her cloud drive so that she would have ready access to her findings from anywhere. *Information this important is too valuable to be left in the hands of just two people in one office. At least on the cloud server it will be safe.*

* * *

A recognition alarm went off in The Ten's Office of Science and Economics. The program monitoring worldwide Internet traffic and cloud storage automatically generated a priority report.

EIGHT

Michael Wroth stood silently at a window in Zurich, staring at the aquamarine waters of the lake beyond. Here in the heart of the banking district in the world's most sacred financial capital, the Office of Economics and Science for The Ten was nothing unusual. No one asked questions about what went on here. In the banking world, secrets were guarded, not flaunted, not even questioned. Certain topics were off-limits in café conversations in the streets below. The Economics and Science division fit the Zurich scene well.

In the two months since his meeting with Sayers, Wroth had survived three more attempts on his life—attempts not even disguised as accidents.

Wroth smirked. The Ten needn't hide the attacks. Terrorist cells across the globe would pay huge amounts for the death of the IC director. Even so, thanks in large part to Sayers, Wroth anticipated the assassination attempts and foiled them with his IC forces.

That was the easy part.

A slight frown creased Wroth's forehead. The challenging part was justifying his presence in Zurich when the demands on him as Director of the IC were overwhelming. Fortunately, Wroth reported only to the President of the United States, so it was not too difficult for him to justify coordinating field research and planning in a neutral European country.

Yet at each spare moment, Wroth would slip away covertly to the Economics and Science office for his mentor training.

At the faint tap on the door, Wroth shifted his eyes to the image in the window. A short Arab, holding a sheaf of folders, walked in, glancing over his shoulder before closing the door.

Wroth's words echoed off the pane. "Number Seven, how are you today? A little late for my tutoring session, aren't you?"

Number Seven sat at the small conference table, spreading the folders before him. "Uh, yes, Number Ten, I was detained by some late-breaking events I had to attend to. Have you examined the economic progress of Southeast Asia as I instructed you?"

As he talked, the Arab pulled out a slim folder and handed it to Wroth who had joined him at the table.

Wroth raised an eyebrow. Though labeled "Southeast Asia," the folder's contents were markedly non-Southeast Asian. He thumbed quickly through the pages. "I'm sorry, but I have been so busy, I haven't examined it."

The Arab glanced around at the walls, feigning anger. "Apprentices! All alike! Don't you realize that you have to sacrifice more? You must be aware of all events. Now! Read the folder quickly. I'll wait. Give me your impression of what we should do."

Wroth finally found the sheet he was searching for.

Three weeks ago, University of Arizona Ph.D. student spotted a large near-Earth asteroid (NEA). Through negligence, supervising professor has failed to notify NASA to institute Project Icarus [near-Earth asteroid deflection project]. Error still undetected.

Earliest Projections [Tentative]

• Size: 10-25 kilometers in diameter.

• Course: pass within a few thousand kilometers of earth, with 83% chance of collision.

• E.T.A.: 493 days.

• Impact: global upheaval in climate, food production, communication, etc.; immediate loss of life within several hundred miles of impact site.

• Estimated time needed to institute Icarus: 500 days. Asteroid currently outside range of detection, but will reappear in 3-5 days.

• Likelihood of detection and concurrence from other astronomical sources: likely within four to six weeks as anomalies are detected in star patterns.

Education & Science Response: Request immediate executive response ...

Wroth paused for a moment. *Undetected! What a break!* The blank bottom portion of the memo requesting a response stared at him. Wroth's mind instantly followed multiple options simultaneously. Time was running out. Silence much longer would cause listening ears to become suspicious of this "private" meeting. Wroth had searched his office meticulously. He was reasonably confident no video surveillance accompanied the certain audio bugs.

Quietly he picked up a pen and scribbled a response. Without a glance, he slid the sheet back to Number Seven.

"Look, Number Seven, I've had a tortuous schedule. It's not like I don't have any outside obligations right now. I've got so much IC work to complete, plus my training with you. Why don't you leave me with the Southeast Asia folder during lunch, and then I promise, I'll be good as new, ready to discuss whatever you want."

While Wroth spoke, Number Seven memorized the response and nodded. "Okay, Number Ten. But I'm warning you. Shape up, or you will have to forfeit your IC responsibilities. Your time is ours! I have a mind to tell Number One about this. I'll be back in two hours."

The Arab exited the room and closed the door with a bang.

The faint hiss from the document incinerator was the only fleeting record of the memo.

* * *

Two days later, a taxi carrying an astronomy professor and his wife sped onto a freeway toward LaGuardia Airport. While merging into the traffic, the cab blew a tire. The taxi driver did a remarkable job of bringing the car under control. He probably would have made it safely to the side of the road if it hadn't been for the big rig that was unable to slow down in time. The resulting collision killed all three occupants in the taxi. The truck driver escaped with a few bruises and lacerations. The police commended him for keeping his truck from jackknifing in the heavy traffic.

* * *

Three days after posting her findings privately on her virtual server, Sue Jenkins was found in her room dead from an apparent drug overdose. A housemate had noticed that she hadn't seen Sue for several days, which wasn't unusual. What *was* unusual was that she hadn't even heard Sue come in during the wee hours of the morning as she usually did.

Sue's death didn't even make the town news, though the school newspaper included a brief obituary. The astronomy department was in mourning over both tragic occurrences. One thing puzzled Sue's friends, however. She had no history of drug use.

* * *

On the Big Island of Hawaii, the observatory was quiet. It usually was, during daylight hours. Nothing much stirred, save for the quiet hum of equipment and computers.

Computers.

One specific workstation woke up, though no one was there to watch it. From a masked location, commands were automatically downloaded over the high-speed connection, altering the code in the latest star mapping software the observatory used—software that compared numerous scanned images of the stars, looking for anomalies.

Only fifteen lines of computer code were changed. From that day's evening onward, the workstation was programmed, in contrast to its designed function, *not* to notify the astronomers of a small blip of light approaching the earth. In fact, the automatic scanning of the huge telescope would almost imperceptibly avoid taking readings of a certain area of the sky.

During the next 24 hours, workstations and computers responded in dozens of observatories around the world. The reprogramming was lightning fast, two minutes or less from login to logoff.

To the astronomical world, the "Jenkins NEA" was no more. It really never had been.

* * *

Several weeks later, Wroth found himself at the Religion and Education office for his monthly mentor training. He and Numbers Three, Eight, and Nine scanned the touchscreen wall in the timeline room.

"Ahem! Why, Number Eight! It seems you've drawn in quite a bit of activity over here." Wroth bent forward to study things more closely, expanding the section in question with a sweep of his hands.

The Indian refused to give Wroth the satisfaction of his attention.

Wroth continued, "Kingdom Preparation Force, huh? Presumptuous fanatics! I told you to expect more from this group."

The Indian turned sharply. "Number Ten, no one had any idea that the group would cause this much impact."

"*I* did! I told you so."

The Indian stood erect. "As I recall, you told us on your last visit that you had anticipated it and that we should have anticipated it. But wasn't that *after* all the commotion in China? And it seems to me that you and your IC group have failed miserably in seeking to prosecute the group." Number Eight bobbed his head slightly. "Why, even your plaintiffs joined the defense. How amusing!"

Wroth turned and glared at the man. "That is not our only strategy. If you had spent even half the time on this problem that I have—I, the trainee—I think you would have neutralized this group long before now."

The Indian smiled. "Neutralize? Why should we want to do that? This KPF is playing right into our hands, doing what we could never have manipulated them to do. Sure, they have placed dozens of teams overseas. And I admit many Christian missions agencies have seen a surge in applications, funding, and activity. But that is all for naught!"

Wroth looked back at the timeline. "I beg your pardon? Thousands of zealous new missionaries are all for naught? Whose side are you on?"

The Indian strode to another section of the wall. "If you had observed the chart more carefully, you would have noticed a rather large split, right about here."

He pointed to a divergence of lines on the wall, then zoomed in. "This KPF is polarizing not just the Christian establishment, but the religious world in general. In the Christian world, churches are hard-pressed right now to decide for or against the KPF's peculiar brand of Christianity.

"The religious world is tired of mindless crusaders, regardless of the religion. Are they not fanatics? Military metaphors and jihadist lingo. Radical and total indoctrination of personnel in a boot camp setting. Sacrifice of many personal possessions. Dangerous living conditions in foreign countries. Intolerance of liberal religion or even mainstream denominations. Granted, I may exaggerate a little, but in many eyes, this is the growing perception of the KPF.

"Admittedly many churches and missions agencies are jumping on board, inspired by the fervor and success of this new type of Christianity. Yet even more are repulsed by it. They prefer a long-term, interfaith approach accompanied by less confrontation and less risk."

Wroth paced a moment then shot back, "So, what are you going to do with the KPF and the others following their lead?"

The Indian looked at his colleagues for support but got no help. Farnsworth and Number Nine were effectively within Wroth's total control. Still Number Eight answered, "Nothing! Absolutely nothing. As I said, their impact is going to be minimal —actually detrimental to their cause. In time the other mainline Christian and religious groups will step in and 'neutralize' the movement. They will not tolerate this for long. Regardless, the movement itself will die out; it can't sustain this amount of high-level energy and momentum."

Wroth turned to the Brit, Number Three, and the Korean, Number Nine. "And what about you two? What do you think we should do?"

Farnsworth and the Korean looked at each other, unsure how to answer. Finally, the Korean spoke hesitantly, "If we follow The Ten's standard operating procedure, we should do exactly as Number Eight has outlined."

"And wait another six hundred years for the Rebirth!" interrupted Wroth. "That's our problem. Fearful of being discovered, we react, rather than anticipate. We wait, rather than move. We hope, rather than guarantee. My friends, we can act secretly, *without detection*, as is within our mandate, and still neutralize this group. We can have our cake and eat it, too.

"Number Eight, you *are* right about the first part. This religious schism will play right into our hands. That was a perceptive conclusion."

The Indian looked up in surprise.

Wroth continued, "But waiting for the KPF movement to be neutralized could take decades, and the damage from their impact will be irreversible. Instead, I think there is another approach from history that might serve our purposes well."

He walked over to the wall and expanded a section normally overlooked. When the other three examined this section of the timeline, their eyes grew wider.

Wroth crossed his arms. "Using this approach, we will so disrupt KPF that the groups who follow their example and approve of their brand of Christianity will become disillusioned with them. The larger religious world and even the fundamentalist Christian establishment will unequivocally condemn them. We will eliminate the KPF, disperse the movement, and step in as the saviors! We will start with what you recommend, Number Eight, but take a giant step further."

Even Number Eight smiled.

NINE

His face and upper torso were bathed in a faint, cold glow as Christopher sat before the computer screen, the only light in his office. Christopher was an early riser. At 5:30 a.m., not much was stirring around the Owens' home/KPF headquarters, though in the basement where the communications center was housed, information gushed in hourly whether anyone was awake or not. But usually there was someone awake. Timothy and Grace had four team members that helped them monitor communications around the clock, as nighttime in California was daytime for many teams.

From the basement, Timothy called him. "Boss, you've got a call incoming from the colonel. He's calling from Afghanistan, and the line could be monitored, so remember, no Christian terms and no specifics about our teams."

"Right, Tim. Thanks." The next voice Christopher heard was Colonel Dunbar's.

"Hello, boss." Dunbar never called Christopher "commander" over monitored phone lines.

"Hello, Win. What's the word?" In the six months since the ordeal with the Grants, the KPF had witnessed a marked growth in its number of recruits and teams sent out. For the last four weeks, Colonel Dunbar had been visiting many of the sixty-three teams in the field. None of the teams had been on the ground more than four months.

"I've got a pretty full report. I wanted to get to you in time for your staff meeting this morning. I'll be brief." The colonel didn't wait for a response from Christopher before continuing. With the two-second delay from one end of the line to the other, two-way conversations became almost unbearable. They found it easier for each person on the phone to talk for a while and then to let the other respond.

"Item one: many teams are demoralized. They expected the company work to be progressing far beyond what it is now. I'll email the specific team reports to Timothy later. Basically, very few teams are seeing any of the spectacular works you saw on your company trip. They have all gone in expecting to see signs confirm their conversation, but there's virtually nothing. Progress is slow; many are feeling there is no way to start any franchises in their area within the targeted time frame of two years. They want to know what to do if they don't see any breakthroughs like you did."

Christopher responded, "They will, Win, they will. But tell them they can't expect it on their timetable. Plus, we may not always see spectacular signs. Breakthroughs may come other ways—in-depth study of the Book, acts of kindness, and clear proclamation. Tell them to be ready for anything."

"Copy that. For the record, the teams that *are* seeing the most immediate results seem to be mobilizing existing national brothers and sisters and equipping or partnering with them to reach the UUPGs in their country. The nationals speak the trade language already and can get to deeper things more quickly. Other than those few breakthroughs, the situation is as I described."

Christopher waited to make sure item number one was done. "Thanks, Win. That helps. I'll relay that helpful strategy to other teams—mobilize nationals. In the meantime, we'll turn our communication network with the Chief Executive up a notch for all our teams. Our network will be talking to Him round the clock until we see some progress."

Static threatened their conversation, but the colonel said, "Thanks, boss. I'll relay that word. Persistence is the name of the game. They'll just have to ..."

Despite the delay, Christopher cut him off, saying, "Persistent *faith*, Win. Many workers in many companies in the field, including our own, are persistent but have lost much of their vision, faith, and expectation. Our workers need persistent *faith*."

"Yes, sir. Item two: Some of our folks are falling out with workers in other companies. You know we've tried to target pioneer areas, but sometimes there are still other workers already there. If not, there are almost always other workers in the same country working with different ethnic groups. Well, it seems that word of our teams arrived ahead of us in many places among people in our line of business. Sometimes that's been good, giving our teams a little respect.

"But other times they have been met with resentment and jealousy. And we're partly at fault. Some of our workers have gone in with pretty smug attitudes, as if just being with our company means they'll produce the same results our first four teams had in Southeast Asia. Whether it's been their cockiness or just the perception of it by others, there have been some arguments and dissension. The divisiveness has caused some of the teams to get sidetracked, I'm afraid."

Christopher was almost irate when he heard this. "Listen, Win. You make this perfectly clear to every worker in the field, all five hundred of them, even those who aren't experiencing this problem. The number one thing I would do if I were the opposition would be to create disunity. We can't see results without humility and unity.

"Tell teams that insofar as it is possible with them, they must be at peace with other workers. No matter who has started the rifts, our team members are going to be the ones to start reconciliation—immediately! This will be our highest priority until these situations are settled. There may be situations where we can't prevent jealousy and hard feelings, but it won't be because our workers haven't done all they could to be humble, loving, and repentant.

"Remember what the Book says, 'If I have a faith that can move mountains, but do not have love, I am nothing.' That's the bottom line.

"Win, this is important to me. Tell the teams I'll be forwarding them my thoughts on this, along with a lot of passages from the Book that they should study and think about. Also, let them know that any worker who displays a proud or uncooperative attitude will be on the first plane back home—at his own expense. It's that serious. There's no other company in our business that is our competitor. We're all working toward the same goal. We need to show that attitude at all times.

"And for heaven's sake, if there are workers with other companies who have been there before our teams, make sure our workers show them the respect they deserve for having been there before us. They probably know the situation better than we do and are due respect for sticking it out in some pretty harsh situations."

Dunbar took this all in stride. He was most comfortable taking and giving orders, and he rarely questioned them. "Yes, sir. Final item: our teams are pretty bold, and the pressure is mounting in many regions. I'll give some specific hot spots in my email to Timothy. I just want to alert you so you can add that to your list of items for the communication network to talk to the Chief Executive about."

Christopher put a finger to the scar on his forehead, which throbbed from time to time, remembering well his own ordeals in China. "Win, we'll start talking to Him about it immediately. Relay that to the teams. Tell them not to fear what might happen. Father will take care of them." He spoke not as an armchair commander but as one who had walked the words he talked. "Anything else?"

"That's it, sir. Hope the staff meeting goes well. If all goes well here, I'll see you in about three weeks."

* * *

The living room was packed for the weekly staff meeting. Christopher started the meeting by sharing the colonel's report with the group. Nic affirmed Christopher's apprehension over the schisms developing on the field. "We've had our share of this here in the States. We can't afford it in the field. Sure, a lot of Christian groups have approved of what we're doing, but it seems like a lot more think we're strange, if not harmful."

Phil shot in, "Yeah, I was listening to KYMS the other day. We just made the bad list of the Cult Watch Association. Can you believe that? They have labeled us 'an aberrant Christian sect' that should be avoided at all costs. My parents called because they heard the program back home in South Carolina. A lot of people respect CWA, and if they label us a cult, we're going to lose a lot of recruits."

Jeanie countered, "I don't care what they label us, we know what we are. We shouldn't expect the world to love us when we try to follow Jesus wholeheartedly."

Chara added, "I agree with you, Jeanie, but it hurts when it's not just the world that hates you, but even other Christian groups."

Christopher continued speaking to the group. "Be that as it may, there is a lot of exciting news. The Southern Baptists and the Assemblies of God have both been working closely with us, as have a number of other mission agencies. They are actually utilizing much of our model and expectation for church planting among the unreached via shorter-term personnel, especially as sent out by churches.

"We're working closely to help each other; we want to not duplicate what the others are doing in the field but rather complement. Plus, they've already been doing some pretty cutting-edge thinking and training in several frontier areas. They're even going to offer us some of that training, especially in contextualizing our CPM approaches for other worldviews— Muslim, Buddhist, Hindu, and so on. They may even help fund part of our work. It's exciting!"

"And sad," interjected the normally bubbly Stacy. "My father just came back from a convention meeting. There's talk that a lot of churches in the denomination are thinking about pulling out if the mission board associates itself with us. How can this happen, especially if we're trying to live purposefully according to God's Word?"

The group was at a loss for an answer. From its infancy, the KPF had striven to be biblical and humble, no matter how radical that might look. As the group pondered this, Christopher rustled the onionskin pages of his Bible, looking for a passage.

"I think it's time we face a sobering fact," he began. "We have all been motivated by the desire to see the world evangelized and to be in that generation that welcomes Jesus' return. But if we actually are the generation, then we need to face the truth that these could be the last days. In fact, if we expect to see Jesus return within the next decade or two, we should expect to go through tribulation. Jesus described those last days in Matthew 24:9-14:

> ***Then you will be handed over to be persecuted and put to death, and you will be hated by all nations because of me.***

At that time many will turn away from the faith and will betray and hate each other, and many false prophets will appear and deceive many people. Because of the increase of wickedness, the love of most will grow cold, but he who stands firm to the end will be saved. And this gospel of the kingdom will be preached in the whole world as a testimony to all nations, and then the end will come.

"We've focused much on that last verse about preaching to all the nations so that no place is left, but what about the verses before that? We should also expect persecution, even unto death, rejection among many people groups and nations, a massive falling away of many so-called Christians, betrayal by those we once thought were loyal to us, false prophets leading people astray, and for many people to lose their love for God. It's going to be rough from here on out—if these are indeed the last days."

"How can that be?" asked Phil. Despite his frequent questions, Phil was zealous for the cause of the KPF. "I thought that in the last days there was supposed to be a massive revival and turning to God!"

Quietly Christopher asked, "Where does the Bible say that?"

Phil began to fidget, being put in the spotlight, "I-I don't know. But it's there. Revelation, I think. Yeah, what about the two witnesses who'll preach?"

"And the earth will celebrate when they die because they won't like their preaching," Christopher reminded him.

"But what about all the people who will turn to God and receive the mark of God on them?" Phil protested.

"And how many more will receive the mark of the beast? Phil, and everyone, I just don't see it in the Word. All I can see is that there will be an apostasy in the last days. Despite the fact that the gospel will go to all the nations, we should not expect a majority of the world to follow Jesus. Instead we should expect a falling away. It won't be a worldwide revival as much as a time of testing and purifying of those who are really God's people."

Phil still wouldn't admit defeat. "But won't the Jews turn to Jesus?"

Christopher answered compassionately, "Phil, I think you're right. Many Jews will become believers. I'm not saying we won't see mini-revivals in various regions. I think we will. Think about the awakening happening among the Tuxiang. But that will be the exception, not the rule. Tough as it may seem, we need to expect organizations, denominations, churches, even families to be torn apart by the stumbling block of Jesus Christ. It's the sober truth."

"Then I guess you guys are ready for my legal report," responded Renee. "I hate to convey more doom and gloom, but I received word yesterday that the International Coalition for the Preservation of World Peace, or the IC for short, will be investigating us."

Gasps were heard around the room. With all that was in the news, everyone was familiar with the group headed by former senator Michael Wroth. "They can't do that!" exclaimed Nic. "We've broken no laws. We're a legal, private organization."

Renee laughed cynically. "I'm afraid they can pretty much do whatever they want. I checked with my firm and did some additional research last night. In layman's terms, they have a special presidential mandate that allows them to bypass normal legal channels and investigate groups they believe are intolerant to the point of constituting a societal danger. That's how they've been so effective. Anyway, I just wanted to let you know. They have the right to interview anyone connected with this organization. If they contact us, we're legally bound to speak to them."

Christopher sighed. "Okay, Renee. Thanks. I'd like everyone to cooperate fully with the IC up to disclosing where our teams are. That is privileged information that we won't divulge, and I'll take the heat for that. But in terms of our methods, training, objectives—be up front. We have nothing to hide there."

The meeting continued as the group discussed various issues on the agenda. Finally, Christopher asked Grace for a report on how new applicants were progressing through the screening process.

"We saw a great spurt of new applicants," Grace began. "Of course, as you know, we have over five hundred soldiers in the field. Those were weeded out from about 2,200 applications. We have many, many more applications that have rolled in since then, but we're facing something we didn't expect. Many applicants started out very excited, but the more they have heard about what we've been talking about today, the more hesitant they've become. Others don't seem to be willing to make the sacrifice to leave family, professions, possessions, and so forth, although they don't state it in such terms. We have to read between the lines. I've been very disappointed that we aren't seeing many of the applicants follow through on their initial interest."

"'The love of most will grow cold,'" murmured Chara. "Christopher just read it to us. Now that people realize just how much is at stake, we should not be surprised that many prefer the comforts of cultural Christianity where you can be a churchgoing Christian and have all the world's pleasures too. Many of our applicants are like the seeds thrown among the thorns in the parable. They're interested in an exciting missions opportunity, but the worries of this life, the deceitfulness of wealth, and the desire for other things choke out their commitment."

Christopher added, "If that's the case, then may God sift out the committed from the non-committed. God knows we can't carry out our mission with anything less than 100% surrendered Christian commandos. At times I worry even about the ones we've already placed on the field."

Finally the meeting was adjourned. As staff were leaving, Christopher called out, "I'd like to see several people in my office immediately. Let's see ... John and Renee, Nic, Timothy, Julie, and Jeanie. The rest of you are free to get back to your work."

The selected group made its way to his office and closed the door behind them. Christopher was quite troubled, and it was apparent to the whole group. "Hey, buddy, what gives?" asked Nic.

"What Renee tells us is quite disturbing. She actually told me yesterday when she first heard about the IC inquiry. I don't have to tell you how serious this might be. Renee, why don't you paint a worst-case scenario for us."

Renee laughed. "If this isn't a switch. Usually you're asking me *not* to point out all the potential pitfalls. Well, the IC has unlimited authority to shut down any group or operation it feels is intolerant of others to a point at which it infringes on their civil liberties. Or, it can shut down any group it feels is detrimental to its own members. Case in point: last month it closed down a relatively obscure mind-control cult in Montana. It moved in with the IC security forces, confiscated all the equipment, froze all assets, and hauled away the leaders. We still don't know where the leaders are.

"It was all quiet and efficient—very hush-hush. But it marked the first time the IC has actually moved to intervene in the activities of a religious group on U.S. soil. It was kept quiet because it could be controversial. Right now, the IC leaders don't want any bad press. It seems that they are moving in a direction of closing down *any* group that might interfere with their mandate of preserving world peace.

"Theoretically, they can come in here, investigate us, and find a number of reasons to shut us down. Namely, we go into other cultures and tell people they have to 'change' if they want to be saved. *We* know it's not primarily a cultural change but a spiritual one. But spiritual changes often cause people to be transformed with respect to their culture. They can probably find justification to shut us down on that issue alone. Problem is, I have no idea how broadly they interpret their mandate. Second issue: they can determine that we are harmful to our members: disrupting families, physical danger on the field—case in point, Ruth Grant—and so on. The long and short of it is, we have no legal recourse if they want to shut us down."

Nic was incredulous. "This is crazy! This is America. Whatever happened to due process and all that? This is a free country!"

Renee continued patiently, "American case law is currently reacting against terrorism as well as groups that don't adopt the new American supreme value: tolerance. America is not the bastion of Christendom any longer."

Christopher interrupted her. "*That* is my very concern. I believe the day is coming when we may find ourselves in a country hostile to biblical Christianity. Remember that during the European Reformation many so-called 'Christian' governments and 'Christian' groups persecuted others that were pursuing a more biblical Christ-walk.

"Let's not be surprised by whatever happens. We've learned how to operate underground. That's what we're doing in most countries overseas. If we have to, we can do it here in America. God help us if America becomes a hostile country. Now, I've called just the few of you here because I want to do something, and it must remain absolutely secretive. I trust each of you implicitly and leave it in your hands about who you will disclose it to. Of course, you will want to discuss these things with your spouses, some of whom I didn't invite to this meeting so that our meeting wouldn't create too big a stir among the rest of the staff. I mean, how important a meeting can this be if my wife and other core leaders aren't here? I'm keeping this small and depending on you to relay the word to the appropriate people, but only those you trust without *any* shadow of a doubt.

"Here's what I want to do, and it must be done within the next week. I want to set up two alternate command sites for the KPF. We will call them Site B and Site C. This will be Site A. The other two sites must be completely 'underground.' And, they must each be fully functional command centers capable of directing KPF affairs all by themselves if necessary. In addition, I want them to be completely mobile in case they need to move fast. Let's modify a couple of old multi-stop delivery trucks—you know, like UPS trucks. I think Nic has access to some. Is this technologically feasible, Timothy?"

Timothy ran his fingers through his disheveled mop of black hair and sighed. "Yes, I guess so. But in a week? Maybe, if I do nothing else but that. And it's not going to be cheap."

"We'll worry about the money later. The second component of my plan is based on what our U.S. military does. I had an uncle who flew on one of the strategic air command airplanes. There is always one in the air that can guide U.S. military operations in case of a catastrophe like a nuclear attack. During the Cold War, we used to keep a third of our air force aloft at all times. With Chara and me, Stewards, Fernandezes, Dunbars, Wus, and several of the single staff—Julie, George, Kellie, maybe a couple of others—we need someone posted at each of our three command sites at all times. In other words, at each of the two secret sites we must have a skeleton crew that alone is capable of running the KPF in case the other two are incapacitated. However we devise that schedule, you will need to come and go from that site in absolute secrecy so that no one follows you there or knows that where you are is a command site."

A few gave Christopher looks of skepticism as he continued, "I know this sounds like something from a spy novel, but I think it is the most prudent action. What would we do if tomorrow the IC walked in here, closed down everything, and arrested us leaders? What would our team members in the field do? We can't let them down, even if that means going underground, and even if going underground means we are part of what the IC labels an illegal organization. We have to obey God even when it conflicts with our laws. If any of you are not comfortable doing this, you're free to bow out of the KPF. For the time being, we can set up the sites. We need to be ready. We face a shrewd enemy who is as old as this earth. We can't afford to underestimate him."

Julie, the command center logistical affairs coordinator, asked, "But Christopher, why keep this so hush-hush with the staff?"

"Because of some of the other biblical passages I didn't read today. Not only will we be persecuted from without but even some of those from within will rise up and betray us. Friendly fire will wound us much more deeply than attacks from outside. Keep the circle small."

TEN

Yijing knocked furiously on door of the small house in the market town of Ban Khong, Laos. Several hands pulled her inside and slammed the door shut behind her. She fell into the arms of the Phunoi sisters, panting breathlessly. One young Phunoi woman stared nervously out the curtained window into the town's only street, watching for the pursuers. Another Phunoi sister brought Yijing a cup of tea and waited for her story to unfold.

"They are rounding up everyone, especially the men. During the Phunoi leaders' meeting, the national police burst through the front door. Not the local police; the *national* police! How could they know we were there? How could the location of our meeting have leaked out?"

Yijing paused to catch her breath and take a sip of tea. Another sister put an arm around Yijing to comfort her. Breathlessly she continued, "We were in the back room. Li Tao and his brother were training the new Phunoi elders. We had just finished making plans for taking the gospel to other tribes in Laos. As soon as the front door slammed open, my husband instinctively knew we were in danger. He only thought of the others and me. He turned to me and whispered in my ear, 'Get the gospel-runners. Send them to these locations. Go quickly before they capture you all, my love. Jesus is coming!' He thrust a piece of paper into my hand and pushed me out the back window while the elders held the inner door shut against the police."

Yijing pulled from her pocket a crumpled piece of notebook paper and held it gingerly. "My last glimpse was of the policemen beating my husband with the butts of their rifles."

Sobs wracked her body, and the piece of paper fluttered to the floor.

After several minutes, she drew her sleeve across her face, drying the flood of tears. Her eyes narrowed. She picked up the list and stared at the fourteen young Phunoi women she had mentored. None was older than twenty-two nor had been a

Christ-follower longer than nine months. But each was completely abandoned to Jesus. A new wave of Christian commandos stood ready for Yijing's directions.

"On this sacred list, purchased with the blood of my husband and your dear relatives, are the names of over twenty tribes that have never received the gospel. The largest of these is the Tai Nua, a tribe the same size as yours. Surrounding them in the valleys are multiple smaller tribes. You Phunoi have faithfully brought the King's news to the other small tribes nearby. Now you must take the message to these more distant tribes that live 200 kilometers to the south. You have been prepared for this. You know what to do. Spread the hot coals from this fire to new places!"

Each of the seven pairs came to Yijing for the names of two or three tribes that were to be their mission destinations. Yijing hurriedly gave them the names of small market towns nearby.

"We do not have much time. Jesus may return sooner than we thought. And the police are following upon our heels. Run as fast as you can. You must stay ahead of them. Stay near the mountain ridges and away from the Mekong River valley where there are so many officials. Do not stop until you reach the tribes I am assigning you. Preach the good news boldly, and expect God to work miraculously. If God has mercy upon us, I will meet you in Luang Prabang one month from today. Now go in the power of the Spirit!"

As she uttered these last words, the woman at the window cried out, "Sister Yijing, the police are here! There is no escape!"

Yijing rushed to the window to and saw that both the front and back doors were surrounded by police. Desperation began to rise up in her heart. She gathered her young sisters next to her, and they began to lift their voices to heaven.

As the police prepared to knock down the doors, the sound of other shouting drifted into the small house. Not the shouts of the police. Rather a mob of Phunoi townspeople came rushing up to the house. The police quickly gathered around the front door to prepare for the onslaught of the crowd. Seeing their only chance of escape, Yijing grabbed the women and ran to the back door. "Your relatives have bought these few minutes with their blood. Make them proud. Flee to the mountains, my gospel-runners!

Flee to the lost tribes! Pray that we see each other in one month!"

While the police beat down the mob in front of the house with their rifles and clubs, the young female Kingdom commandos escaped into the night followed by their trembling, husband-less leader.

ELEVEN

The office of John Steward, Associate Professor of History, was small yet normally fastidiously clean and neatly organized. But not so in the wee hours of this Tuesday morning. The office opened into an adjacent room of the same size where two graduate students sat on the floor sorting papers and occasionally fiddling with the Mac on the small desk in the corner, waiting for printouts.

An overweight Ph.D. student named Hal, the department fixture for the last six years, sat as close to a shapely brunette as he dared. Alicia, the newcomer of some three months, paid him only enough attention to get the job done, especially in light of his flirtatious glances. Actually, Alicia had stirred the hearts of all the male students in the department and even those of a professor or two. She was a definite distraction but remained icy toward most men.

This coldness disturbed John, who figured she must have had some painful experiences with men in her past. Strangely, she was quite open and genuinely warm around him. Of this he was glad, since he was her supervising professor. John hoped that her openness to him might allow him to witness to her in a fatherly way. John mused to himself that this was probably the deciding factor in why he had selected her from among his students to assist him at the history convention in San Diego the upcoming weekend. It didn't hurt, however, that she seemed to be the most ambitious and focused Ph.D. student he had ever supervised.

John's phone rang. "Hello?"

"Hey, John. It's Christopher."

"I figured it had to be you. Who else would call at 1:15 a.m.? Surely not Renee. She has gotten really absorbed in all the legal ramifications of the IC investigation. She called me earlier and said she would be working most of the night at her office."

Christopher sighed. "Yeah, I know. You both are burning the midnight oil tonight—again. Listen, I'm calling to see if you want to break away and pick up the colonel at LAX. His plane arrives in an hour."

John looked at the mess on his desk, the mess on the floor in the other room, Alicia who was watching him, and Hal, who had packed up and was walking out of the office, closing the door behind him. "Christopher, I can't. You know I have that convention this weekend. I'm going to be one of the major presenters, and I really have to finish a few slides."

"Okay," said Christopher. "Wish you could. I'm sure the colonel will have a lot to tell us about, and I want to get the scoop first."

John could hear the disappointment in his voice. "Me, too. Wish I could be there. Call me in the morning, and we'll have coffee together. I'm sure I'll still be awake."

Christopher hesitated briefly then continued, "John?"

"Yeah?"

"Is everything okay with you and Renee? Everything okay at home?"

John smiled at his friend's expression of concern. "Things are okay. They just feel a little disjointed right now, but I think it's because we've both been working under some tough deadlines."

"I know. I feel partly responsible. Renee is donating so much of her time to KPF in addition to her normal caseload. As soon as this IC thing blows over and your convention is finished, we're going to figure out how to let you two get a little second honeymoon together."

John sighed. "That'd be nice. Salute the colonel for me."

As he hung up the phone, Alicia came to stand unusually close to John, handing him a flash drive with the latest version of his PowerPoint presentation. John avoided her eyes. "Thanks, Alicia. I noticed Hal packed things up for the night. Why don't you pack up too? I can finish here."

She plopped down in the chair across from him and caught his attention, holding his eyes with hers. "Dr. Steward, I can't leave until we're finished. You can't do all this by yourself. I know how important this presentation is to you. This could be your big break in academia, an opportunity to build a name for yourself, and I want to help you if I can. You'll probably do the same for me one day. That's why I was so honored you picked me to be your grad assistant this weekend. I'm going to stick with you to the end."

Getting up, Alicia reached over and patted his hand, then left to work in the other room. "By the way, can I make some more coffee? We're going to have a long night."

John avoided eye contact with her as a frown creased his forehead. "Yes, that would be nice, Alicia. And please open the outer door to the hallway. You know my policy."

* * *

The colonel's confident, special force's gait was unmistakable as he walked up the ramp in the international terminal at LAX, looking around for who might greet him. Jeanie and Christopher both waved and then embraced him. The colonel said, "Commander, I'm surprised to see you here."

Jeanie chided him, "Don't be, Winthrop! Soldiers deserve a soldier's welcome."

"Even in the middle of the night," laughed Christopher. "But where's the rest of your luggage?"

Win carried only one medium-sized duffel bag. Jeanie answered for him. "Commandos travel light, Christopher. Come on, let's get in the car."

Christopher walked a little apart from the other two to give them time to renew their relationship. Finally in the car, he peppered the old soldier with questions. "Okay, Win. So give me the whole story. What's your read on the situation with our teams?"

The colonel craned his neck around to look at Christopher.

"Hold on, Win. If you are going to turn and look at me the whole way, your neck's gonna get discombobulated. Just put your visor down and look at me in the mirror."

"Whatever you say, sir. Overall I'm pleased with the progress of our teams. Of course, I wish we had had more time for training before they hit the field, but we really needed them out there to stay on pace for NoPlaceLeft 2025. As I was leaving, a few of the teams were starting to see some salvations. As you told me, I relayed to them to be patient, have faith, and take a few risks. I pounded into them the importance of unity and humility. I think things are going pretty well in that area. They're even fasting weekly to ensure they stay humble."

The colonel paused for few moments, concern registering on his face.

"But something's bothering you, right?"

The colonel looked up and met Christopher's eyes as he glanced in the mirror. "Absolutely. Somehow things are not right in many areas. The teams seem to be in an unusual amount of danger."

"Win, there's a reason most of the unreached areas are unreached. They're tough. Really tough. That's why we're there. We're commandos, and so there are going to be casualties. I know that doesn't make it any easier. Actually it makes it harder, because we know that wherever we send these teams, it's where the fight should be the toughest. But the members know that. They know it's risky. They've decided to accept that risk. This is what *you* have been preaching to me since you joined the KPF."

The colonel didn't say anything, but from behind the steering wheel came the needling voice of his wife. "Winthrop Dunbar, are you going to withhold information from your commanding officer? I'm surprised at you. What's the *real* issue?"

The red-faced giant turned away. "Aw, Jeanie. Don't do this to me. I don't have any more information to give, just deluded hunches from an overly jaded old colonel."

Christopher spoke urgently. "Win, one of the things I admire about you is your brutal honesty. I want to hear *all* your unfiltered hunches and scatterbrained ideas. Let me hear your 'feel' for the situation and make my own judgments."

Win looked over his shoulder at Christopher. "All right, sir. It's not the risk that's bothering me. I know more about risk than any of you. I am concerned, however, about a new variable in the equation. Sir, in light of the exposure we got in our first mission ventures and then with the Ruth Grant affair, we have exercised more caution and secrecy than we ever dreamed we would need to. We have sent team members out of this country in ones and twos rather than as teams so as not to attract attention. They've gone into most countries the same way. We've sent them out of different stateside airports—L.A., San Francisco, San Diego, New York, Washington, DFW—all so they wouldn't be traced to the KPF. In some especially sensitive countries, the teams are never together as a whole so that they attract less attention. We've got great visa platforms for most to be in their respective countries.

"Commander, for most of my life my job has been to ensure the secretive, unnoticed insertion of special ops teams into sensitive situations. I think I know what I am doing. Yet, despite these and other precautions, many of our teams are under intense scrutiny and suspicion. I don't understand it. There is absolutely no reason I can find for them to be suspected of anything connected with the KPF."

"But they're witnessing, aren't they, Win?"

"Yes, sir, of course. But most of that is done discreetly or behind closed doors. Still they're eyed with suspicion. I hate to say it, sir; it's why I didn't say anything earlier, but ..."

"What is it, Win?" Christopher prodded him.

The colonel finally blurted out, "I think we have a leak! It's the only thing that makes sense. I remember one time I took a special ops team deep into North Vietnam during the conflict. No one knew we were going in except for three administrative personnel at HQ. Not even my soldiers knew until we were in the air. I'm talking *total* secrecy, sir. We got into our landing zone smoothly, no hitches. No one could have seen us. But when we arrived at our target site, the enemy troops were waiting for us. They surrounded us, completely cut us off. Out of the twelve of us, only two survived. Years later, we found out that one of the three trusted officers at HQ was working for the Viet Cong.

"I have the same feeling now, sir. There have been certain situations where they couldn't have known we were KPF or missionaries or even Christians, but somehow they knew the KPF connection. Someone's tipping them off. We've got a Judas."

The car was silent as it sped along the Century Freeway. Christopher broke the silence. "That's a weighty charge to make."

The colonel listed factors off in a tight voice. "Item one. Before we inserted one of our Middle Eastern teams, we examined the strategy of a team with another organization in the same general region. After learning the hard way—persecution— they limited groups of local believers to six or less. So, we sent our team in with the same guidelines. Same country, different people group.

"First few converts began to meet. Soon they multiplied, but our team members were so concerned about the local authorities that they limited the groups to four individuals each. Plus, only one team member would meet with each group to teach them and that only every third meeting.

"On one of those third meetings, our KPF team member was late, thank God. As he was walking up the back alley to the apartment building, two police cars screamed past him and halted at the building. He waited in the shadows to see what would happen and shortly saw the four new believers handcuffed and driven off. He heard the police questioning them about where the fifth member was, but the believers said nothing. Commander, they were after *him*—trying to catch him in the act.

"Item two. One of our team members in Southeast Asia was arrested and taken into the local police station. The sergeant who arrested him asked him about his companions, his studies in the local university, etc. Our team member handled himself honestly and respectfully without disclosing any important information. The sergeant, growing frustrated with his inability to gain any useful information and losing face, since his superior officer had just walked in, stood right in the face of our team member.

"He said, 'We know who you and your teammates are! We know what the KPF is. You're going down.' He was going to say even more, but his superior officer pulled him away and slapped him a couple of times. The impression our team member got was that this was information the police didn't want to let on they had. The superior officer apologized to the member and let him go, presumably to watch him and crack down at a more opportune time. Need any more examples, sir?"

"He was sure that the officer said 'KPF'?"

"Absolutely."

"And no one on the team could have slipped and said something about KPF before that?"

"Absolutely not."

Christopher sighed in frustration. "Then I have to agree with you. Somehow, someone knows about our teams ahead of time. But who could have told them? Perhaps one of the team members said something before leaving the States, and a parent or friend inadvertently leaked the information."

The colonel disagreed. "No, sir. It's too widespread for that. I could give you ten more examples. There's inordinate suspicion in many fields. I think the problem has to be somewhere here at HQ. It must be with someone who knows where the teams are placed. How many people have access to that information?"

Christopher counted in his head. "It's hard to say, really. The only ones who know for sure are the people who work in the communications center. That's Timothy and Grace plus a couple of their helpers, Phil Young and Cassandra Brown. In addition, the core leadership team would know."

The colonel was a little surprised. "Phil Young? Wasn't he on your original team? I would expect him to be leading a team by now."

"I would too, but he was really shaken up by what happened to our team—especially to Ruth. He was disillusioned and confused for a few weeks. He even wondered about his future with the KPF. He's a zealous young man, however, and when he found out he could help significantly at home with the safety of our teams abroad, he felt he had finally found his niche. He's been very effective in communications. No way he'd betray us."

"And the Wus. They have access to everything, right?"

"Of course, Win, but they're completely reliable. There's no way in the world either of them could be the mole."

"Okay, sir, you said it's hard to say how many people have access to the team locations. What do you mean?"

"In the last three weeks, we've experienced a lot of transition. It's one of the reasons I insisted on you coming back for a while. We've set up two more command centers in secret locations."

Christopher described for him the uncertainty he felt about the IC probe and how he had initiated the new changes. "We've had a number of people training to command the various sites. In addition, there is the core staff that has always had access to and made decisions in the war room: the usual folks—us, the Stewards, the Fernandezes, plus a few of the singles, especially Kellie, Julie, Lance, and George from my original team. Win, I can't imagine who might be leaking information."

"The *whole* core staff has access to this information, not just the communications personnel?"

"That's right."

"Well, sir, you can see why I was so reticent to leave the field when there's a Judas and our teams are in danger. Sir, the circle with access to sensitive info is much too large. The traitor must be someone close to us who is disgruntled. Probably someone you named already. It can't be a new recruit—been going on too long."

"Win, I trust them all implicitly." He glanced at the colonel in the mirror. "What? What is that face?"

"Permission to speak freely, sir?"

"Of course!"

"What do you know of Dr. John Steward? Frankly, sir, from the time I joined this outfit, he's always the first one to object to new ideas. He seems to counter you at each turn."

"He can be a little, uh, ..." Christopher's phone startled all of them. He picked it up and read the number. "Hmm, comm center calling at this hour?"

The voice at the other end of the line was Phil Young's. "Christopher? This is Phil. I'm the only one at the comm center. Just got here an hour ago. No one else was here when I arrived, which is very strange. Something terrible has happened, but I don't think I should talk about it over the phone. Everything's falling apart!"

"Okay, Phil. We're heading north on the Harbor Freeway and should be there in twenty minutes. Where's Timothy?"

"I don't know. No one was here when I started my shift."

"No one was there?"

"No, Christopher. No one!"

Christopher hung up and dialed Timothy and found him at Site B. "Hey, boss. Where are you? I've been here for four hours waiting for you just like your note said."

"What note?"

"The one you left telling me to leave Site A immediately and join you at Site B."

"You've waited for me for four hours? I didn't leave you a note. Why didn't you call me?"

Timothy was as startled as Christopher. "Boss, you're note said don't call you. It was too sensitive. I was to wait for you at Site B until you called."

Christopher was so frustrated he wanted to scream. "We're going to Site A. Phil's there, and he said something terrible has happened. Join us there immediately."

He hung up the phone and turned to the colonel. "We've got a traitor, alright. From the emotion in Phil's voice, it sounds like the damage is already done. I just hope he was able to isolate the impact. Jeanie, step on it!"

TWELVE

Jeanie sped into the Owens' driveway just ahead of Timothy. Christopher, the Dunbars, and Timothy all ran downstairs to the comm center two steps at a time. Monitors, maps, whiteboards, countdown timers, and the hum of the two servers surrounded the trembling Phil Young. "I'm so glad you're here. Something strange is happening. I just got here at two this morning and found this."

"Two?" cried Timothy. "What do you mean? You were supposed to be here at 11 p.m. to relieve me. That's the only reason I was willing to leave a bit early to meet Christopher at Site B."

Phil stuttered, "Y-y-yes, that's right, but you left a note on my door last night telling me to not come in until two. See?" He held out a sticky note with Timothy's signature at the bottom.

Timothy examined the paper with a puzzled look then glanced defensively at Christopher and the colonel. "This isn't my signature. I didn't leave the note."

The commanding voice of the colonel cut in, "It doesn't matter right now, soldier. What's the problem you called us here for, Mr. Young?"

Phil, white-faced, looked at the colonel. "In the last four hours, two of our teams have been arrested."

The colonel looked to Christopher, who deferred to him. "Mr. Wu, please close the door. Mr. Young, which teams have been arrested, and why do you say that?"

Phil sat at the nearest computer terminal and made a few keystrokes. In a few moments, a speaker spit out the recording of a muffled telephone call. "Hello? This is Team 47. I don't know why you're not answering, but we're in trouble. I repeat, we're in trouble. Right now the police have broken in the front door and arrested two of my teammates. They'll find me in the back room soon. I don't ... " A door burst open in the background and shouts filled the room. Then there was dead silence.

Phil bowed his head into his hands and moaned. "It's just like it was for us in China all over again! Exactly the same! And no one was here to get their call! Someone is always supposed to be here to take the call! *Always!*" Sweat drenched his shaking body.

Timothy walked over to Phil to comfort him. "Phil, there was nothing you could have done if you had been here."

Phil pushed him away. "Get away from me! Like I said, there's *always* supposed to be someone here, and there *was* someone here when they called. That person listened and did nothing!"

Colonel Dunbar stepped up and barked, "Explain yourself, soldier!"

"I checked the time the phone call was made. Team 47 called in at 12:39 this morning. I checked the system to see where Team 47 was and discovered in the download manager that someone had downloaded the complete names and addresses of all members of Team 47 to a computer within that country at 11:09 p.m. our time. I also noticed that at 11:12 p.m., the same information was downloaded about Team 26. For the last hour I have tried reaching Team 26 on their secure line but have received no response."

Timothy was incredulous. "This is crazy! I built impregnable firewalls into the system, and the whole network is encrypted. No one can get onto the system and download that kind of information without a password unique to each individual."

The colonel probed further. "Mr. Young, where was Team 47?"

Phil stared at Timothy and hissed, "Ask him! Every download, every inquiry, every encounter in our system is identified by someone's initials. Like he said, everyone has a unique password. The initials next to the downloads for both Team 47 and Team 26 were Timothy Wu's!"

Timothy looked like a caged animal, eyes wide with fright. "What are you saying? I would never do that. I *didn't* do that. They couldn't be my initials—I was at Site B, just like the boss told me."

Phil brought up the download list for the last twenty-four hours. Next to the two most recent entries—one to North Africa, the other to Southeast Asia—were Timothy's initials.

Christopher looked at Timothy pityingly, trying to hold back the emotion. "Timothy, go to my office upstairs. I want to talk to you before I dismiss you. Jeanie, accompany him upstairs." Shoulders slumping, Timothy slunk up the stairs like a whipped dog.

Christopher eyed the stairs and waited until the soundproof door was shut. "Thanks for your help, Phil. I'm sorry you, of all people, had to be here when it happened. The colonel and I were just talking on the way over here that we felt there might be a leak somewhere. We don't know where this is all going to lead, so the colonel will stay here with you to monitor the situation. Keep trying to reach those two teams. Win, you round up the critical staff we need right now. I'll be back down in a few minutes."

When Christopher entered his office, Timothy was sitting on the couch in a daze with Jeanie next to him. As Christopher entered, Timothy looked up with tears in his eyes, "Christopher, I swear to you on everything I believe in: I didn't leak that information!"

Christopher sat on the other side of him. "I know you didn't. Jeanie told me she was with you at Site B until 11:20 p.m. There's no way you could have made it back and sent those downloads, my friend. Is it possible that someone could have gotten your password?"

Hope filled Timothy's eyes. "What's 'possible'? Anything is possible in cyberspace. Our password protocol is very advanced. But any encryption system can be hacked if enough forces are brought to bear on it. But what did you say a minute ago about dismissing me ...?"

Christopher smiled. "Oh, sorry. I did that for Phil's benefit. At this point in time, other than you, I don't know who I can trust outside of Chara, Jeanie, and Win. I would like to trust everyone, but we have a leak. If I know I can trust you, then I'm going to use that to smoke out a fox. If your ego can handle it, we need for people to suspect that you're the traitor for a while.

"In the meantime, I *am* dismissing you and Grace—to Site B. This site has been compromised. Hopefully Site B won't be compromised, because you and Grace are going to man it round-the-clock. Might as well move a mattress into the back of that old delivery truck!" Christopher said. "And from now on, although it will appear that we are controlling things from Site A, I want them really run from Site B. Can you arrange that?"

Timothy became his usual flabbergasted self. "Wow, boss. That's a tall order. You want me to intercept all communications both directions and alter them as you see fit, yet never let Site A know what is happening, right?"

"Something like that. Site B will be a shadow command."

"Okay, boss. I'll be there first thing in the morning."

Christopher spoke very seriously. "No, Timothy. I need you there now. Grace can pack up your stuff and join you in the morning. If you haven't forgotten, we have two teams to try to save. I want you at Site B in twenty minutes.

"Your first order of business is to get a message to every team out there. As soon as they get the message, they are to take an immediate vacation from their field site. They will call us only from public phones or new disposable cell phone numbers on our secure line. We will instruct them as we go."

Jeanie added, "Timothy, in the military we call this 'damage control.' We don't know if we can save Teams 26 and 47, but we need to save the other teams and do it quickly. I'll be joining you at Site B in a couple of hours, right after I take Winthrop to the airport. Am I right, Christopher?"

"I'm afraid so, Jeanie. Sorry, but we need Win out there. I'd rather go, but ..."

She scolded him, "Oh, don't be silly! You're on the blacklist in most limited access nations. This is the calling of the officer's wife. At least I know it's for a good cause. And if any human being can help those teams, I believe it's Colonel Winthrop Dunbar."

* * *

All Christopher and the KPF leadership team did for the next four days was wait and watch. Though an assortment of individuals manned the Site A comm center at headquarters, Christopher depended most on Timothy at Site B. Tuesday showed no news anywhere on the international networks of either team being arrested. All Timothy could give Christopher was his best guess. It appeared that all eight members of the

North Africa team had been arrested the night before, but apart from the fragmented call the KPF had received, nothing more was forthcoming. By early Thursday morning, Pacific Standard Time, the colonel had arrived in the North African state and immediately began pressure through the diplomatic channels for the team's release. His first call back to the KPF indicated that the government had no knowledge that any team members had been arrested. The second call was much more alarming, however. Christopher was waiting at Site B when the call arrived.

"What's the situation, Win?"

"Pretty bad, sir, and let me remind you this is not a secure line. There's a good reason the government has no knowledge of their arrest. It turns out they were kidnapped by a guerrilla group—you probably know the one—it's in the news a lot. There's a lot of turmoil here in country. The word from the terrorists is that they want a confession from our group stating that we are a subversive group trying to upset Muslim cultures throughout the world. They also want assurances that we will not send people into this or any other country that has a Muslim government or a majority Muslim population."

Christopher pulled at his hair. "We can't do that, Win. Every member of our organization knows that our unwavering policy is that we don't negotiate with terrorists. Nor can we make a promise or a statement like the one they want. What do they say they'll do if we don't negotiate?"

The colonel hesitated and then replied, "Execute them at midnight local time, which is 3:00 p.m. for you."

"Win, isn't there anything you can do, you know, like how you helped me in Asia?"

"Sir, I can't say. My resources on such short notice are very limited. I will try to press for an extension. That's all I can do. In the meantime, I will see if the government can do anything more."

"Thanks. By the way, no word from the group in Southeast Asia. It's near your old stomping grounds. I'll let you know as soon as we have word."

For several hours nothing transpired. It was the worst kind of waiting. Christopher would almost rather have bad news than no news as he agonized over the fates of sixteen Christian commandos in the two different countries.

At 5:00 p.m. word came from Southeast Asia. The eight team members had been found guilty of espionage and proselytizing. They were all being sent to prison for sentences ranging from two to eight years.

Christopher immediately got in contact with Win and relayed the information to him. The colonel responded, "Sir, we just reopened a consulate there, and an old military buddy of mine is on the new staff. I'll call him and see if we can't press them for a straight deportation."

The next day most news sites included breaking stories of both developments. Pictures of many of the sixteen team members were included, along with brief biographies. News of the terrorists' threat was played up, and on the front page of every news site and newspaper was the picture of Seth McGorman, who was in his early twenties. The terrorist group in North Africa had indeed granted a forty-eight-hour extension, but only after executing McGorman. Already the group had uploaded a gruesome video of the event onto the Internet.

America was appalled—not only by the terrorist group's actions, but also by the apparently reckless nature of an upstart organization called the KPF.

Christopher received a phone call from Win confirming Seth's death just minutes before the news broke publicly.

KPF members were shell-shocked over both the death and the way their organization was being maligned by the media. Accusations of abuse and mind control resurfaced, along with calls for some sort of government intervention to stop the whole organization.

Pacing in Site A, where he had to keep a high profile now, Christopher threw both hands up into the air. "Our second martyr in such a short time! What are we doing? Why Seth? He was so young!

"And where did the press get these pictures and bios? How did they get their names? That information is kept on an encrypted server!"

Chara wrapped him up in her arms. "Honey, I'm sure they got them the same place the terrorists and governments got the names. We all knew there was this risk."

Christopher pulled away and bent over double. "No, we didn't. We knew there would be a normal risk, but this is the risk that comes by having a traitor in our midst. This young man died, and others may also, because of a *traitor*, not because of the inherent risk of being a KPF missionary!"

He stumbled to the adjacent room. "I-I've got to call Seth's parents."

Other front-page articles confirmed the report Win gave them about Team 26. The government of the Southeast Asian country had tried and found guilty the eight team members in that country, but out of generosity and as a gesture of goodwill, it had decided to waive their jail time and deport them.

Renee muttered to Chara, "Makes their government sound like the epitome of mercy and kindness, the way our press interprets it. Not one word of how the colonel pressed them until they waived the jail time under diplomatic coercion. We come out looking like the bad guys, not them!"

No sooner had Christopher finished with his call than Phil emerged upstairs. He stared at his leader's disheveled hair and bloodshot eyes. "Christopher, we're getting dozens of calls each hour—parents, our blog readers, you name it—all urging us to negotiate with the North African terrorists."

Grabbing his head with both hands, Christopher groaned. He shouted, "We're not negotiating! Got it? Everybody here got it?"

The room went silent. The team had never seen Christopher lose control. Feeling conspicuously ashamed, he turned and left the house to walk—just to walk—anywhere.

The others watched. No one wanted to say anything. Chara broke the silence. "Phil, how long before the terrorists are supposed to execute more of our people?"

Phil stammered, "Uh-uh, tomorrow, 3:00 p.m. our time."

"Okay, then, let's go downstairs. I'm going to dictate an urgent prayer request for you to send out to our prayer network immediately. And where is Nic?"

Phil consulted the ubiquitous clipboard he carried around. "He's flying back from a New York business trip this very moment. Should be in town around four o'clock this afternoon."

Chara wasn't used to running things. "All right, leave him a message to come here as soon as possible. Christopher needs him. And where's Julie? She's been strangely absent the last two days despite the call for all leadership to report for duty."

Phil replied, "She called in to say she's been deathly sick and in bed the last forty-eight hours."

"Well, we'll need to get her out of bed. I need her here to run the office while Christopher is gone. No one, outside of Timothy, knows the system here like she does. If I need to nurse her back to health, I'll do it. The rest of you, do what you're supposed to do. If you have nothing else pressing, pray. As a matter of fact, unless you are helping to solve this problem logistically, please pray. Come on, Phil, we have a message to send."

* * *

Standing in the American embassy in the North African nation, Colonel Dunbar almost barked over the phone. "Jerry, what do you mean? You boys have no information about where these terrorists are? How can I organize a team to get them out if I have no information?"

The voice at the other end tried to appease him. "Sir, you know I'd find it for you, of all people, if I could. Either the government doesn't know, or the information is being blocked. I have run into a concrete wall here. No info. Nothing. Sounds like the State Department is taking over."

Though he was fuming, the colonel avoided disconnecting the phone. "Okay, Jerry. But if you could ever work on a problem with all your resources, this one is it. There are seven innocent kids out there who are going to be dead in twelve hours if I don't get that information, plus a chopper and a few good men."

All that Saturday afternoon, the day of the scheduled executions, the colonel labored. For the first time he could remember, however, his every effort was stymied—whether in getting the location of the team members, or recruiting a group of commandos, or procuring a helicopter. Win Dunbar had somehow met his match. His call to KPF at 7:00 p.m. local time arrived in Site B at 10:00 a.m. Pacific Time.

Christopher was there, numb, though surrounded only by the Wus, Jeanie, and Nic.

Christopher had never heard Win like this. He was a defeated man. "Sir, I've failed. There is nothing I can do. I have no information. Even if I got it now, I could not get a rescue team in time. All we can do now is—is—pray. I think we'd better face the facts. They killed one young man already. They are willing to kill again and have vowed that there will be no extensions this time."

THIRTEEN

From 30,000 feet above the desert floor, a bomber dropped four torpedo-like bombs, the wind whistling by them as they sped to earth. At an altitude of 5000 feet, the faintly whirling propellers and stubby wings on each bomb cooperated with an onboard computer to guide it above a small village. Skimming at a thousand feet above the village, each issued a profusion of gas that, together with that from the other bombs, blanketed this nervous desert village late in the evening. Just as silently, the computers guided the smart bombs to a desolate area ten miles away where they quietly embedded themselves in the surrounding dunes. By morning, they would be covered by the drifting sand.

The colorless, odorless gas sank lazily over the town and seeped into every room and crevice. People who were not asleep already began yawning and closing their eyes. In five minutes, the whole town of 700 slumbered.

Fifteen minutes later, gas-masked soldiers in desert fatigues stole into town along the silent streets. They noiselessly made their way into a three-story building just across from the mosque. Inside they found and carried away eight bodies—seven alive but sleeping, one dead.

The village's inhabitants enjoyed a good night's rest, though only 692 people awoke there the next morning.

* * *

Christopher walked for hours. Finally, he wended his way to Site B. At exactly 3:00 p.m., the monitor in the modified delivery truck flashed a special CNN news report. The little group in Site B watched in deep concern.

"This is a special report from Washington, where a press conference has been called by International Coalition for the Preservation of World Peace Director Michael Wroth. Now, here is Director Wroth."

"Thank you for joining me at such short notice. I will make a brief statement. Approximately one and a half hours ago, IC forces rescued the remaining seven members of the KPF group being held captive by terrorists at an undisclosed site in North Africa."

Cheers erupted in the vehicle. "Quiet," yelled Timothy, "There's more."

"They also recovered the body of the one member, Seth McGorman, who had been previously executed. Since the start of the kidnapping, the IC has been tirelessly working to obtain the group's release. When diplomatic means failed, we decided it best to act covertly. The group was rescued less than two hours prior to their execution time, which incidentally is this very hour.

"While I cannot disclose the methods the IC used, I can say that the IC worked to preserve the dignity of both sides, and no one was harmed. The seven KPF members are now safe and on their way home.

"The IC regrets not being able to prevent the loss of young Mr. McGorman, but this action underscores our commitment to make this world a tranquil one, free both from terrorists and so-called peaceful organizations that, in fact, use subversive means that infringe upon the rights of good citizens. All eight KPF members were, I believe, victims of a handful of leaders in the KPF organization who are acting in violation of the newly enacted legislation that forbids acts of intolerance; this law also authorizes the IC to deal with those who violate it.

"Even as I speak, an investigation is being made into the KPF by IC investigators. If they find that the group is subversive, the IC will act immediately within our authority to close it down and help all its members abroad get home safely to their families at our expense.

"At the same time, we did not take any harmful steps against the so-called splinter terrorist group that took the KPF members captive. Though they did execute this one man, we feel that they were provoked by the KPF. Their group's religion and way of life were seriously threatened. While we do not agree with their actions, we believe they would not have acted in this manner without such provocation. We are giving them another chance to prove that, in the future, if they are upset over groups like the KPF, they can appeal to their government or the IC, and we will do our best to help them preserve their cultural heritage. That's all I have for now. We're just glad to have these kids headed home." Though barraged by a thousand questions, the IC director simply smiled and left the room.

"Praise God!" shouted Jeanie. "Our prayers were answered!" Everyone laughed with relief and cried tears of joy.

All except Christopher. Nic turned to him. "What's wrong, buddy? This is great news!"

Christopher didn't look up. "Yes, I know it, but something's still not right here. The IC investigates us but rescues our people? Why didn't they let them be executed? That would have given them a lot more ammunition to use against us."

Grace gasped. "Christopher! You can't think that the IC would resort to such dirty dealing when it was in their power to rescue our people? Who would do something like that? That would be inhumane!"

Though a little embarrassed, Christopher continued, "Inhumane or not, it's not above what I would expect from them. Something is not right. Not everything that goes our way is a victory."

He looked at the other four in the truck: Jeanie, Timothy and Grace, even Nic. Each wore an expression of disgust that he wouldn't share in the joy over the release of the team members. Christopher himself felt disgusted over his attitude, but something gnawed at his soul.

Christopher felt he must get away, so without a word he left the truck that was parked in a grocery store parking lot and ran until he could run no more. Several blocks away he collapsed in a park. Though children played around him, he didn't hear them. The world was spinning around him.

* * *

On a secure line at IC headquarters, a caller reached Marlene Hayes. In a nervous voice just above a whisper, the caller hissed, "I can't stay here any longer. You didn't tell me anyone would get *killed* when I sent you those names. We didn't agree to *this*. I just wanted you to stop them from sending out more innocent people. Someone will find me out soon. I have to get out—*now!*"

Marlene asserted forcefully, "You will stay there until we tell you to leave. In a couple of weeks, there will *be* no KPF, and you will be working with us here. But you must prove you have the stuff it takes to work with us. You must learn to do exactly as you are told. That's Director Wroth's way. And if you decide to pull out early, your name and picture will be plastered across every headline of every newspaper. You'll be known forever as the Judas who betrayed fellow team members, leading to the unfortunate death of one. My friend, you'll go to prison for the rest of your life. We can arrange that without any problem. We're in control, and you know it."

The caller thought for a few moments. "Okay. But I can't wait forever. It's getting too risky! I'm worried they might suspect me."

"Remember the risk you take in not obeying us!"

"Just do what you have to do, and do it quickly. The sooner I'm out of here and in Washington the better. Please! How much longer?"

"Is all the information in place?" Marlene asked.

"It's all here. Every name. Every location. Everything. I can't upload it to you anymore. The computers are watched too closely now."

"You won't have to. Just hold on two more weeks until we confiscate it, and you'll receive your reward."

* * *

Nic looked as if he had run a marathon. Among the homeless people scattered around the park settled in for the night, he found one man curled up in a fetal position on a bench. Recognizing the clothing, he shook him.

Christopher stirred. "Nic? Ugh! Where am I? I feel like I've been sleeping on concrete."

A grin greeted him. "Not far from it, buddy. I've been looking all over for you."

"What time is it?"

"One in the morning."

Christopher stammered, half awake. "One! I can't believe I s-s-slept so long. I f-f-feel totally drained and hopeless. What's happening?" He closed his eyes again.

Nic shook him again and helped his friend up. The two of them began walking back to Site B. Finally Nic broke the news to him. "I'm afraid I've got more bad news for you."

Christopher looked concerned. "What is it?"

"I don't know. John just called in from San Diego, distraught. I tried to get him to tell me what was wrong, but he said he had to talk to you first. Christopher, he was crying—weeping! I've never heard John cry."

Back at the truck, Christopher called John at his San Diego convention hotel. He was met with sobs. "John, you've got to control yourself and tell me what's wrong."

For three or four minutes, the sobs continued. "Christopher, I've ruined everything."

Christopher wracked his brain, wondering what could be wrong. Surely his good friend wasn't the traitor in their midst. Though that idea didn't seem logical, it somehow seemed to stick.

John finally spoke again. "How will I ever dig us out of this hole?"

Christopher insisted, "John, tell me exactly what happened."

"Tonight after the convention, I was on cloud nine. My presentation went flawlessly. M-my a-assistant Alicia helped me with the PowerPoint and everything. For two hours afterwards, I was the big man at the convention as dozens of people asked me questions and rubbed shoulders with me. And everywhere I went, Alicia was by my side—as my grad assistant *only!*"

John paused before asking, "You remember Alicia Price? She's that girl who has made us coffee a couple of mornings, one of my new Ph.D. students. I didn't think she ever had a father figure, so I was encouraged by the deep talks we've had. After the convention was over tonight and everyone had left, we were alone and decided to have dinner—*in a public place.* You know the boundaries I've set up.

"It was late when we finished, so I escorted her to her hotel room. I purposefully booked us on *separate* floors. That's my protocol, per our accountability process. You know that. Anyway, I walked her to her room to make sure she got there safely since it was late. As she opened her door, she turned around and gave me a hug. I thought it was a sweet gesture, until I noticed that she gave me a suggestive look. She took my hand in hers and began pulling me gently into her room. She said, "John, why don't you come in and let's finish the conversation we were having in the restaurant."

There was silence on the end of the line. A few sobs came over the line. Christopher just waited.

"Am I completely blind, or what? It was then I realized that something wasn't right. I jerked my hand away immediately and got out of there—ran back to my room—as fast as I could. All I could think of was Joseph fleeing Potiphar's wife. As I ran up the stairs to my floor, I heard her shouting from her room, but I couldn't make out what she said. I closed the door to my room and tried to calm down. I couldn't shake off the creepy feeling of the whole affair, so I sat up in bed to read my Bible.

"Just a few minutes ago I heard a strange noise at my door. I got up to see what it was and found a large manila envelope slid under the door.

"Christopher, in it—," John stammered, "—in it were pictures of Alicia and me in the restaurant, pictures at her hotel doorway, pictures of her hugging me and holding my hand in the doorway inviting me in. Who would have done such a thing? It must have all been set up from long ago."

Christopher paused then asked in measured tones, "John, listen to me carefully. Nothing—more—happened? You never went into her room? You did nothing, absolutely nothing, more than you told me?"

There was a long pause on the line. "Christopher, I promise you, nothing more than I told you happened. Christopher, what am I going to do? How can I face Renee? Who's going to believe me? What will this do to KPF? I can just see it now in the headlines, 'KPF Leader Commits Adultery with College Coed'!"

Christopher was almost speechless. He could only answer as honestly as he knew how. "I don't know what will happen to KPF, and right now I don't care. All we can do is tell the truth. We can't make people believe us. As far as Renee is concerned, you should have called her first. Call her now. Tell her everything you told me. Get back up here first thing in the morning and beg her forgiveness for being at the convention by yourself with just a college coed. I don't know what'll happen. Just get home as fast as you can."

Christopher prepared to hang up but stopped suddenly. "Wait, John, hold on a minute. Something's not right about this whole incident. What do you know about Alicia? Where did she do her undergraduate work?"

"University of Colorado. Why?"

"Had you ever met her prior to agreeing to supervise her graduate studies?"

"No."

"Isn't it normal for you to interview applicants before accepting them as Ph.D. students?"

"Well, quite often a professor meets prospective candidates ahead of time. But when Alicia's resume and recommendations came across my desk, I accepted her. Her credentials were *that* good."

"Too good, to my thinking. I think that you're right that this was set up long in advance. John, is it okay if I talk the situation over with Nic and Timothy?"

"Yeah, I guess so. There's going to be no hiding it in the morning. Someone sent me those pictures to send me a message."

"Thanks, bro. God's going to work things out; don't worry. Now call Renee!"

Christopher hung up, jotted down some notes, and handed the slip to Timothy. "Find out what you can about this young lady, Alicia Price, right now."

Christopher and Nic walked outside the truck into the deserted parking lot. Christopher told him everything. "I don't understand it. Something's rotten in the state of Denmark. Nic, how could everything fall apart in one week? I have always believed KPF could handle any onslaught, but never in my imagination did that include betrayal and scandal in our ranks. A house divided against itself cannot stand."

"Listen, Christopher," Nic began. "You're emotionally drained. I don't think you've slept in the last seventy-two hours, except for your brief stint on the park bench tonight. Come on, I'm going to take you home."

The two of them made their way back around the truck to where Nic's car was parked. As they were getting in, Timothy called out from the truck, his face ashen. "Christopher, Chara's on the secure line. It's urgent!"

Christopher ran to the phone. Chara spoke quietly, though children in the background were crying instead of sleeping. "Christopher, IC soldiers just burst into the house half an hour ago. They had a warrant and everything. They knew where *everything* was—your office, the comm center, the files. They carted off every piece of equipment and every document in the place. They even knew about a couple of hidden compartments in the redwood paneling *I* didn't know about. They didn't even try to be quiet. The kids are hysterical, and the neighborhood is awake. That's not all. Cassandra, Phil, and Julie were in the comm center. They arrested all three and took them away. They were going to arrest me, too, but I guess they decided not to because of the kids."

Christopher's head began swimming. He sat down. "I'll be right there!"

"No! That's the one thing you must not do. They're looking for *you*, above all people. If you come back, they'll find you and arrest you. Stay away until this blows over. We'll be okay.... I love you."

Chara began to cry. The world collapsed around Christopher. His heart tore apart as he listened to his sobbing wife, feeling powerless, knowing he couldn't wrap his arms around his own wife and kids to comfort them. And, he couldn't stay on the phone much longer. Even though it was a secure line, it could still be traced with the right equipment. Of that he felt sure.

"I love you, too, Chara." He ended the call. "Timothy, get this truck moving. I'm sure the IC will try to trace that call. They can probably track its point of origination. I've got to leave for a while. I'll call you later."

He and Nic got into Nic's car. As they drove around aimlessly, Christopher withdrew deeper and deeper within himself. His ever-optimistic friend tried to pull him out of his depression. "Listen, Christopher. Renee's at her office tonight. There's no way the IC can get to her there, not in a prestigious law office, unless they have more judicial clout than I thought. I'll call her and have her start fighting this. The IC can't just shut us down. They'll see."

"It doesn't matter," murmured Christopher. He felt broken beyond hope. "It doesn't matter, don't you see? We've been beaten! Every name of every KPF member was in those computers. They even found the encrypted backup drives we hid. Before tomorrow's over, those names will be in every paper, on every news site. Then what will happen to them? The week we've just finished will be repeated dozens of times over as local governments hunt them down and imprison them. No, we've been beaten. Tell Timothy to contact every team tonight and call them back to safety if there's still time.

"Monday morning I'll call a press conference. I'll tell the media that we're disbanding the KPF. We had good intentions, but the world is not ready for our brand of Christian commitment. If we don't stop now, we'll stain every reputable organization with the name 'Christian' attached to it. We're dragging God's name through the mud. This is the best way. It's over. It was an amazing ride, but it's over. Maybe someone else will one day do what we only dreamed of."

Those were the last words out of Christopher's mouth that night. Nic pleaded with him but got no response. "Listen, buddy. You're just going through a spell of despondency. It will pass soon enough."

Still there was no acknowledgment from Christopher. "I'm actually shocked at you," Nic continued. "What happened to that victorious spirit I thought we were supposed to have? Who can stop us if God is for us?"

Still no response.

"I know what you're thinking. We shot ourselves in the foot. Betrayed ourselves. Well, let me tell you, Jesus had His betrayer and went on. Joseph was framed and trapped in a scandal and rose to be second in command in Egypt. God is watching out for us."

Heedless, Christopher sat motionless as light from the streetlights they passed danced on his face.

"Christopher Owen, there are sixty-one KPF teams still out there doing their best to bear witness for Jesus Christ despite what happens here. They need you. They need me. Well, actually they only need the Lord. But I imagine the Lord is going to put some skin on and use somebody to support them and meet their needs, and I intend to be one of those people. I hope you will also. When Jesus knew He was about to be betrayed, He had His Gethsemane—He prayed. When things came crashing down, He was still victorious.

"Christopher, I know for all intents and purposes, it seems like everything has come crashing down. But God is still in control. If the plan to get to *no place left* is really His, it will prevail. And if we are faithfully a part of that, God will see us through."

Christopher still stared ahead catatonically.

Nic swerved into a local motel. "You need some rest, and you need time alone to pray and listen to God. I'm checking you in here, primarily because they'll probably be following my car as soon as they spot it. Stay here. Get things worked out with God. I'll come get you later."

Nic checked him in for a couple of nights, paying cash only, and helped the dazed director of the KPF into bed. When Nic turned out the light and closed the door, his last image of Christopher that night was of him lying in bed, glazed eyes staring at the ceiling. "Hastening? Hastening? No, it's over! It's over," he was mumbling.

Six blocks away, a police car spotted Nic's SUV. Nic spent the rest of the night in a jail cell.

FOURTEEN

Christopher awoke late Sunday morning feeling like he was still in a stupor. *It must have all been a bad dream.* Then he looked around at his small motel room. The depression set in again, and he turned over to go back to sleep, to insulate himself from the real world—but something inside him forced him to get up. *What time is it? 10:20 a.m.* He decided there must be a worship service on television. He wasn't ready to face a real church in person. Not yet.

Christopher reached for the remote control and flipped through the channels. He stopped on a news network. An attractive young brunette was recounting a harrowing tale of an attempted rape the night before by her professor, the co-director of the Kingdom Preparation Force.

"For three months, he has drawn me closer to him emotionally, often coercing me to work with him late into the evening, even after other students have gone home. He purposefully chose me to go to this conference alone with him, even though I'm his newest and least experienced student. Does that make sense if he didn't have some ulterior motive? He knew I came from an abusive background and that I was becoming emotionally dependent on him."

She choked back tears.

"I trusted him! Last night he came into my hotel room after our presentation. For a while I went along with it, flattered by his advances. But then I came to my senses and forced him to leave. I even shouted a couple of times until he backed away. As quickly as I could, I packed up my things and checked out. I can't believe a professor would do that to his student, and he calls himself a *Christian* professor!" She hid her face in her hands and began to sob.

Following this came a series of photos from an amateur sleuth. "Yeah, I followed this Dr. Steward after all I heard about this KPF. He seemed just a little too friendly with that gal. I used my telephoto lens to capture some shots, and wouldn't you know it, I was right!"

Pictures of the restaurant and the doorway scene kept flashing on the screen, especially the ones of the couple hugging and holding hands.

After showing a picture of John Steward, the reporters switched to the testimony of two individuals who saw someone resembling Steward's description hurriedly leaving Alicia's room quite flustered while another person admitted to hearing her shouts.

It was too much for Christopher, who flicked off the set. He lay back down to sleep the new tidings away, yet sleep eluded him. Finally, he forced himself to get up. *I've got to pray. God, if You're there and You're really in control, I need some help. I admit, I don't even want to pray. I'm so burned out! I'm in such despair. I don't even have my Bible!*

He checked himself and the room but again realized he had nothing but the clothes on his back. He surveyed the room and was struck with an idea. He hurried over to the dresser as if it were a treasure chest, opened the top drawer, and gazed in. Ever so gently, he reached in and cradled a small brown Bible in his hands. *Praise God for the Gideons!*

* * *

The hours ticked by. as Christopher plunged from one level of despondency to another. His world and the mission were falling apart. *"No place left"* seemed further away than ever. The cost to cross the finish line was proving too great.

O Father! We have the resources, but do we have the resolve?

Hours of reading and praying seemed to be of no avail. At times he paced the room and prayed out loud; at other times, he simply lay flat on the floor face down, waiting. Twilight settled, and the room began to darken.

Utterly fatigued, famished from days of fasting, Christopher collapsed on the bed. Despairing thoughts passed through his mind. *Perhaps sleep is what I need.* He closed his eyes, yet as he did, a strange luminescence filled the room. He cracked open his eyelids. He couldn't call what he saw a light—it was more of a glow or aura. He convinced himself it was simply some reflection of the sunset and began to close his eyes again, until he saw a faint glimmer, a movement in the corner.

He bolted straight up, eyes focused as the glimmer began to take shape. A brightness filled the room, emanating from the luminescent shape which took a man's form.

Christopher's eyes widened more. "Oh God, oh God, oh God! I'm seeing an angel!" he kept muttering in fear. As fast as a five-year-old, he jumped off the bed and hid his face on the carpet.

The angel called out, "Christopher, don't be afraid! Look up."

Christopher looked up into the kindest face he had ever seen, one that put all his fears to rest. The angel took his hand and helped him sit back on the bed. Christopher said nothing.

"You must not fear what is happening. All this has been foretold by the Lord Himself. Remember when He prophesied how His own disciples would be scattered: *'I have told you these things, so that in me you may have peace. In this world you will have trouble. But take heart! I have overcome the world.'*

"Mighty warrior, what is happening to you is nothing new. Times of increasing trouble lie ahead, but you serve the One Who has overcome this world. He will always be with you. Trust in Him, and you will find victory. He *will* be exalted among the nations.

"Who is there who can thwart Him and His purposes? Your enemy has been defeated, though he tries to deceive many into believing he has more authority than he really has. Resist him, firm in your faith. Now, get up. The people of the Almighty are waiting for your leadership."

The angel touched him, and Christopher felt the fatigue wash away from his mind and body. The light from the manifestation slowly faded to a faint glow and then was gone completely.

Christopher rubbed his eyes. He knew angels existed, of course, but to actually see one with his own eyes and hear one with his ears? That type of encounter was something he normally reasoned away as simply sensationalized hallucinations by Christians on the fringe. But he couldn't deny this experience.

Heart racing, he paced around the room in silent amazement which soon gave way to shouts of praise. When his heart rate returned to normal, Christopher went to the phone and dialed a number he had memorized by now. Timothy answered from Site B. "You still moving around, Tim?"

"Yes, boss. What happened to you? You sound different!"

"Yeah, let's say I've had an illuminating experience." He smiled to himself. Somehow, despite his lack of food, Christopher called upon new reserves. "Where's Nic? I'm kinda stranded."

Timothy sighed. "Arrested, boss. Right now we can almost count on two hands all the people who *haven't* been arrested."

Christopher rolled his eyes and actually chuckled. "They don't know what they got themselves into if they arrested Nic. I imagine his cellmates are followers of Jesus by now. Timothy, you'll have to pick me up. We have a lot of work to do."

"Now, boss, that's more like it!"

"Oh, and Timothy? Can you grab me two double burgers, fries animal style, and a chocolate shake—no, make it two—at In-N-Out Burger? And a Coke! I'm famished!"

"No problem, boss. I'll pick you up ASAP. Now where are you?"

* * *

As Christopher sat in the back of the converted delivery truck that housed Site B, he gave instructions while stuffing his face with burgers and fries. He gave a muffled yell toward the front. "For Pete's sake, Jeanie! Don't you think we can stop this thing for a while? We're going to bust our budget with gas costs alone! And come back here for a conference. We need you."

Jeanie laughed. "Whatever you say, Christopher."

Christopher turned to Timothy and Grace. "Now, first thing we've got to do is contain the damage we've received. First item of business is to get our teams back home somehow." He grimaced. "If only the IC hadn't confiscated all those computer files with the names and locations of our teams!"

Timothy and Grace grinned at each other, as did Jeanie, who had just joined them.

Christopher looked at all three. "Okay, is someone going to let me in on the secret?"

Grace beamed at Timothy. "*You* tell him."

Timothy beamed back. "Well, you see, boss, we've been a little secretive ourselves. We figured that if we had a traitor back at Site A, he could still get that information out to the IC. So, when Grace and I left, we took a few classified personnel files with us from the filing cabinets. Then, we remotely manipulated the computers at Site A so that we erased all the names and locations of every team member from the hard drives. Though it was designed to protect against remote manipulation, I had left myself a couple of back doors."

Grace chuckled. "Erased isn't really the right word. We totally wiped all that data so that no one can recover it. We completely reformatted the hard drives one at a time and then remotely re-installed the original programs minus the information."

"Plus, I switched out the backup drives that we had hidden. I've got the real ones with me here."

Christopher looked at them in astonishment. "Then the computers the IC investigators confiscated were ..."

"Totally useless!" finished Jeanie. "The three of us have worked night and day to erase any trail that could lead the IC to our teams."

Christopher sighed in relief then caught himself. "Oh, no! I already gave the order for all of our teams to exit their countries! The IC will identify them pretty easily when there is this mass exodus. They can put two and two together." The other three looked at each other sheepishly. "You *did* carry out my order, didn't you?"

Timothy and Jeanie said nothing, but a frustrated Grace answered, "Look, Christopher. I know you and the rest of the KPF like thinking of yourselves as a spiritual army and such, but at times that can get in the way of common sense. Jeanie and I went back and traced all downloads from our computers. When we realized there had been no more information leaked about the teams, we just ignored your order. It didn't make sense, and you were under a lot of stress! Sometimes I think you men blow everything out of proportion." She crossed her arms with finality.

Christopher turned to Jeanie. "You're a soldier's wife, and you agreed to disobey orders?"

Jeanie just shrugged.

Christopher laughed and took a big slurp of his chocolate shake—his second one. "Thank you, God, that we have a few folks around here with cool heads! Okay, so our teams are still in place and secure, as long as our traitor didn't *hand deliver* the information about them."

Jeanie and Grace looked in surprise at each other as they realized that tiny factor they had forgotten. "We'll just have to assume he or she didn't, since that isn't the pattern we've discovered so far," Christopher continued.

"Next item: the IC confiscation of our property and arrests of many of our leaders. Any word from Renee? And—oh, I forgot about this whole stink with John in San Diego. Better forget that route for a while."

"On the contrary, Renee's handled things remarkably well," replied Jeanie. "She's at her office waiting for your phone call."

"On a Sunday night?"

"Yep!"

Christopher picked up the phone and called her. "Renee? Hey, I'm so sorry about all that has happened."

Renee cut him short. "Don't worry about it, Christopher. John's here, and we've talked a lot about it. I know he didn't do anything except act stupidly. Here's what we're going to do. We're going to bail the KPF out of this mess legally, then we're taking a week off together in the mountains where no one can reach us. We're going to talk things out and do some damage control of our own—on our marriage."

"I'm so glad to hear that. Now what do you mean by 'bail us out of this mess'?"

"I've had a whole team of my associates who have put in a lot of hours pro bono to help me research the constitutionality of what the IC is doing. One of them has argued several Supreme Court cases. The folks at the IC are in way over their heads. Everything they did this weekend was unconstitutional, but they will try to justify it by citing the recently enacted Peace Preservation Act.

"They don't have a leg to stand on, and they probably know it. They raided our headquarters over the weekend because they knew we couldn't go to court for a restraining order until tomorrow morning. They want to scare us, and they want the information from our files and computers before they conveniently return them to us."

Christopher was dumbfounded. "So how can you get around their legal justification of intolerance in the PPA?"

"Remember, all of our personnel have signed waivers acknowledging they are of age, are aware of all the inherent dangers of the job—including death—and are taking full responsibility for whatever happens to them. They've signed hold-harmless agreements concerning KPF, releasing us of liability. In a court of law, any judge will immediately overturn IC grounds for invading our headquarters. They may fight it out in court in the long run, but I doubt it. I think they are just after our info and are trying to intimidate us."

Christopher was thinking fast. "But those hold-harmless agreements. Weren't they in the files they confiscated?"

Renee laughed. "Christopher, I'm afraid you'd better face up to the fact that a lot happens behind your back that you don't know about. We moved the agreements to a safe-deposit box months ago, if for nothing else than as safekeeping from fire and theft. I'm going to pick them up on the way to the courthouse in the morning. We'll have our people and property home by noon. Count on it. Until then, *don't go home!*

"By the way, John and I will both issue a statement to the media about the incident in San Diego. In addition, we've already contacted several witnesses who will vouch that Alicia came on to John, not the other way around. I'll talk to the D.A. tomorrow. She doesn't have a case if she pursues some sort of assault or attempted rape charges, but she's creating the smudge on John's image and on KPF's that she intended to."

"Thanks, Renee. I guess we'll talk tomorrow. Then I don't want to hear from either of you for at least a week. Okay?"

Christopher ended the call, wiped the last remnants of food from the corners of his mouth, and turned to the trio.

"Next order of business: the two teams returning home. Any update on when they'll be back?"

Timothy punched in a few keystrokes on one of the computers and consulted the screen. "Team 47 has left the Mediterranean already on an IC transport accompanied by the colonel. They should be back in L.A. Monday, tomorrow evening. Team 26 had to fly commercially out of Bangkok. They will be home midday tomorrow."

"Very good. Look, we need to make these guys feel really special. They have suffered for the sake of the gospel and deserve extra honor. Can you work on something that we can do to show our appreciation and respect?"

Grace beamed. "Already been working on that, Christopher!"

Christopher shrugged. "You guys don't need me; you've got it all under control." Now he hesitated and looked around, just to make sure nobody could eavesdrop on them. "But the next thing I have for you should catch you off guard. If it doesn't, then we are in big trouble. Timothy, can anyone listen in on what we're talking about?"

Timothy thought it over and shrugged. "Yes, anything is possible if the equipment is high tech enough. But I have an idea —if you don't mind typing. We can link four of these computers together on our local network and type our messages to each other. No one can read that." He and Grace took a few minutes to set up the systems. The four took their places at four different laptops. "Go ahead, boss, type."

CHRISTOPHER: I want to set up a new organization—a secret one within the KPF. Call it whatever you want— Trailblazers, Pathfinders, Closers, etc. If we've got a mole in our midst, there's no telling what kind of damage he or she can do in the future. Even if we root him out, our profile is too big. Plus, if we have a mole, I suspect there is some sort of plot—weird as it sounds—to discredit or damage our effectiveness. If we just disband KPF and start over, it'll be obvious. But if we let the KPF gradually decline, perhaps whoever is trying to interfere with KPF will slack off some. That make sense?

Everyone nodded.

CHRISTOPHER: In the meantime we build this new secret NoPlaceLeft organization with the same purpose. But this one is the ultimate in low profile. We only take recruits who can work in a clandestine, though legitimate, organization. The others can still work through KPF, though the risk to them is more open.

JEANIE: I recommend we only take recruits that have been vetted thoroughly, preferably already with field experience with KPF.

CHRISTOPHER: Perfect! The downside for those in the clandestine wing is that they will have less visible support. Above all, no one except a few select leaders can know about the new wing. It will not be talked about openly, even within the KPF.

GRACE: We'll have to figure out a way to develop the same prayer support without letting on that there is a new organization.

CHRISTOPHER: Right. If worse comes to worst, and somehow KPF does get shut down, this other organization can keep functioning. Our present leadership can take time in shifts away from normal KPF duties to train the new teams in an alternate training site.

TIMOTHY: That shouldn't be difficult, though it will mean longer hours for us.

CHRISTOPHER: I want these new teams trained to act completely independently of our central command structure if need be. Once they leave here, they need to be on their own—able to function independently, make strategic decisions, even initiate work in new countries and new people groups based on our priority UUPG list. Reporting in will be done very secretively. We will have to assume that everything we do and say is susceptible to surveillance. I want you all to get the ball rolling in setting up this new parallel structure.

JEANIE: Somehow our select leadership inner circle will need to maintain contact with them by way of encouraging podcasts, email, or whatever we can make work.

CHRISTOPHER: Exactly! But ultimately they must be able to operate independently.

TIMOTHY: Shouldn't be too difficult since we have Sites B and C already set up. You, Nic, John, and the colonel can all just spend a little extra time away from KPF to devote to it.

CHRISTOPHER: Right. And you and Grace will be doubly busy. I want you ALONE to monitor communications for the new group. I don't want anyone else who has touched the comm room to be a part of this. We don't know who to trust. Plus, on top of that, you'll still need to intercept communications for KPF.

JEANIE: Christopher, that is a lot of work. Isn't there someone else you can trust to help them? They do need some time alone as a couple.

CHRISTOPHER: Sorry! You're right. I forgot about that. I'll assign Julie Konami and Kellie Davies to help you some. If I can't trust them, I can trust no one. On second thought, when school gets out, I'll let Joshua come help also.

The other three looked at him in astonishment. Christopher's son Joshua was only eight years old.

CHRISTOPHER: Really, I mean it. He's been bugging me to get to do more in the comm room. He's going to be in the fourth grade next year but could be going into sixth or seventh. He's that bright and mature. Plus, I think it will build vision in him. He can keep a secret, too.

GRACE: Good idea. He's already helped me out a lot. He knows computers pretty well. And he's good company. Has faith like his daddy!

Christopher tried to ignore that comment, though he still blushed a little.

Grace faced Christopher and spoke out loud, "Christopher, it's good to hear you talk like this. This is the man of faith we joined up to work with. I know you've been under a lot of pressure, but it's good to see you have such hope again." She leaned over and hugged him.

Jeanie got their attention and began typing:

JEANIE: Winthrop has a good friend who has been in the CIA for quite a number of years. Old Marine buddy. Friend is semi-retired from CIA now. Unclear if he is a Christian or just a very "good" person. I think he would be willing to help us set up new wing of KPF if Winthrop asked him. He knows a lot about being covert!

Christopher laughed.

CHRISTOPHER: With God on our side and consultants from the special forces AND the CIA, how can we lose?!!!

Christopher finally spoke out loud again. "Now I only hope that Renee's prediction about getting our folks out of jail really pans out. And that the real files were not hand delivered prior to our discovery of the mole."

FIFTEEN

"**What do you mean** the court overturned our shutting down of the KPF?" A red-faced Michael Wroth stormed around the office, waving his arms yet with hardly a wrinkle in his immaculate suit. He turned to glare at Marlene, who half cowered in front of the closed door, notepad in hand. She could only recall two or three times she had ever seen her boss this irate. Normally he received bad news with that stoic look of his, processed it, and spit out an amazing solution.

This issue, however, had hit a nerve somewhere. Wroth liked to be in total control, and here was one group that so far had eluded his grasp despite his indirect orchestration of the deaths of two of its members—the one part Marlene felt uncomfortable with. They hadn't agreed on *killing* innocent people.

Pulling herself together, Marlene straightened. What did she have to fear? She was simply the message bearer. "The lawyers said the PPA does not give us liberty domestically to shut down an organization like this in which the members have been fully informed of the dangers and have signed waivers of liability against the organization."

Wroth paced in front of her. "Let me guess. Those waivers weren't in the files we confiscated."

"No, sir. Not any more than the names and locations of the team members were in the computer databases."

"What? You mean to tell me that this raid was for nothing? We *still* don't know where the teams are located? It sounds to me like we're no better off than we were before the weekend."

Marlene ventured, "Well, we did intimidate them."

Wroth blew up again. "Intimidate them? We showed our hand! They're probably laughing at us right now."

Wroth slowly walked the perimeter of the room, fingertips touching, brows knit together.

"What about the model, you know, the coed, the one whose past we wiped and credentials we faked? Surely a girl that attractive succeeded in her mission!"

Marlene stammered, "S-Sir, she tried—really tried. Our photographer was in place. The problem is that she never got the professor to actually come into her room. At the last moment, he panicked and fled the scene. She improvised after he left, but without more incriminating photographic evidence, it is just her word against his."

Marlene braced herself for the tidal wave of anger.

Wroth grimaced, paused, and then laughed. He sat down in his plush chair and took a sip of his drink.

Marlene blinked in surprise.

"This group is smart, Marly. Shrewd. Not the pushover Christians we thought they might be. They have outsmarted us so far, but that's not the worst of it. What upsets me is the weakness in the Peace Preservation Act. I thought we were assured it gave us legal justification to shut down groups like the KPF. But now you're telling me that the courts aren't interpreting it that way."

He closed his eyes in meditation for at least two minutes. When he opened them, his voice was confident again. "Not only were we not able to shut them down, but we couldn't have announced our intentions any louder with bullhorns. Now the KPF and every other missions group, even some more subversive groups, will breathe easier. The IC doesn't have the clout they had feared we might.

"Fine. Let them relax. Let them think we've lost some of our punch. We can wait. Michael Wroth can wait when something better is coming down the road. In less than a year, we'll have so much authority that every group like the KPF will be kneeling for mercy. They'll be operating on our terms. Less than one year. Less than one year." He kept murmuring that phrase under his breath.

Marlene didn't know what it meant, but she did know her boss was changing, growing, metamorphosing.

SIXTEEN

In a remote mountain village of central Laos, Yijing sat among the growing band of gospel-runners. The faces of young people from the Phunoi, Tai Nua, and Pong tribes stared at her in the torchlight of the dirt common area. Very few young men sat in the group. Most men in the poverty-stricken villages in these mountains had headed to the cities to find work.

The flickering torches cast wavering shadows upon the determined face of Yijing. "Today, after months of uncertainty, I have finally received definite news that my husband, Li Tao, is dead. Though he was tortured by the national police, he did not betray even one of us. His reward is great. Jesus is very proud of him."

Yijing pulled from her pocket two sheets of notebook paper. A sister brought a flashlight and shone it upon the pages. "Today, the day I received news of my husband's death, I have also received from foreign colleagues the names of twenty tribes in the south that have yet to receive the light. We haven't much time. Everything around is signaling that Jesus may return soon. You twenty teams must run swiftly to these lost tribes. Take the good news with you. Their dialects will be different, but you will be able to communicate in Lao. God will open a door; do not give up. In two months, those of us who have escaped the clutches of our pursuers will gather in Pakse to evaluate the status of the Kingdom advance."

Yijing's briefing was interrupted by a faint hum that grew to a louder rumble, which crescendoed into an earthquake that shook the buildings violently. Homes collapsed. A deafening boom reverberated from the mountainsides.

The small band huddled in fear and covered their heads.

"Sister Yijing, what is happening?" someone shouted above the roar.

"The end is coming! Jesus is nearer than we thought! Wait not until tomorrow; now is the time! Flee, my gospel-runners, flee! We must lose no time to get the gospel to them!"

SEVENTEEN

Christopher gathered his core KPF team for a high-level retreat one early December week on the central coast of California at a spacious, beachfront home donated for their use by a wealthy businessman.

Behind him, the spray from the tumultuous Pacific surf blurred the view from the windows. Christopher and the group listened as Renee gave a report.

"In the summer and autumn since the IC raided our headquarters, several groups previously sympathetic to KPF have withdrawn their support. What's more, three cult watchdog groups have issued statements that, while not condemning our movement as heretical, come quite close to it.

"More Christian groups, however, were offended by the allegations made by Alicia Price against my husband, even though there was nothing to them."

Renee grabbed John's hand and drew closer to him.

Clearing her throat, Grace picked up the report. "Even so, the NoPlaceLeft movement has grown. There is an expanding coalition of churches and organizations globally racing toward the mark of completing the task by 2025 and preparing for Christ's return. Impromptu iron-on-iron gatherings have popped up around the world to foster this new unity among Great Commission groups."

As the wind howled outside, she tapped her tablet a few times. "The names of the UPGs that remain unengaged have been circulated. The number of groups that are unengaged has decreased while the numbers in the mission ranks have increased despite growing persecution. The countdown app continues to keep partners aware of the remaining task."

Nic grinned and spoke above the noisy surf. "NoPlaceLeft has been a starfish! The coalition has multiplied even when arms were cut off. We are a movement, not an organization. With Jesus alone as its leader and a *no place left* vision at its core, this movement is racing toward the finish line!"

John stood up. In his best professorial manner, he hooked his thumbs in his waistband and said, "Even so, the religious climate in America is morphing. Hostility mounts daily toward any religious or moral ideology that sounds intolerant of other lifestyles or religious beliefs. Conservative Christian groups find themselves under increasing pressure to soften their stances on social issues. Centuries-old values are being jettisoned in the span of a few years.

"Scathing attacks are being leveled against any group that openly declares a policy of seeking the conversion of Jews, Muslims, Hindus, Buddhists, and so on. Declaring that salvation is in Jesus alone is viewed as 'intolerant.'

"Religious leaders of all faiths are calling for an attitude of working together and combining our religious traditions, taking the 'best' from all." He pulled out a legal pad and consulted his notes. "Many nominal Christians have switched their church membership to churches that are more 'open-minded.'"

Nic interjected, "Well, buddy, I can tell you in business and political circles, 'intolerant' ideas or association with 'intolerant' groups is spelling death to deals and careers. For most people it's easier to switch than to fight. In many cases, churches and clubs have simply been a vehicle for them to be involved in their communities anyway!"

Timothy walked over to a chart he had created and taped to a wall. "The KPF itself has seen new enrollment drop to some extent. Some team members have become disillusioned with the events of the previous months, including more intense persecution, and resigned."

A few sighs could be heard despite the crash of the waves outside.

The colonel stood up and strode to the chart. "However, resignations have minimized due to the intense training that our recruits receive before being deployed in the field. Through reading *Foxe's Book of Martyrs* and the book of Revelation so many times, they have come to expect much of this opposition, as have many of the new converts among the various people groups.

"What is more encouraging, however, is this. Flip the page, Mr. Wu." Timothy revealed a new chart underneath the old.

The old soldier continued as he pointed to the graph, "The growth and emergence of *2414* has been nothing less than phenomenal. *2414*—the name—was the brainchild of none other than Lance Chu, much to my chagrin."

He chuckled. "In his words, it was something like, 'Dudes, like, why is this so hard?'" The group laughed as the colonel mimicked Lance's southern California vernacular. "'You want something non-religious yet descriptive, right? Like, isn't our theme verse Matthew 24:14? Just call the new group *2414*.'"

Lance stood up and waved his arms in the air. "Dude, that is *not* what I sound like!"

"No! It was perfect!" yelled George.

The team continued laughing and doing their own Lance impersonations until tears streamed down their cheeks.

Win wiped his own eyes and said, "Good thing we're sending you 7,000 miles away to lead our Central Asia work. Not sure I could handle having you around much longer, Mr. Chu." He winked at Lance and sat down.

During the following lull in the discussion, eyes began to turn in Christopher's direction. He rose to his feet and addressed this group of people he loved so much.

"Well, we've seen good times and bad times," Christopher began, "but Father knows what He is doing. Many of our teams are experiencing amazing success, and a few church planting movements are emerging."

Christopher cleared his throat and continued, "Yet a number of us—the Stewards, the Fernandezes, Chara and I—have sensed we may have gone as far as we can without a fresh work of the Holy Spirit in our lives. Just like the missionaries and their national partners a century ago were renewed in the famous Shandong Revival, so we too need a fresh work of God. I do not expect to mimic that revival. I only know we need to go to a deeper place of seeking God. It must start with us and then filter out to the teams on the field and their national brothers and sisters."

For four days, with no agenda, the KPF leadership family humbled themselves before the Lord and His Word in prayer and fasting. On His own timetable, the Father descended upon the little group in a powerful way. Confession of sin was abundant. Forgiveness was limitless. Re-surrender to God was rampant. Joy was overflowing.

The Spirit rekindled a first love that had waned for some amidst all their toil. The Spirit filled the members afresh and knit them more closely than ever in unity. The team emerged from this time of revival like the early disciples in the upper room— ready to take on thousands and tens of thousands. They pledged to call all the members of the KPF to fast and pray together for similar revivals in each of their countries of service.

On the fifth day of the meeting, everyone slept in, exhausted from the emotion and ecstasy of the previous days. Late in the afternoon, gale force winds howled outside while the team huddled in a glassed-in family room. Though the sky was darkening outside, the glow in the faces of the KPF family was bright.

Fifteen trusted leaders gathered around the circular fire-place in the center of the room: Christopher and Chara Owen, John and Renee Steward, Nic and Stacy Fernandez, Timothy and Grace Wu, Win and Jeanie Dunbar, newlyweds George and Julie Konami Yang, Kellie Davies, Lance Chu, and Tal Gillam.

Tal was a wiry man of seventy-two who was the colonel's friend from the CIA. In the changing religious milieu, he had come to Christ after being challenged to evaluate what he was really living for. He had spent many years as a bachelor living a clandestine life, but many of the ideals he had worked for were lying in dust now.

In the months of searching for answers, his friend Win had introduced him to Christ, saving him from the path of cynicism and disillusionment many of his former coworkers had taken. When he came to Christ, and eventually to the KPF, he had been anxious to leave his cloak-and-dagger lifestyle. Instead, he found Christopher encouraging him to keep his contacts in his former profession and transfer the skills to help the KPF covertly and humanely accomplish something truly worth fighting for. Christopher had told him that none of his legitimate skills or training should have to go to waste in the Kingdom of God.

Christopher stood before the group. "Family, the timetable is more urgent than any of us anticipated. To help us address this situation, the colonel and I have brought into our ranks Tal Gillam. Tal has decades of experience in the CIA and has worked hand in hand with the colonel much of that time. Although he is fairly young in his faith, we are hoping he can help us with the new wing of the KPF—*2414*.

"We are trying to follow Jesus' words to be as wise as serpents. We are not advertising *2414* or acknowledging it publicly, even within KPF. Everything we do through it will be morally and biblically sound—just low profile. Tal, brief us on the status of *2414*, please."

Tal rose from his chair, his eyes quickly assessing everyone. He spoke seriously but a bit uneasily as the team focused on him.

"Okay, this Christian stuff is new to me. I'm a young Jesus-person, less than a year old, though I've been trying to make up for lost time. But I do know clandestine operations, and this is what you've asked me to help you with. First of all, let me say that everything we share in this room is confidential. It must not leave the room. This house has already been swept for bugs, so we're safe here."

His cat-like form stepped about quietly.

"Normally I wouldn't share these things with so many, but Christopher tells me everyone can be trusted. I sincerely hope so. If any of you talks about these things, even carelessly, lives could be lost, as they already have been."

His intense eyes made contact with the group briefly.

"Christopher also tells me that things are going to get real tough soon, in terms of persecution. The measures we are taking are to try to minimize our exposure to that. We have already started setting up *2414* and are about ready to insert our first teams. Some of the new recruits are trusted team members in the KPF who will transfer over to this division, though the others in KPF will simply believe they have retired. Others in *2414* are intensively screened new recruits—people we ourselves have approached.

"Every team of six we send in *2414* will be completely autonomous. The members will have a broad guideline of the primary people group they are to catalyze a movement among. After accomplishing the task, they will report back for the next assignment. We are, however, preparing for the worst-case scenario, which is that KPF headquarters is closed down and all home communication cut off. To prepare for that, each group will not only have the authority to act on its own but also will have a list of five other high priority UUPGs in its region to which it can proceed, plus a new region it can move to if the first is too hot. We will have fallbacks on fallbacks."

John rose to his feet in exasperation and butted in. "Really, Tal, this sounds like overkill. How can things get that bad?"

Before Tal could speak, Colonel Dunbar stood up. "John, both the Bible and history make it clear that things will get worse than we can imagine from our current peacetime world. As a student of history, you should know this better than any of us."

The professor nodded grimly and sat down.

Win motioned to the ex-CIA operative. "Go ahead, Tal. Speak freely. This is a safe group."

"To preserve the secrecy of the endeavor, we will have to sacrifice some record keeping here at home. Team members will not be known by real names, only code names. No one in the organization will know all the team members' real names, not even Christopher. Even if someone confiscates all our computer and paper files, they will not be able to track down 2414 teams. Teams will train here separately from each other so that even *they* will not know the other teams' members. At the most, two or three teams will train at the same time together."

Grace chimed in, saying, "Recruiting is very hush-hush. All applications still come to KPF, and we approach individuals in that pool that we think would consider working through 2414. In addition—and this is highly confidential—through the help of some of our friends in Pasadena, Colorado Springs, Sydney, and Singapore, several missions agencies that I will not name are funneling some of their best recruits to 2414 covertly. These agencies want to be a part of the type of work we are doing, but the pressure from the public and even their constituencies hinders them from doing it publicly. It's really exciting, but unfortunately we can't tell anyone about it."

Tal nodded. "That's one of the downsides of covert work. Another downside is that the *2414* teams will have less contact and support from headquarters. We will visit them less often because we have to assume that we may be followed every time we go to them. That means discouragement is a greater risk. To compensate for that, we have built our teams of six to contain a balanced mix of personalities and spiritual maturity. Hopefully, the teams themselves will be diverse and mature enough to operate indefinitely on their own. Another disadvantage is that the groups will send in fewer reports, so we won't have as much info as we want to be able to pray for them and rejoice with them."

Lance interrupted Tal. "Dude, like, that's not really very good news—that they will have less staff support. When George and I were in jail and then our brave commander joined us," he said, winking at Christopher, "we would never have made it through without the colonel coming to our aid."

The colonel spoke up. "Overall, the teams will have fewer visits from staff. However, several of the staff are spending larger and larger chunks of time at several undisclosed locations to intensely train the new teams. Publicly, we are giving the truthful appearance that the KPF is in decline—which the main organization is—so that our leadership can spend less time with the main KPF members. But the staff will be *more* available for crisis intervention and training *2414* recruits. If we play our cards right, *2414* will grow, and no one will know a thing. But the fact is, soldier, these teams will need a lot of God's grace."

Lance responded, "Well, I understand that, and it's cool. Let's just pray these *2414* teams have a beastly amount of God's wisdom and presence."

The fifteen stopped to pray toward that end before going on.

Colonel Dunbar concluded, "Here's the crux of the matter. We not only have to increase operations at Site B and Site C, but we need to intensify training over the next several months. The commander feels we may have less than a year to train and deploy these teams before we are in danger of being closed down. The IC is ratcheting up pressure on groups like ours. Renee, you might want to share about that."

Occasional forceful gusts rattled the windows. The sound of breakers crashing on the beach outside competed with the discussion in the villa.

Renee raised her voice slightly. "You all know how close we came to being shut down by the IC several months ago. The legal resources were almost there to do it. For several months, the IC has been strangely inactive in regard to peaceful 'intolerant' groups. Many interpret that to mean they have *backed off* from shutting down evangelistic groups.

"We don't think so. Instead, their lobbyists have very subtly been massaging the legal apparatus to bend it more and more to their desires, giving them greater and greater authority. As long as they do this quietly, they don't attract opposition. It's not anything big, like instituting martial law. It's just a little law here and a little one there. Closing loopholes. I think that within a year, they'll have built a tight case against groups like ours. They won't need any trumped up charges to close us down."

George asked, "How can they do that? Makes no sense. I thought we had a free country."

A few others murmured similar things. Renee waved her arms to hush them. "Don't tell me they can't do this, that this is a free country. The legal system doesn't work that way. They're doing everything constitutionally, that is, the way *they* want the U.S. Constitution to be interpreted. And the courts may very well go along with them on it. You see, in this era, it's not Congress that creates the law so much as powerful judges who interpret it the way they think it should be. Case law is everything. The courts are creating 'law' through their interpretations. The IC has been grooming and installing new judges favorable to their views in addition to creating new legal justification for themselves."

Many of the staff shook their heads. Christopher stood before them. "My dear brothers and sisters, we have to face the facts. We know that the end times will involve persecution. We have to be ready for that. The reason I have gathered you here is to help us all prepare for what we may go through and to call us all to unparalleled sacrifice to train as many 2414 and KPF teams as we can, while we still have time. We must make one final, life-sacrificing push as the final assault on the gates of hell. We are still a long way from *no place left*. Will you do it? Will you risk the persecution of the Great Tribulation for an eternal reward?"

"Great Tribulation?" John muttered, "Is this really what we signed up for?" Renee took his hand in hers.

Christopher said, "In my most despondent moment, the Lord brought me to this realization. We have the resources. But do we have the resolve? Are we willing to be the Revelation generation?"

No one said anything while the weight of his words entered their minds and settled all the way to their toes. Like the sudden blast of a cold shower, the words sobered them to the reality of the cost. The team members thought they had already chosen to give up all to follow Jesus and fulfill His purposes, but now they realized the stakes were even higher. The stakes were their lives, their comfortable lifestyles, their cherished citizenship, their occupations, their vacations, their retirement, their kids and grandkids, their health, their reputations. Everything they held dear. The end times scared them.

Nic and Stacy were the first ones to nod. Across the room another nodded. Then another, until the whole room was nodding in assent.

Tal Gillam, who understood all too well the dangers, nodded with the others, then shook his head in disbelief. He murmured, "Are we all fools?"

Nic, sitting next to him, jabbed him in the ribs. "Fools for Christ! By the way, did I tell you about the guy I led to faith while I was in jail?"

The meeting adjourned until the evening prayer time. Tal watched as Win's giant frame lumbered unevenly to an exterior door. The colonel trudged through the onslaught of the gale toward the breakers. Tal grabbed his own coat and followed the silhouetted figure. The colonel stood for a few minutes atop a dune, oblivious to the spray, then collapsed.

Tal scrambled up the dune and rushed to his side. He felt the colonel's pulse and grimaced. Perhaps twenty years earlier he could have lifted the colonel's 230-pound frame, but no longer. Dozens of contingency plans flitted through his mind, but these thoughts were interrupted by a movement in his peripheral vision.

Tal jumped off the crest of the dune and slid down its side. He wrapped up Jeanie in his overcoat and shouted in her ear. "He's had another attack! Worse than before! Where's the medication?"

The soldier's wife pulled a small pill out of her pocket and put it in his hand. She shouted back, "Force it through his lips! Quickly! He may not have much time!"

Tal clawed his way up the dune face and plopped himself next to the crumpled form. He pried apart Win's lips and pushed the pill in. "Chew this, you old galoot!" He raised his eyes to the sky. "Oh, God. Oh, God. Don't let us lose him. The movement needs him. *I* need him."

Jeanie crested the dune and placed an arm around each of the men. "Don't worry, Tal. God has heard your prayer—our prayers. He won't take Win until it's time."

Together they huddled over the unconscious soldier to protect him from the spray and waited for the medicine to do its work. Five minutes later, the colonel stirred. He looked up into the face of his friend. "Hmm, this must mean I'm not in heaven yet."

The former spy smirked. "Not yet, my jarhead friend. Not yet. You came close this time. But remember, you're gonna have to look at this mug for all eternity now that I'm in the Kingdom."

Win muttered, "I guess it could be worse. We need to get back to the meeting. Help me up."

With his diminutive helpmate on one side of Win and Tal on the other, the trio gingerly made its way back to the villa to continue the assault on the gates of hell.

* * *

The KPF didn't have a year. Dozens of teams were sent out over the next few months by *2414*, until there were twice as many *2414* teams as normal KPF teams. Christopher rejoiced with every team sent out, but he felt a twinge of sadness with each one also. It wasn't the sadness of saying good-bye. He didn't know why, but it felt more like the sadness of signing someone's death warrant. As he looked into the brave, eager faces of the people in this diverse group—young couples, college students, retirees, even a few mid-career families—he ached, knowing that the world they were going to evangelize was rapidly changing. These were faces he might never see again on earth, and he didn't know if it would be his own imprisonment and possible death or theirs that would be the cause of it.

Yet still he sent out the teams with tearful words of encouragement and warning. "We send you out, despite the risks, to carve out one more niche of God's Kingdom on earth among a people group. You do this not because you are special and not because the people group deserves it, but because Jesus Christ deserves the full reward of His suffering—people from every tribe, tongue, nation, and people to stand before the throne praising Him for His glory. You leave from nations that have had the gospel so long it is no longer counted as a blessing. And you go to nations, peoples, and tribes that will listen in awe, wondering why someone hasn't ventured there sooner with such astoundingly hopeful news."

With each launch of a team, he kept up a brave face, but afterward, during those evenings at home in the arms of his wife, sobs racked his body.

Even so, *2414* teams from many nations—a varicolored coalition of the global NoPlaceLeft community—joined the growing flood in the final assault on the gates of hell.

One particularly painful winter evening after sending off a team to Central Asia, Christopher confided to Chara. "How long will the KPF have until the International Coalition closes the final loopholes and swoops down like a bird of prey? How long before we lose contact with these precious servants of Christ?"

Chara hugged him tightly. "Honey, Renee thinks we might have a year—tops. Remember Psalm 90. Let's number these days to present to the Lord a heart of wisdom."

They hoped for a year, but they didn't have it.

In a moment, the whole world changed.

EIGHTEEN

The following spring never arrived. Instead, what rushed in would be remembered as March Madness. Not college basketball, but true, unnerving, chaotic madness.

On March 1, Director Michael Wroth sequestered his team in a cluster of suites in Buenos Aires, hatching plans with top aides. Marlene scanned her surroundings. These secret offices in Argentina had always been the backup to the backup offices, should the worst happen. *Well, the worst must be here.*

With Marlene at his side, Wroth leaned forward, elbows on a massive table, mapping out the critical month with a few trusted officers. "The asteroid should hit exactly when and where, Ethan?"

Marlene knew that Ethan Farnsworth—Number Three—had taken quite a step to join them in Buenos Aires, risking the wrath of the Prime Director if he was discovered. Beads of sweat formed on his forehead.

"Nine days from now, on the tenth. We still don't know where it will hit. Economics and Science hasn't yet been able to pinpoint it. Eighty-seven percent chance it will be somewhere in the northern latitudes."

Wroth interrupted, "And you're sure no one knows about it?"

"Economics and Science—that is, our coalition *within* Economics and Science—has effectively blocked out all the data about the approaching asteroid. It's big, chaps. Twenty kilometers in diameter. No nation on earth possesses a nuclear warhead that can approach the magnitude of the blast its impact will create."

Wroth relaxed in his seat. "This will be the key to our accession to power. There's not a government in the world that will be prepared for this cataclysm, but we will be, right, Jake?"

Jake Simmons, the head of IC security forces who had come through it all with Wroth, nodded shrewdly. "Our forces have secretly tripled over the last year, numbering over three hundred thousand crack troops, not counting auxiliary troops we partner with around the world. We've amassed huge stockpiles of munitions, weapons, trucks, tanks, planes, choppers, ships—you name it. Supplies are stored all over the world in secret bases. Our troops are dispersed over most of the southern hemisphere so that no matter where the rock hits, we won't be adversely affected. But we'll be close enough to step in and take control. We're ready to bring order to a world plunged into chaos." He smiled wryly. "*Our* kind of order."

Marlene shuddered as she listened. She and the others were about to profit by refusing to warn the world of a danger that would kill millions. Her mind convulsed again at the thought, but she blocked it out as she had many times before. She had a job to do, and she *would* do it, unswervingly. The greater cause demanded it.

The secure phone in the room rang. Simmons picked it up, listened, and hung up quickly. "Sir, I think we'd better turn on CNN, right now."

He flipped on a monitor. The first blurry images were now coming in over the air as a reporter a hundred miles from Washington, D.C., sped away from the capital in a news van. A shaky image from the camera pointing out the blown-out back window came to them. The viewers couldn't tell if the camera shook from nervousness, the rough ride, or trembling under the ground. What *was* clear on the image were several mushroom-shaped clouds billowing miles into the atmosphere.

Marlene gasped. She struggled to hide the tears that wanted to stream down her face.

The reporter tried desperately to control her emotions as she spoke into the microphone. "Washington, D.C., is no more. I repeat, Washington, D.C., is no more. What you see are the blasts from what we conjecture to be several missiles that hit the entire capital area. Even now, a hundred miles away and speeding as fast as we can go, we are not sure we will escape the blast and fallout ...." The image faded, then came back. "... uncertain as to the missiles' origin. Initial speculation is that they were launched from a submarine. Otherwise, there would have been more warning. It appears that the whole city was caught off guard. As far as we know, the president was in Washington at the time. Congress was in session and ...."

Wroth's team watched as a sudden flash lit the screen. After a few seconds of blackout, a news anchor came into view, face ashen.

"We are back in our L.A. studio. Apparently we have lost contact with our reporter on the highway in Pennsylvania. More disturbing news: we have been unable to reach our New York studio. Reports indicate that the same type of what we are assuming to be nuclear blasts hit the entire Eastern Seaboard from roughly Richmond to Boston, with the heaviest blasts in the Washington area. Our military analysts conjecture that if missiles were indeed launched from one or more submarines off the eastern coast, the survival rate in the coastal cities is likely to be extremely low. What is shocking is how sudden this is. It makes Pearl Harbor look like a parade. Military analyst Hal Holcomb is here with us in the studio. Mr. Holcomb, thank you for coming on such short notice. What is your read of the situation?"

"Our best guess, and please understand it is preliminary, is that this is not the work of any nuclear superpower. We know all too well where their missiles are. In addition, our intelligence keeps a very tight surveillance on their nuclear submarines. Our best guess is that this is the work of a terrorist regime that somehow gained access to both submarines and nuclear missiles ..."

Marlene suddenly flinched.

"Turn it off!" barked Wroth. "Ethan, why didn't our Politics office notify us of this? Surely they knew every move of this group, whoever they were!"

Farnsworth fidgeted nervously. "Where's your office, Michael? Where does every person outside of this room think you are right now? Where does *Number One* think you are right now?"

Wroth glared. "He wouldn't dare! He would never kill millions of innocent people just to get me."

Farnsworth laughed. "Michael, listen to what you are saying. In nine days, *you* are going to let millions of people die from an asteroid collision so *you* can assume power. Why shouldn't Number One do the same? Except, this way he wipes out you, the IC forces, *and* the most powerful government on earth—the one that can most likely resist the ascendancy of The Ten. You have to remember that Number One heads up the Politics division. His right hand man is Number Four, the Russian. *He hates you, too.* Only Number Five, the Latino, is sympathetic to you, but he would never countermand the other two. He's under their thumb, though none of The Ten are supposed to be. We're all equals, right?"

Wroth leaned back in his chair and laughed. "As Sherlock Holmes used to say, 'The game is afoot.'"

Millions of people on the Eastern Seaboard are dead, and he is laughing. Again Marlene shuddered. *For him it actually is a* game, *and now he has verbalized it.*

Wroth sat up. "Ethan, pressure our South American colleague on Politics to tell us where the submarine or submarines came from. I'm going to need that information to expose this attack. Jake, it's time to shut down every terrorist group and fringe group we've been targeting. I want the world to see that the IC is still in place. Commit only as many troops as can effectively get the job done. The rest must stay in hiding."

Again the secure phone rang. Dr. Larson Sayers was on the line. "Hello, Michael. It has started. You might want to read the biblical book of Revelation, chapter eight, before you do anything." Then Sayers hung up.

Wroth set down the phone. "What? Who has a Bible?"

In the entire group, no one owned a Bible, or at least no one wanted to admit it. Sheepishly, however, Marlene finally produced an old King James Bible from her purse. "It was my mother's. I guess I carry it as a sort of good luck charm with all the flying we do."

She checked the table of contents in the front, turned to Revelation 8, and handed the book to Wroth.

He read mechanically when he reached the middle of the chapter:

and there followed hail and fire mingled with blood, and they were cast upon the earth.

"Well, I'll be. He was right." He continued reading about a second trumpet:

*a great mountain burning with fire was cast into the sea:
and the third part of the sea became blood.*

And then on to the third trumpet:

*there fell a great star from heaven, burning as it were a
lamp, and it fell upon the third part of the rivers, and upon
the fountains of waters.*

Jake tried to lighten the moment. "You're not getting religious on us, are you, sir?"

But Wroth didn't laugh. "You have no idea, Jake." He paused. "The result of the first trumpet could very well be a nuclear attack just like we're witnessing. The third is obviously our asteroid. But there's another one coming before that. A mountain burning with fire. My God! Ethan, are there any more asteroids or other such objects heading toward earth?"

Farnsworth thought. "Not that I'm aware of. With the asteroid coming, we've scoured the skies bloody well. I should say we have as certain an idea of any other dangers as we could ever have."

Wroth paced a moment. "Jake, are any of our troops stationed anywhere near volcanic regions?"

"Volcanic regions? I have no idea. What difference does it make?"

"Find out, and get all our troops hundreds of miles clear of any active volcanoes."

Simmons stood, uncertainty and confusion on his face.

Wroth shouted, "Now! I want them out now and *not* by ship. Only by air. Now! We don't have any time to lose. Otherwise, don't move any of our troops. We don't have time to arrest the terrorist groups, so forget those orders. Tell everyone to hunker down and hold on, and as much as possible, to stay away from coastlines. This world will be just as ripe for picking in a couple of weeks as it is now."

The cluster of suites was a buzz of activity as troops were redeployed and the IC responded to the nuclear attack. For the sake of the dream, Marlene shoved aside her emotions as she had done a million times before. She moved into automaton mode, translating her boss's every wish into reality with uncanny efficiency.

Within hours, reports flooded in to the IC's temporary headquarters about the millions who had died in the eastern U.S. Those who hadn't died instantly now faced the agony of dealing with nuclear fallout and famine. All food and water had been tainted, and few people were prepared. There had been no time to implement the evacuation plan for the president and his cabinet in Air Force One. No time to evacuate the U.S. Congress to its secret subterranean fortress.

In an instant, America's top officials had been wiped out, and the symbol of world freedom—Washington itself—was no more. In an instant, the financial and trading power center of New York City was erased off the map. Within hours, the entire eastern third of North America struggled in the clutches of a nuclear holocaust.

Within just those few hours, the world's most stable, powerful, and hope-giving nation was transformed into a chaotic nightmare.

Communication networks were down across the country. Much of the population along the coastal regions of the South and the West fled inland in case they were targeted next. As a result, the inland areas were overwhelmed with refugees; in the days that followed the attacks, the infrastructure of roads, stores, and living accommodations crumbled under the pressures of providing for these millions of people.

Meanwhile, on the southern and western coasts, the remaining foolhardy souls began a plundering spree that decimated many cities and towns. Police, emergency workers, and the National Guard didn't know where to start to contain the chaos. After two centuries of bliss, "America the Beautiful" was transformed almost overnight into a Third World nation in disarray.

* * *

March 3 found other nations contemplating how to take the greatest advantage of the sudden leadership vacuum created by the collapse of the United States. Japan was poised to seize the economic opportunity when something like "a great mountain burning with fire was cast into the sea." It was actually a long inactive volcano on one of the southern islands of Japan.

This one didn't erupt. It exploded, like Krakatoa in 1883. Only this explosion was much more massive, and unlike 1883, the world was much more populous now. Children in India 3000 miles away were awakened by a strange exploding sound from the direction of the Land of the Rising Sun. The detonation itself killed, maimed, or injured roughly a quarter of the Japanese population. Across the Korea Strait, the blast killed thousands of South Koreans.

A tsunami 130 feet high spread throughout the Pacific, flooding countless shores in Indonesia, Thailand, the Philippines, Micronesia, Hawaii, and even the West Coast of the U.S., though it had mostly subsided by that time. Hundreds of thousands died.

Throughout the northern and middle Pacific, thousands of sea-going vessels in or near seaports surrendered to the wave's fury, virtually obliterating Pacific trading. Overhead, hundreds of planes within a 200-mile radius succumbed to the ash that clogged their engines. In a single day, one blazing mountain plunged into the sea and brought an island economic powerhouse to its knees.

The Land of the Rising Sun emerged in as much disarray as the Land of the Free.

During the next several days, the IC prominently showed itself to be in the vanguard of the nations bringing disaster relief to the U.S. and the Pacific. Marlene activated every communications link she could find to keep IC forces in play.

The world itself was relieved to see that Michael Wroth, who had supposedly been in Washington during the nuclear attack, was not only alive but very much in control of the relief effort.

At his side was former Vice President Philip Bowen, a man whose rise to power had been orchestrated by Dr. Larson Sayers. Bowen, who had been in the Midwest during the nuclear attack, was now sworn in as the new president of the crippled nation. President Bowen threw all his support to Director Wroth.

Marlene not only had to manage her boss's every wish but also found herself trying to buoy the spirits of the shell-shocked new president and his staff. She exuded more confidence than she felt, hoping that Bowen's staff would follow suit.

IC troops everywhere brought food, clothing, medicine, and above all, order. They flew in medical personnel and set up portable hospitals. Everything seemed to be moving along as well as could be expected, despite the fact that more people had died in four days than in two world wars combined. For five days, the IC and various nations labored in joint relief efforts.

* * *

On March 4, Julie Yang rushed inside the Site B truck and shoved a printout into Christopher's hands. Out of breath, she gasped, "We-we've got to take refuge immediately!"

Julie rested in Grace's hug while Christopher asked, "What do you mean? Calm down, and take a deep breath."

"You-you remember Sue Jenkins?"

"Sue Jenkins. I seem to remember her. Wasn't she an undergrad student at our church years ago?"

Julie nodded her head vigorously. "She was my roommate. She moved to Arizona to work on her Ph.D. in astronomy. A while back, she died mysteriously—they say of an overdose, though I know she never used drugs."

Scanning the sheet in his hand, Christopher asked, "Then how could you have received an email from her today?" He handed the sheet to Timothy to observe the time and date notation.

Julie shook her head. "I don't know. The email was short and very cryptic. Perhaps Sue set it to be sent out automatically."

Timothy read it out loud:

Dear Julie,

If you get this, it means that something has happened to me. It means that word never got out about a large asteroid that may impact the earth sometime during the first two weeks of March. It means that Project Icarus was never initiated to deflect it. Tell everyone you know to take refuge in basements with any supplies they can gather. It will mean global destruction like you have never seen.

Much love, Sue

The team in the truck looked at each other in silence. Christopher awoke them from their trance. "Timothy, get the word out to all our teams about this. Have them warn everyone they can. Publish anything you can online. People need to know about this."

"I-I'll try," Timothy stammered. "But much of the Internet is down. Satellite communications are somewhat intact, so our sat phones and some cell phones will work. I'll get the word out to our teams, but I don't know how widely we can spread this to the global community. We'll do our best."

The KPF staff moved into overdrive, contacting teams around the world. Most of the global community, however, ignored the apocalyptic predictions from the much-maligned religious group.

* * *

On March 10, Michael Wroth and IC troops quietly retreated back to their dens, leaving their global humanitarian effort. It would have been more noticeable had March 10 been a normal day. Instead, it was the next installment of March Madness. No one noticed the soldiers' withdrawal into their hideaways. No one knew that Wroth and his cronies huddled in a cluster of suites in Buenos Aires.

"Marlene, call President Bowen," Wroth ordered. "Tell him to hunker down in the deepest bunker he has, and I'll contact him in a few days."

Marlene looked up in amazement. *What has this world come to? I, the aide to the IC Director Wroth, am giving orders to the President of the United States?* She picked up her phone, stepped into the next office, and made the call. When she returned to the planning room, she nodded at Wroth.

Wroth asked, "Jake, are we done here?"

"I believe we've done all we can, sir. Time to evacuate the staff to our subterranean vault."

Wroth stood up.

Immediately Marlene escorted the small staff to the waiting choppers. Within an hour, the team was hunkered down, like IC forces around the globe, to await the next phase of cataclysm.

Instead of noticing the absence of Wroth and his IC forces, the world riveted its attention on a solitary boom heard round the globe. The point of impact for the Jenkins NEA was a remote forest north of Moscow. At 10:36 a.m. Moscow time, an asteroid twenty kilometers in diameter plummeted to earth. The forest where it hit was flattened in a moment by a force greater than any atomic weapon created by mankind.

Northern and Eastern Europe immediately experienced not only the force of the impact itself but also the earthquakes that followed. Equally devastating was the climate disruption the blast created. A cloud of smoke and ash, so large that it blocked out a third of the earth's sky, plunged much of the world into darkness. Spring never sprang. Instead of spring showers, March rained acid into the water systems of Northern and Eastern Europe. More people died in the subsequent weeks from poisoned water than from the initial blast. The darkness that followed, as well as the acid rain, prevented crops from being planted or grown in much of Europe and Asia.

Wroth and the IC forces emerged from their burrows to help with the relief effort once more. The entire world seemed to be reeling under the catastrophes in the eastern U.S., East Asia and the Pacific, and Europe. Planet Earth convulsed under the effects of the climatic changes. Spring and summer never arrived. A perpetual winter settled in, even in the tropics.

Wroth was ready to assume control of the situation and made several premature attempts to do so amidst the worldwide disarray. In the entire world, it seemed that the regions least hurt were in South America and parts of Africa.

Marlene worked at his side trying to rebuild communications links, but the majority of their efforts failed. Their well-laid plans were increasingly frustrated by the unplanned and unforeseen earth-shattering events. Just as Marlene felt they might be gaining the upper hand, a new disaster occurred.

Wroth gathered his team together, surrounded by a cadre of elite scientists. He spoke barely above a whisper as the nervous researchers leaned forward. "I *must* know what this swarm of hell's hornets are and where they came from."

One balding scientist ventured, "Sir, we can only conjecture at this point. It's possible that this plague emerging from the Amazon Basin was triggered by the climatic changes and radiation drifting southward from the U.S."

"Out of the uninhabited recesses of the Amazon," said an entomologist, "have swarmed billions of insects—sort of a mutant hornet or locust. Swarms of these hornet-locusts have somehow crossed the southern Atlantic and plunged into the western coast of Africa. Others are sweeping up through Central America into the U.S., Canada, and up to Alaska. Crossing the Aleutian Islands to Russia, these fist-sized creatures are poised to circle the world. It could be months until we find a way to stop them. Our best hope is that perhaps they will die out on their own."

Wroth sat in his swivel chair and said nothing.

"The sting of these Amazonian hornets sends excruciating pain throughout the entire body," added a physiologist. "Fever, muscle and joint pain, itching, stomach cramps, even epileptic fits ensue. It's too early to establish a strong case history, but it appears that most people will feel the effects for four to six weeks, though there are a few recorded instances of deaths. Instead, most victims experience a living death for a period of about a month."

Wroth nodded once. Marlene knew her cue. She ushered the scientists out of the room and returned to the inner sanctum.

Jake was the first to speak. "Sir, I think we have to prepare for the worst-case scenario. This insect plague rocks the world and drives everyone to try to isolate themselves. Based on the lifespan of these creatures, we think that normalcy should return about five months from now."

Wroth laughed grimly. "Normalcy? There will be no normalcy until we usher in the Rebirth. The world will descend into chaos before it emerges glorious." He tapped his fingertips together. "Okay, we wait. Marlene, give the orders."

The world's population remained in self-imposed quarantine for those five months, locked in their living quarters, except for attempts to get the items necessary to survive. International commerce stopped. Business shut down. Food production ground to a halt.

Marlene's blood pressure rose. Her boss was good at waiting, but she was better at acting. Director Michael Wroth couldn't gain control, no matter how great his charisma and his resources.

His troops were too busy trying to survive. The situation frustrated her, but what options did she have?

As the months crept by, Marlene took note of a phenomenon little observed among outsiders but evident to many within the Christian church. Of the various members of churches globally, a great number of the more radical Jesus-followers were not attacked by the hornets.

* * *

The KPF staff struggled to maintain contact with teams. Christopher gathered his team at the beachside villa. As they discussed the growing global confusion, he pondered about whether to share his hunches with them.

John walked up to him and wrapped him in a bear hug. "Well, our diminutive leader, it's obvious to us all that something's eating away at you."

"Yeah, there's no fooling us," said Nic. "Remember that you promised to share with us what was in the deep places of your heart, even before the ideas were fully hatched."

Chara stepped up next to him and squeezed his hand. "It's okay, honey. We're all in this together. Tell them what you've been thinking."

Christopher ran his fingers through his hair and studied the group. As his eyes gazed on each eager face, his heart swelled with pride. *Why do I always underestimate them?*

"You guys, I can only conclude that we're going through the plagues of Revelation, chapter eight."

The whole group began murmuring and turning the pages of their Bibles.

"If you look through Scripture, you'll find that God often protects his people during plagues. Just look at the Israelites in Egypt before the Exodus. That must be why many Christians are immune to the hornet attacks."

John protested, "But how can that be? I thought we were supposed to be raptured out, you know, just like the bumper sticker, 'In case of rapture, this car will be unmanned.'"

That got a laugh from the weary team, but the group soon sobered.

Christopher said, "If there was any doubt in anyone's minds, it should be erased now. We are in the Great Tribulation. God never promised to rapture us out before it, although I think a lot of us secretly hoped He would."

Nic spoke up. "Yeah, better to be prepared for the worst and surprised by the best, than prepared for the best and surprised by the worst!"

The KPF team digested that for a minute.

Christopher continued, "Tribulation or no, I believe God is protecting us from this particular disaster. This plague is a divine opportunity. If believers are the only ones who won't be stung, then think of the opportunity and responsibility we have to minister to the rest of the world during these coming months. Let's notify our teams about this. Get the word out, however you can. Perhaps it is what God will use to turn many to faith. Time is running out. We must press in till there's *no place left!*"

The colonel stood up and started pointing with his finger. "When bombs are falling and bullets flying, it is easy for a soldier to get distracted. The first thought in his mind is to run for cover. One of the counterintuitive tactics of my special forces teams has been to advance into the teeth of the enemy at such a time. When all hell breaks loose, so do we!

"While the world is reeling, this is our chance to show the sterling quality of our love for the lost and zeal for the King. All teams must advance! If there is fear, we must trust the promises of God. Things will not get any easier from this point on. Remember, the King is worth it!"

The KPF and 2414 teams and, in fact, much of the Christian community did just that. As true believers toiled to keep the world functioning—producing food, carrying on business, ministering to the suffering, healing the sick, and comforting the hurting—much of the population was touched by their compassion. Indeed, many non-believers turned to Christ, both in the established church and among unreached people groups.

NoPlaceLeft teams around the world tuned out the growing turmoil and pressed in to the spiritual battle. The age-old enemy sought to waylay them through his schemes, yet each week, new people groups were touched by the love of Christ. The momentum of Kingdom advance into hard-to-reach places increased.

Even though many came to Christ, the hearts of many more were hardened during this time. Instead of welcoming the ministry of the believers, they resented them for not being touched by the plague. In addition, many nominal 'Christians' fell away, for they were not immune to the stings. Some prophetic voices proclaimed that only *true* believers were immune to the insects' stings. That sharp word stung these churchgoers more deeply than the hornets. In many regions, the public turned on the Christians.

Michael Wroth brooded during those months, resentful at being delayed in his plans and even more resentful of the Christians who strode about freely in high visibility. In his lair, he schemed and adapted to the ever-changing situation.

Marlene frequently heard him muttering under his breath, "My time will come. My time will come."

Even the activities of The Ten were largely halted for five months. The plague of hornet-locusts began dissipating first in China. Most of China was free of the pests a month before the rest of the world.

It was then that China, the slumbering giant, awoke.

NINETEEN

During midsummer, Michael Wroth and his team prepared to assert control again. But a month before they could safely launch their plans, a new earthshaking event frustrated them.

While the rest of the world writhed in agony, thinking only of their own suffering, Chinese leaders, fully recovered a month earlier than other nations, thought only of their unique, long-overdue opportunity. The Middle Kingdom decided that for the first time in human history, its turn to dominate the entire world had come.

In an uncharacteristically rapid time frame for the septuagenarian Chinese leaders, they decided to amass their army on the western and southern borders and invade Central Asia, the Indian subcontinent, and Southeast Asia. China's multi-decade accumulation of so-called defensive armed forces was released. The Middle Kingdom didn't have to worry about any threat from Japan or Russia, who were in survival mode and no longer major powers. Instead, those nations prayed fervently that the Chinese would ignore them. During the dog days of July, the bulk of the 200-million-man Chinese army advanced in high speed jeeps and all-terrain vehicles equipped with machine guns and, more strategically, chemical weapons. In Beijing, leaders reasoned that with the largest army in the world and weapons that could wipe out whole populations, the world was theirs for the taking.

It was. Chinese armies swept through Southeast Asia, India, and Central Asia. They followed the paths of the retreating hornets, especially along the Silk Road. Everywhere, the Chinese juggernaut overran cities, towns, and villages still incapacitated from the hornet stings. Specially modified Chinese vehicles rolled through the streets; it was a simple task to shoot chemical weapons ahead while the troops remained in airtight vehicles or donned gas masks. Sometimes the chemicals led to death, at other times to temporary paralysis. For four weeks, the Chinese met little resistance as the troops rained down artillery and chemical weapons on every place in their path. The only thing that slowed them was the need to set up bases along the way to resupply their millions of troops.

The hornets had caused worldwide panic for months, but the news of the invincible Chinese blitzkrieg struck fear into the remaining national powers. In four weeks, the Chinese had gained control of Southeast Asia almost to the tip of Malaysia. Singapore remained one of the few holdouts leading the Pacific Rim resistance. The majority of the Indian subcontinent stood firmly in the Chinese empire; only the lowest portion from Madras southward remained free. Most of Pakistan, Afghanistan, and the former Soviet republics of Central Asia gave allegiance to China. Russia, still decimated from the asteroid, was not a threat.

During the second month of conquest, Chinese troops moved through Iran and across the Euphrates River, which had dried up due to the great climatic upheaval. The juggernaut halted just past the Euphrates in Iraq, considering its next move. Pockets of resistance remained in areas, but the army generally advanced on schedule. In its wake lay a chemical and military holocaust. No one wanted to believe the reports of the numbers of victims. Like the holocaust of Nazi Germany, reliable information was not readily available to the outside world. But the numbers of casualties still circulated, usually in the hundreds of millions. The Chinese had rampaged mercilessly, unleashing their centuries-old rage. Asia Minor, the Middle East, Africa, and Europe waited in fear for the hammer to fall. In which direction would the military force move? With 200 million troops, it could move in all directions.

Marlene could see it in his eyes. Wroth was worried, genuinely worried, for perhaps the first time in his life. The Chinese eruption had been on no one's radar. All his hopes rested on being able to assume control with his IC forces. Most of those soldiers were only just recovering from the hornet stings. What could he, with only 300,000 troops, do against an army 200 million strong?

In Buenos Aires, Marlene summoned a staff meeting of Wroth's military and political advisors. As they gathered around the situation table, Wroth polled them. Before them lay a map diagramming the Chinese troop movements and predictions as to their next moves.

Huddled over the map, the director first turned to his political advisors. "Can we negotiate with the Chinese? Strike an agreement?"

"Are you kidding? The Chinese are in a position of power. Why should they negotiate with anyone?" said one consultant.

Wroth countered, "Even with President Bowen's unilateral support of the IC?"

Another advisor spoke up. "The Chinese have waited for this for 4000 years. With all their pent-up frustration of being the underdog for so long, they won't stop until someone stops them."

Wroth pivoted to look straight at his military advisors. "Then do we have any hope of resistance? Who can we count as allies?"

One officer replied, "The Americans are out despite Bowen's sympathetic support. What military forces they have left are trying to restore order to their own country. Same in South America. I imagine they'll sit back and wait. They don't think the Chinese can make it across the ocean, and they're not about to commit troops badly needed at home to an overseas venture."

Wroth drummed his fingers on the tabletop. "Then who can we count on to help?"

Another officer weighed in. "The advantage the Chinese have is that they are walking in as other countries are trying to restore order to their nations. To restore that order, these nations have to divert their military to domestic needs.

"Fortunately, we have a couple of things going for us. It has taken longer for the Chinese to advance than they expected. The hornets have been gone long enough that many nations in the Middle East, Europe, and Africa are starting to recover. I imagine we can get most of those nations to send troops. If we can get the Brits to commit, too, then we may be able to form a sizable force. But we have to move quickly. Make a stand in the Middle East or Turkey. We can't let the Chinese out of the region. We must keep them bottled up before the roads diverge."

Wroth picked up a large marker and questioned the officer. "So let's assume you gather the forces all these nations can spare. What kind of numbers are we looking at?"

The officer looked around the room at the other advisors. "Who can say? It depends on how urgent they see this. For instance, the Brits probably aren't too worried since China basically has no fleet to cross the English Channel. Nevertheless, I'd guess—" As he paused, Wroth prepared to write the number on the map. "I'd guess we could muster perhaps 25, maybe 50 million troops."

Wroth dropped his marker. "25 million troops! Against 200 million? Sure, let's just toss in our 300,000 IC soldiers to frost the cake! This is suicidal!"

"Not necessarily," declared a deep voice behind Wroth. It was Jake. "You have to remember the Chinese are now spread thin across thousands of miles and numerous mountain ranges from China to the Middle East. Despite their successes, they *have* suffered some casualties and have had to leave some troops posted in garrisons along the way. Also, the bulk of these troops are poorly trained and hastily assembled. They've simply taken advantage of disorder along the way and used their chemical weapons, which has given them an inordinate advantage.

"Our intel tells us, however, that one reason they've stopped is they're low on chemical weapons, as well as food supplies. You have to remember, this has been a scorched-earth strategy. Somehow they still have to feed 200 million troops. I'd say that what you have in Iraq are about 75-100 million poorly fed, exhausted troops with little ammunition left. You might be able to beat that kind of force with 25 million fresh troops. Get some of the pockets of resistance on their flanks to rise up and cut off the supply lines, and we have an even better chance at victory."

"You'd have a much better chance of success if you thought about how the Chinese *think*," said a soothing voice from the shadows in the corner of the room.

Marlene turned, suddenly reassured by the voice. She felt her tension level subside.

Dr. Sayers stepped out into the light. "What is an empire without a capital? What is an empire when its heart is destroyed? The identity of the Chinese people is wrapped up in the symbolism of Beijing itself, the seat of government and countless emperors of time past, home of the Forbidden City, of

Tiananmen Square, of the People's Assembly, of Mao's mausoleum, even of the Olympics. The place Chinese have always looked to for the mandate from heaven.

"No matter where the empire expands, *that*, my friends, is China. Take away the heart of China, and its troops will melt away. That heart is ripe for the picking. Sure, gather the nations in the sands of the Middle East for a showdown, encourage freedom fighters to cut off supply lines, but, Michael, send your IC troops secretly to Beijing. Take Beijing, and you'll crush the empire. The ancient city awaits you, unafraid and unsuspecting, because it believes all its former major threats—Russia, Japan, and America—are immobilized. You will use the same strategy that China used, and they'll never suspect it. Just as they rose from nowhere to launch a merciless attack, so you will emerge from nowhere to strike where no one dares strike."

Marlene found herself nodding along with the others.

Wroth stopped to consider Dr. Sayers's words. "You want me to persuade a coalition of nations to risk their small forces—25 million though they are—against a minimum of 75-100 million Chinese battle-hardened troops with chemical weapons? Troops who have charged across Asia in just over a month, flattening all resistance? To risk those men without any hope of assistance from the Americans, Japanese, Russians, or Indians? To face the world's largest army all on the hope that we can mobilize three hundred thousand troops and have them all converge on one city in China in a surprise attack?

"You think I can convince them to take a stand in the sand and fight as long as possible, hoping that the Chinese will melt away when and *if* they hear that their beloved Beijing has fallen? Do you really think I can convince them? And do you think we can do all this within two to three weeks before the Chinese start rolling again?"

Everyone in the room sensed the foolishness of the concept. A few even chuckled from the back. Dr. Sayer's spell had been broken.

But Sayers hobbled slowly forward, and as he did, the crowd in the room parted. With his eyes fixed on Wroth, the elderly peacemaker moved within inches of Wroth, handed his cane to

Charles, his steward, and placed both hands squarely on the Wroth's shoulders. He whispered so only Wroth could hear. "With me at your side, we *can* convince them, because we must." Then more loudly he announced, "If anyone in the world can do it, *we* can!"

Wroth grinned confidently. "Yes, of course we *will*." Then looking around the room he asked, "Why is it that no one else here believes but this one dear friend? We will make our stand in the sand! We will stop the Chinese army. Then the entire world will know that I am the savior of this generation. This will be my defining moment!"

Marlene looked up, shocked by the words coming from Wroth's lips.

A few murmurs of approval began to rise until Sayers spoke again into his ear. "No, Michael. This will be a glorious moment, which will catapult you to the top. But your defining moment is yet to come. Then, the whole world will worship you."

TWENTY

"Please, uncle, take us aboard your boat." Yijing and twenty gospel-runners stood on a remote dock near Pakse. Flames from dozens of buildings in the city cast a yellow glow in the night sky. Sounds of gunfire drifted ever closer to the gospel band. These were all the gospel-runners Yijing had been able to find before fleeing the region.

An old boat captain with gnarled hands held the dock lines, preparing to shove off. The running lights of the fishing boat remained darkened in an effort to escape the notice of the Chinese advance. "Little sister, I already have too many people on board and too few hands to help. My deckhands have all fled the Chinese assault. You must find another way of escape."

Yijing gave orders to the gospel-runners. "Quickly release those ropes from the pilings. Push the boat into the channel and jump on board." Then, turning to the captain, Yijing beamed, "*We* will be your deckhands. We will do your bidding. Just take us with you."

Gunfire split the hushed conversation. Soldiers of the People's Liberation Army came sprinting down the muddy road leading to the dilapidated dock, threatening to cut off the boat's escape. To the soldiers' surprise, Yijing shouted in perfect Mandarin, "We are friends and not enemies. Stop your firing!"

The Lao captain looked at Yijing with astonishment. Her continued shouting bought a short lull in the gunfire. Without waiting, the captain ran to the pilothouse and gunned the motor. Diesel exhaust billowed in the air around the fleeing boat. Yijing jumped up on the gunwale while continuing to yell in Mandarin. Two gospel-runners held onto her tightly as she hung off the side.

As if awakening from a slumber, the Chinese soldiers ran to the riverbank and began firing again in the direction of the dark shape disappearing into the mists of the Mekong River. The gospel-runners pulled Yijing safely up on the deck where she cowered behind the gunwale with the others as bullets whizzed about them.

As the gunshots grew fainter, Yijing summoned the fearless band to her side. "You must make yourself invaluable to the captain. Obey his every order. Only by working in unison will we escape. While onboard we must serve the needs of the passengers. Many are wounded. Do your best. We must love them and nurse them back to health. Quickly now!"

Yijing climbed into the pilothouse and peered with the captain into the dark, swirling mists as the old boat chugged through the muddy waters. "You did not tell me you were Chinese!" he hissed.

As the moonlight shone upon his face, Yijing spotted the doubt in his eyes.

"I am from China, but I am not Han Chinese. I am from a tribal group like yours." Yijing continued gazing into the murk in front of the boat. "How can you see?"

"Little sister, I have grown up on this river. I do not need to see. I know every bend of this ancient mother."

"But uncle, where will we go to escape the Chinese army? I hear rumors that they line the banks for many kilometers."

"Darkness and fog are our friends, little sister. Soon we will be in Cambodia and then from there on to the Delta in Vietnam. We can only hope that the Chinese devils have not beaten us there. But if they have, perhaps your Mandarin will come in handy again."

The slur against her fellow countrymen stung Yijing, but she ignored it. "Perhaps. But more importantly, my friends and I will pray that the angels of the Most High God will escort us safely through. If they do, where then from the Delta?"

"That, little sister, is a question I cannot answer. This little boat has been into the open sea to fish, but never far from land. Where will we go? Wherever there are no Chinese. Malaysia? Indonesia? Only your God knows! Pray for calm seas."

TWENTY ONE

Christopher clapped his hands in glee. "Win, tell me more!"

Win and Tal had just returned from a covert trip abroad to visit the KPF and *2414* teams. "We almost didn't make it back, sir. With the U.S. military just recovering from the recent disasters, especially the hornet invasion, we couldn't count on transportation from them. And of course there have been few commercial flights in the last several months. Those seats that are available are being scalped at up to fifty thousand dollars for a trans-Pacific flight. But ...," Win paused, grinning a little, "I do have some old buddies that are now with IC. I know that the IC's not too favorable toward us, but my buddies don't know who I work for."

Tal elbowed him. "Don't know? Why, you old hound, I'd say you've become almost as sly as a CIA spook—almost, I say. Sure you haven't been fooling me all these years?"

A larger grin turned up the edges of the colonel's lips, but he continued. "All I can say, sir, is that I am utterly amazed. While the world has been reeling from the plagues, mission teams from numerous groups like ours have witnessed unbelievable success. Time after time I talked to teams that labored in hard areas. When the locals saw how these faithful Christ-followers were not affected by the hornets, they knew God must be with them. Their god or gods didn't protect them, but Jesus protected our people! Sir, the teams are seeing some entire villages convert! This is unprecedented."

Christopher questioned him further. "I assume you've already given Timothy the data?"

"You must remember," said Tal, "that information technology is my specialty. How's that program I obtained for you, Mr. Wu?"

"Amazing!" Timothy piped in from his seat in front of a console in Site B. "Boss, take a look here!"

Christopher looked at a computer simulation on the screen in front of him. No other eyes had ever seen this unique simulation, simply because the information was potentially damaging to the teams in place. Nevertheless, Christopher felt he needed to know the exact placement of his teams so he could understand the status of reaching the remainder of the unengaged unreached people groups.

He had had Timothy plot all the data week by week, though virtually all the staff were unaware of this. A handful of trusted collaborators from other organizations around the world supplied data to the KPF and received data they needed in return.

Timothy stored the data in a tamper-proof file on a computer not connected to the Internet. Only a complex coding system could retrieve it. Timothy's program was an adaptation of a CIA version that Tal had obtained for them.

Christopher watched a display of the progress of the last two years, as increasing numbers of the over three thousand UUPGs gradually were shaded in with different colors: red meant a team was present, orange meant a breakthrough was occurring, and green indicated where churches were reproducing past four new generations in multiple locations.

Christopher held his breath as he watched the world moving toward green, but there was still such a long way to go, even with the plotting of all known NoPlaceLeft initiatives in the world.

A more generic version of the same time-lapse simulation was distributed to a few confidential sources in other missions agencies so that together a concerted effort could be made. Movements were starting, but the gap to *no place left* was still large. Even so, the progress was breathtaking.

As Win, Tal, Christopher, Timothy, and Nic watched the display, Tal spoke up. "Christopher, as exciting as this is, there's more news. I don't think this is very accurate—this simulation, that is."

"What do you mean, Tal?"

"Well, an unusual thing has been occurring on the field. Many of our teams have traveled to remote areas that have been opened up due to lax security by their local governments who are temporarily distracted. While the rest of the world is mourning all the recent world events, this lax security has been a real boon to the quest."

Tal's expression became even more intense, and his voice lowered to a whisper. "Here's the strange thing: as the teams have gone into previously unpenetrated areas, some of which have taken several days to reach by truck, then horseback, and so on, they have had villagers tell them of rumors of similar teams who have been in even more difficult-to-reach neighboring areas with the gospel. Many of these teams are from other continents."

Christopher shouted, "Praise God! We knew other churches and groups around the world were still sending teams but not the full extent. You know how most regular communications have been down, what with the nuclear attack, the asteroid, and all the other recent crises."

Tal's face had a sour look. "Could be, Christopher, but the teams pretty much know what's happening in their areas. They've never heard of these groups, and then suddenly in the deepest, darkest interior regions, they hear about them. It just doesn't add up. Color me skeptical."

Win coughed. "Uh, sir, Tal does have a propensity toward painting a worst-case scenario. Even so, the evidence does not look too promising. "

"There must be a simple explanation—," Christopher began, but he was cut short by the frantic rustling of pages in a Bible.

Nic spoke up enthusiastically, with his large Bible flopped open. "What if the reason they have no explanation is that this is a supernatural occurrence? It could be that God is dispatching teams there we don't know about. Or, what if they're really *angels?*"

The four other men raised their eyebrows in response.

Tal said, "Angels? Uh, I don't think so. Not in this day and time."

Remembering his motel room experience, Christopher said, "Well, Tal, let's not completely discount this idea. Go ahead and share what you've got, Nic."

The entrepreneur spoke rapidly. "Listen to Revelation 14:6 and 7:

*Then I saw another angel flying in midair, and he had the
eternal gospel to proclaim to those who live on the earth—
to every nation, tribe, language and people. He said in a
loud voice, 'Fear God and give him glory, because the hour
of his judgment has come.'*

"What if these are *angelic* teams?"

Christopher shook his head. "Nic, that may be, but I find it a little farfetched. I always have interpreted that passage to refer to God empowering His people to proclaim the gospel to every group."

Nic wasn't daunted. "Could be. You know more about Scripture than I do, but you have to admit that *my* interpretation is *possible*."

Christopher laughed. "Okay! Okay! It's possible. Maybe the KPF can retire now."

"What? And miss the end-times party? No way!"

The colonel spoke up. "Sir, I hate to spoil this party, but there's more news. Not all of our teams have had it easy. Even with what you're calling God's divine protection, some have lost their homes, many are hungry, and some have been attacked. We lost some teams to the asteroid and the volcanic explosion, though we still don't know the full extent. As you say, the communication is difficult. It's pretty disheartening in those areas.

"With the Chinese troops rolling over Central Asia the last month and a half, a lot of our teams have had to evacuate before the onslaught. Lance Wu, who is in charge of our Central Asian teams, reports that our teams are in hiding until the troops pass. You wouldn't believe the destruction they find when they go back."

Tal looked at Win, who nodded, and then added to the colonel's assessment, "There's more. My confidential sources have informed me that there's going to be a major showdown in Iraq between the Chinese and a coalition of nations. There are going to be some major fireworks in the Middle East. Not only that—and this is *top* secret—there may be a major invasion of Beijing by IC forces at the same time. We've been pretty fortunate with our personnel so far, considering the circumstances, but as much as we might dislike doing it, we may want to attempt to withdraw them from those regions, at least until the military threat subsides."

Christopher sat down. Though he had rejoiced for a few moments, a look of consternation returned to his face. His brow had increasingly worn this concern over the last several months. When he spoke, it was not with the tone of a triumphant commander but of a sobered strategist.

He sighed. "Do you realize that in the last six months, some estimates put the loss of life at as high as one quarter of the world's population? That's almost two billion people! Will this fighting never stop? Christians around the world are witnessing and seeing unparalleled numbers of people come to Christ, but the number of people *losing* their lives to war and disasters is increasing even faster."

Christopher breathed deeply. "It seems we advance three steps, then retreat two." He paused again. "Okay, have the teams withdraw from those locations until they decide it's safe to return. It just seems we'll never catch up."

He sat back and put his head in his hands.

Nic walked over to the coffeepot and returned with a steaming cup. He set it in Christopher's hands. "Come on, buddy, I know there's something more bothering you. What's up?"

Christopher didn't even raise his head. "Persecution. It's going to get worse. A *lot* worse. In fact, if I read Revelation right, we Christians have had it pretty good so far. But God's about to remove the protection. We're going to be like sheep going to the slaughter. We wanted to be like Christ. Well, we're going to have the opportunity to follow Him not only in life, but also in death—droves of us. *That's* what concerns me."

When he looked up, tears were streaming down his face. "The faces of hundreds of team members that looked so expectant as they boarded their planes—those faces haunt me. Those are the faces that are heading toward prison and the gallows. And soon, as we pursue *no place left* there will be *no SAFE place left*. Not there, not here. We will all be hunted down. It is the price of being the last generation, of being allowed to have our robes washed by the blood of the Lamb as we walk through the Great Tribulation. Life will never be the same again."

Christopher looked up into the colonel's eyes. "Tell them, Win. Tell the teams what's coming. Warn them. Tell them there will come a point where they cannot hide from persecution. Tell them to endure to the end."

And then, as if it was a passage he had not only memorized but had been meditating on for some time, he quoted the sixth chapter of Revelation in a ghostly voice:

> *When he opened the fifth seal, I saw under the altar the souls of those who had been slain because of the word of God and the testimony they had maintained. They called out in a loud voice, "How long, Sovereign Lord, holy and true, until you judge the inhabitants of the earth and avenge our blood?" Then each of them was given a white robe, and they were told to wait a little longer, until the number of their fellow servants, their brothers and sisters, were killed just as they had been.*

No one said a word. No one questioned him. The hair on the back of their necks stood up.

Win nodded and stood. Tal stood with him. "I will, sir, I will. We will advance into the teeth of the fight until there is *no place left.*"

A grimace spread across Tal's face. "Like always, I guess."

* * *

World War II's D-Day had involved only one million Allied troops landing over a three-week period on the Normandy coast. Now, along an imaginary line in the sand just west of the dried-up Euphrates River, a joint force of 9,340,000 troops from fifty-three nations dug in, waiting for the Red Storm, as the Chinese assault had become known. The allied force had been thrown together in less than three weeks' time—*too* much time, in Marlene's opinion. And apparently for her boss, who paced back and forth.

The Chinese had had time for a partial resupply, though this was a daunting task for a functional army of 87 million. But no less daunting were the logistics of gathering together this allied force. It had taken all of the persuasive powers of both Wroth and Sayers to convince the nations to send any sort of sizable force to the Middle East when every soldier was needed to help settle the unrest back home in the allied countries. Nevertheless, three weeks later the battle had not yet begun.

Wroth stopped pacing and stood in the sand next to his tent. Marlene knew he didn't want to be here. He wanted to be with his IC forces, which were *hopefully* going to invade China in time. The trusted allied commanders fervently hoped that the Chinese would wait to press the attack in Iraq until the strike on Beijing could be assembled, but there was no guarantee of it. The focus of where Wroth should make his stand had been debated in the secrecy of the inner circle.

Marlene sat in the Hummer next to where Wroth stood. Wroth gestured toward the Red Storm forces. "Marlene, why do they wait? There is no reason. The longer they wait, the more allied troops and equipment will arrive."

"I don't know, Sena-, uh, Director. At least our troops are fresh. Whenever the Chinese attack, we'll just have to hold out, hoping that Jake and the IC forces can get to Beijing in time."

That night, few slept. Marlene awoke at 3:00 a.m. to find Wroth already pacing in front of his tent.

Sunrise revealed that the Red Storm's advance had begun, with the rumbling of a third of the Chinese tanks and the roar of a smattering of Chinese artillery. Most of the all-terrain vehicles equipped with the chemical weapons rolled forward.

"Ah, it's started, Marlene. So that's it. They don't have enough fuel for all their equipment, but they don't dare wait any longer. Here we stand in the middle of oil fields, and still there is not enough refined fuel to power their tanks."

As formidable as the tanks were, it was the fast-moving chemical weapons vehicles that concerned the allies the most.

The allied commanders urged their troops to hold the line despite the coming chemical attack. Gas masks donned, the troops waited anxiously. The chemical weapons were fired. The allied troops cringed as the shells exploded all around them. As they waited for the invisible gas to be released, they could only hope that all their gas masks were functional and resistant to the chemicals.

Marlene clutched her mask, though she stood beyond the theoretical limits of the nerve gas.

She waited. The army waited. Yet nothing happened. No burning. No wheezing.

It was only a bluff, a feint. Apparently, the Chinese had no chemical weapons left but hoped that the firing of the empty shells would unnerve enough troops to cause a break somewhere in the battlefront. Apart from a few isolated spots, the troops did not panic, and the long line in the sand held fast.

Regardless, the bulk of the Chinese army surged forward.

Marlene began to shudder, but Wroth spoke reassuringly. "Remember your history, Marly. The British 'Thin Red Line' held back the Russians during the Crimean War. Today will be no different."

The ensuing battle raged all day. It might have been over more quickly had the Chinese spread the battlefront more, but they were content to fight along the front given them by the allies. Though the allies were not enveloped, virtually all of their troops were engaged, while the Chinese continually replaced tired units with fresh ones.

When night fell at last, the guns went silent. The next day, the battle raged again along the now-jagged battle line. For three days the allies fought, yet gradually, inevitably, they gave ground to the Chinese.

Wroth rode the circuit of the battlefront. Wherever troops wavered, Wroth appeared out of nowhere in his camouflaged Hummer to encourage them.

Marlene marveled to see how the soldiers' spirits were buoyed by his words. Knowing Wroth's eyes were upon them, the military units renewed their resolve and fought as maniacs. She gazed at the figure at her side, speeding along the battlefront with his hair blowing in the wind. *He's a new Napoleon! They worship him. Let's hope this isn't his Waterloo.*

Yet when the fourth day dawned, hope seemed to fade for the allies. For the first two hours, the intensity of the battle grew feverish as the Chinese threw everything against the remaining allies. The allied line began to be beaten back. A rout appeared imminent.

Wroth's spirited cries could only summon so much resolve from the exhausted troops.

Then it happened. A few Chinese units in the rear turned and began a rapid retreat. As difficult as worldwide communications were, news had just reached the Chinese commanders: IC forces had entered Beijing in a surprise attack! All resistance had been swept away. The ancient capital was in flames! The area around Tiananmen Square—the Forbidden City, the government headquarters, Mao's mausoleum—the entire center of the newly emerging Chinese Empire was burning. Officials fleeing the capital of the Middle Kingdom sent out a panicked cry for help.

These abrupt and unexpected troop movements sent waves of panic among the remaining Chinese forces. Unclear communication led to the perception that the army was retreating. In moments, the whole Chinese force collapsed into a self-induced rout. The allies, seeing an opportunity, regained fresh vigor and pressed the attack upon the fleeing Red Storm.

Wroth shouted at his driver to keep pace with the pursuit. But it soon became clear that they were passing the leading edge of the allied advance. A colonel assigned as an aide for the director barked at the driver. "Too far! Too far! You'll endanger Director Wroth!"

With a visage of stone, Wroth stood oblivious to the danger, grasping the front windshield. Suddenly bullets whizzed past him as the Hummer flew forward.

Marlene tugged the director and forced him to sit. The driver swerved the vehicle and returned to safety.

Exhausted troops streamed by, shouting at the tops of their lungs with renewed fervor. The allies released an Allied Storm upon the Red Storm.

Retreat led to massacre. The Chinese army that didn't have enough fuel to send all its tanks into battle realized too late that it also lacked enough to fall back. One by one, Chinese transports, tanks, and other vehicles ran out of fuel and fell behind, only to be overcome by their pursuers. Worse still, the Chinese possessed little air support, and without mobile ground-to-air missiles to cover their withdrawal, their fleeing army was simply target practice for the allied planes.

Before the day was over, the Chinese army was not only defeated, it was for all intents and purposes *eliminated.*

Eventually the Hummer rolled to a halt. As he stood atop his vehicle, Wroth was mobbed by the victorious allied troops and hailed as a hero. The men and women in this force had stared death in the face for three days, and that had followed six months of turmoil and powerlessness by their own governments. But now they had found a man of strength who had finally halted the unstoppable tide and promised to bring the world back into order.

Somehow, amid the teeming troops, another Hummer pulled alongside with Dr. Sayers inside. Though he spoke in a normal voice among the cheers, Marlene heard him perfectly.

"It's time, Marlene. Give the word."

Marlene signaled key IC staff to begin the covert distribution of millions of silver triangle patches, the IC insignia. As one, the troops under the influence of Wroth and Sayers tore off the insignias of their home countries and replaced them with IC patches.

While this change of insignia spread through the millions of troops, Marlene listened as, on cue, Wroth repeatedly shouted over his loudspeaker for them not to do it. Yet the more he insisted, the faster the troops acted.

The troops began chanting in unison, "Michael! Michael!"

Marlene shook her head in disbelief as several million soldiers from dozens of nations switched their allegiance to Michael Wroth. *How could Sayers have known it would play out like this?*

Finally, Wroth shrugged in acquiescence and told the chanting troops he would accept their allegiance if they would give it in the cause of establishing world peace.

One by one, most of the major world powers had been eliminated or their armies had pledged allegiance to Wroth. Michael Wroth now stood alone on top of the heap, with the largest, best military force in the world—a force that now would die for him.

No one questioned his sudden rise to power. Instead, the intimidated leaders of the world jockeyed to see who could curry the most favor with him. The world was ready for peace—at all costs—and Wroth promised peace.

For two weeks Wroth remained silent about the political situation, strategizing with Dr. Sayers in their mountain hideaway. He didn't need to speak. For two weeks, his huge army of IC personnel—civilian and non-civilian—and almost the entire weight of The Ten's resources devoted themselves to rebuilding the world's infrastructure and establishing law and order.

All the world knew was that, at the end of two weeks, Michael Wroth would appear in a worldwide broadcast to speak about the future. How that would happen, no one could guess, since most communication systems were still out of commission.

* * *

At the end of those two weeks, due to the amazing amount of effort put into it by the IC and The Ten's forces, a basic worldwide infrastructure was in place. With the hidden resources of The Ten alone, Wroth could work wonders no other man on earth outside of The Ten could. Combined with the resources of the International Coalition, the transformation was miraculous. The world stood again in some semblance of order.

On a chilly night in England, Marlene stood on the platform examining the packed stadium. IC personnel held the crowd at bay as they struggled to catch a glimpse of Director Wroth. She spoke into her microphone, "Jake, is everything ready for Director Wroth's appearance?"

In her earbud, the voice of the man on the other side of the stage said, "As ready as we'll ever be. Signal the team to bring the director out."

Marlene gave the word, and in an instant, the lights of the soccer arena went dark. The crowd gasped in unison.

A low, rhythmic melody began crescendoing until it reverberated through the stadium. Spotlights shot out and lit up the stage.

A figure emerged from a trapdoor in the stage. Michael Wroth strode forward alone, illuminated by the light.

A cheer erupted from every lip. The stadium shook.

The world's attention was focused on this one man, immaculately dressed in a black suit, standing at the podium under the glare of spotlights and the watchful eye of restored worldwide video streaming.

For minutes on end, the crowd shouted, "Michael! Michael!"

Unlike the rest of the world, the people in the stadium had no screen to watch. Instead, in a feat never before attempted in a public arena, three-dimensional holograms of Michael Wroth, fifty meters high, suddenly appeared at the four corners of the arena. They moved in exact unison with his figure on stage.

The crowd gasped in astonishment and then grew silent as the images motioned for them to listen.

Not until one could hear a pin drop anywhere in the world, did Michael Wroth, Director of the International Coalition for the Preservation of World Peace and former senator of the United States, speak.

"My beloved fellow citizens of Earth, how I have longed for the day I could cradle you in my arms as I do today. I had hoped it could come before now, before all the destruction of the past six months. Indeed, for several years, my every waking moment has been devoted to you, my brothers and sisters of every race, who, like myself, long for a world that dwells in true peace— something the world has not experienced in history. My heart breaks over the millions who have died, deprived of the right to see this day.

"But today I whisper to you words of affection and news of a plan for your welfare that has never before been discussed publicly yet has grown up over the last sixteen centuries. The peace you experience today is not due solely to the combined force of the International Coalition and the allied nations. What you see before you today is unexplainable by any humanly known plan—except for one."

Marlene stood in the shadows, following Wroth's oration on her faintly illuminated speech notes. She mouthed the words with him, as familiar with the script as he was.

Wroth had the crowd in his grasp.

"Almost sixteen hundred years ago, a group of ten influential men—men who loved this world more than their own little empires—rose up and implemented a plan to reach their dream. They dreamed of a world born anew, a time of Rebirth. They dreamed of an age in which the whole world would know peace, possessing all that was needed for life and happiness. Rather than see the world continue in cutthroat competition or aspire to substandard plans such as we would see later in communism, these men set about withdrawing from society and helping to order world events to bring about this plan for the welfare of the world."

* * *

Number One hobbled around the triangular table rasping, "He *must* be stopped! He is eroding the strength of our invisibility!"

The fire in the hearth crackled and sprang to life, casting gargoylish shadows upon the tapestried walls.

Number Four responded in his Russian accent. "Do not worry, Prime Director. Plans are in motion."

* * *

People around the world listened, as transfixed as the crowd in the arena. As one might follow the speech of an enemy, the Owen family listened to Wroth. Christopher focused intensely. *If for no other reason than to know what to expect from the evil one.*

* * *

The fifty-meter holograms of Wroth gestured gently, almost touching the upturned faces.

"These men have been the silent overseers of the world, the caretakers of human society. Through the last sixteen hundred years, the baton has been passed from man to man, and during that time, the influence of The Order of The Ten has grown immensely. Few individuals have known about the group, and never has it been spoken about publicly until tonight. No president or king has ever heard of The Ten, yet we—yes, I am one of them—we possess more authority than any government in the world. We decreed that we would never speak openly of our group until," he paused, "the Rebirth—the time when the world would be born anew.

* * *

"He is announcing the Rebirth!" shouted Number One. "He is destroying everything!"

Number Eight, the Indian, responded matter-of-factly. "I have always mistrusted and hated this man. Do not worry, Prime Director. Today his schemes will backfire on him."

* * *

The holograms raised their arms 25 meters into the air.

"My brothers and sisters, this is that day! Today the world is reborn!"

The crowd erupted in cheers.

Marlene began crying. *Finally! Finally! All our plans are finally leading to that glorious dream we had when we were young. Surely the end has justified the means in this case.*

Wroth continued to speak. "Only a handful of governments in history have truly had the welfare of their people at heart. Unfortunately, none has ever possessed the power to *guarantee* the welfare of its people, and none has had the interests of the whole *world* at heart. How can any nation live in a blissful state when it competes with other nations for resources and territory?

"But in the last six months, divine judgment, yes, *divine* judgment has fallen on our world. Call it a *purging* if you will, a catharsis, but in the last six months, a purging has wiped away every legitimate power that could oppose the divine plan to give birth to a world imbued with peace and happiness. Yes, I say divine, for every man, woman, and child must surely recognize, as he looks into his heart, that the events of the last six months have not been natural. No, they have displayed the very finger of God!"

Murmurs spread through the crowd, and people began nodding in assent as Wroth's holographic gestures appeared to touch the stands.

Marlene looked up in surprise. *He's gone off the script! What is he doing?*

"Not the God of Christianity or Islam or Buddhism or Hinduism or Judaism alone. No, but the one Most High God of all religions has smiled upon us. He has purged all parties that could oppose The Ten. Today, we witness the Rebirth of the world. Now may The Ten come out of hiding and stand before you publicly as your devoted servants. Your welfare is our only concern. Let me share with you the names of The Ten—

* * *

"Fool! Fool!" The grizzled old Italian danced from foot to foot. "How stupid can you be?"

* * *

"—as well as the list of the remainder of the six hundred sixty-five members of The Ten who have come before me. I would ask every one of you around the world to stand out of reverence for these selfless servants who have worked silently and without recognition for your well-being."

* * *

"Quickly! Quickly! There is no time to lose!" The Prime Director hurled a drink into the hearth, and a flame leapt up to consume it.

* * *

Without hesitation, the crowd stood to its feet in silence.

Dr. Sayers watched in admiration as Wroth held the crowd spellbound.

Marlene looked from him to Wroth and back to Sayers. *You two planned this long ago. You chose to take a route none of us anticipated.*

Wroth motioned for one of his personal aides to bring him the list of names to read from. The whole world watched as one solitary figure moved through the crowd toward Wroth with a rolled parchment scroll in his hands.

* * *

Christopher and his family watched the monitor in silence and dismay. *I can't believe this is happening,* Then Christopher said aloud, "Don't you see how this man holds everyone in his grasp?"

Joshua chimed in, "But what he is talking about are good things, Dad, aren't they?"

A close-up of Michael Wroth showed on the screen as the Owens talked in hushed voices. Chara answered, "Honey, it depends on how he wants to accomplish these things. If he tries to do good things in a bad way, then what he is doing is *not* good."

Elizabeth was puzzled. "Mommy, the kids in the neighborhood say Mr. Wroth is a good man. They say that without him, our world would still have lots of problems and millions of people would be starving."

"Yes, dear, I know. He's done lots of good things, but we need to see *how* he does them to evaluate him as a person. Just because your friends—and the whole world—think he is a good man doesn't make him one."

Christopher interrupted, "Hush, everyone, listen!"

The image on the screen continued. "—as well as the list of the remainder of the six hundred sixty-five members of The Ten who have come before me."

Chara and Christopher exchanged suspicious looks, and both mouthed, "666!"

While Wroth waited for the aide to bring him the scroll, Christopher commented to the kids, "See, kids. He doesn't talk about the God of the Bible, but something different. He's violating ..."

His jaw dropped. All six family members stared at the screen in horror. Chara, trying to cover the smaller children's eyes, whispered, "Oh, Lord!"

* * *

The solitary figure's stately march brought him up the steps of the stage to Wroth's side. His hands unfurled the scroll, and out of its hollow interior he drew forth a long blade. Before anyone could respond, the aide-turned- assailant slashed Wroth across the forehead, splitting his skull.

Wroth collapsed upon the stage. The assassin crumpled beside him, five bullets shot through his head by IC marksmen. Medics and aides rushed to Wroth's side and felt for a pulse.

Michael Wroth, the hope of the known world, was dead.

TWENTY TWO

"He is dead, Prime Director, as you ordered." An aide took a step backward after delivering the message to the leader of The Ten.

The Italian's eyes widened, and a grin spread from ear to ear. Standing up, he flapped his arms like wings and cackled, "So shall be every enemy of The Ten! The glorious Rebirth will proceed on *our* schedule."

The loyal members of The Ten stood and shook hands. They had chosen the right side. Champagne was passed around, and for a moment, their hearts were filled with mirth and relief.

The Prime Director turned to Number Two, the Chinese gentleman. "Initiate the rest of the plan. We must contain the damage created by that fool Wroth. The Rebirth *will* come but will now be delayed even longer due to his lunacy. Let this be a lesson to all of you!"

* * *

The entire crowd convulsed at the sight of Wroth's fallen body and then rushed for the exits in pandemonium. IC security forces blocked the exits and futilely tried to restore order. Several of Wroth's staff tried to approach the microphone to urge calm and order, but the mob swarmed the platform as one more avenue of escape.

The world watched as its one hope of restoring world peace lay on the stage.

Crowds rushed around the fallen figure, but no one trampled it in the tumult.

Instead, a lone figure in white stood over the body of Michael Wroth to guard it from desecration. The body of the assailant had long since been seized and disfigured by the crowd. Each successive minute brought more chaos, but still the small figure of Dr. Sayers quietly stood over the crumpled body of Wroth, hands upraised to heaven, eyes closed.

It began as just a small breeze, but increasingly a wind blew through the arena. The thousands milling around in the stadium began to quiet down as a strange peace descended upon them. The wind's velocity increased as it swirled, pivoting around the very spot on the platform where Sayers stood. Gale force winds soon knocked people back to their seats or knees, dust swirled through the stadium, and few were able to even stay planted in place. But in the eye of the growing vortex that allowed no man or woman to stand, stood Sayers, not a hair blowing in the stillness.

The audience around the world continued to watch in disbelief.

*   *   *

Christopher's phone rang. He saw John Steward's name flash on the screen.

"Hey, Kemosabe, you watching this?"

Christopher responded, "Who isn't?"

"You thinking what I'm thinking? Read Revelation recently?"

"Every week! Let's keep watching to see if it plays out. If so, we need to put all teams on high alert. Don't hang up."

*   *   *

Sayers was not standing near the microphone, but when he spoke, the whole stadium heard his quietly soothing voice, and the winds began to die down. "Peace. Do not be afraid, little children. Don't you see that it must be this way?"

Sayers still stood, eyes focused upward, almost rolled back into his head. His jaw dropped, but his lips formed no words as he spoke. The whole crowd sensed that this was not Sayers speaking, but he was rather some sort of conduit. The message continued, "Listen to the voice of the mighty one, the god who has always been and always will be. Stand back from the one who dared assail my servant while I render judgment!"

The crowd, in shock, backed away from the mutilated body of the assailant that lay on the turf of the stadium. When sufficient space was given, Sayers lowered one arm, picked up his cane, and stretched it toward the body. A dazzling flash of fire descended from the sky, hit the cane, and shot out toward the body of the assassin. Instantly, the body was consumed in the fire. A tremor of fear shot through the crowd.

The voice continued from Sayers's mouth. "Thus shall I treat everyone who mocks me or my servant! What did you come here today to see? A mighty man who has brought peace to the earth! Michael Wroth has been the servant of my choosing in these last days. And, my children, you have waited a long time, millennia, for my rule to come on earth, but today it comes. No longer will you see Michael Wroth the man; henceforth I will live in Michael Wroth. No longer shall he be a mere mortal; today, I, your god, come to you, to restore my kingdom and to bring peace that will never end."

* * *

"Uh, Christopher?" asked John. "You know I like sci-fi, but is what I'm seeing for real?"

Christopher shook his head in bewilderment as Chara herded the kids into the adjoining room where she could listen in without them watching. "You're seeing what I'm seeing. The events of Revelation have to play out some fantastic way no matter how you read them, right?"

"Uh, I guess so. This is freaking Renee and me out!"

* * *

The voice continued speaking through Sayers.

"I am the fulfillment of all your religions. The god you worship—be you Christian, Jew, Hindu, Muslim, Buddhist, or any of the many children who have looked to me in various forms—I am he! All of you have been seeking me, and now will you find me. For millennia, you have been seeking me in veiled form, hoping against hope that you had the right system of belief. Yet, your hearts have been right. No longer shall I speak to you in dreams and visions or written words.

"No. Instead, I will speak to you in person, for I will take on the body of Michael, my servant, and dwell among you. If I were to dwell with you unveiled, however, you would all die. I will be with you forever! And I will be ministered to and especially work through my prophet Larson Sayers, a man after my own heart. Because you are unable to bear the glory of my face, he will speak to you words of wisdom and of comfort."

The words coming from Sayers's mouth were the most loving and comforting ones the listeners could imagine. During this message, a strange phenomenon occurred around the world. In countries everywhere, translators stopped translating the message, for everyone heard the words in his own language.

The voice came again through Sayers. "I will lead you through these two men, though I myself shall be in Michael. Watch and see the coming of your god!"

* * *

Christopher had put the phone on speaker. "John, hold on while I add the colonel and Nic to the call."

Sixty seconds passed.

"Guys, you on?"

"On, buddy. Both Stacy and me."

"Same here, Commander. Jeanie, Tal, and me."

Chara joined Christopher. She whispered, "The kids are doing okay."

Nodding, Christopher said, "We've got no time to lose. We must initiate the next phase of the plans toward *no place left*. We must immediately—"

His voice trailed off as everyone on the conference call stared at their screens.

* * *

Sayers's head slumped forward, and he backed wearily away from the body of Wroth. All others on the platform dispersed so that only Sayers and the bleeding figure of Wroth were there. Sayers stretched both hands toward Wroth and threw his head back once more.

This time no fire came. Instead, the clouds themselves parted in the night sky as a gigantic angelic figure descended. No one watching that evening would ever agree on an exact description, for it was not exactly a bodily form; in each conscious mind, the recognition came that this was a supernatural being. The glowing, heart-settling figure descended toward the slain form until it hovered over it. The blazing eyes of the glorious figure pierced every heart, searching them all, and as the radiance grew almost blinding, a mighty voice bellowed, "See me this once, my children, in my true form! You will never see me in such a glorious state again, or you would die!"

The population of the world felt the truth of those words, yet no one diverted his or her gaze, for the sight was supernaturally beautiful. Many later remarked that they would rather die looking at the figure than look away and live. The figure itself then knelt onto the body and laid itself into the still form of Michael Wroth until it was no longer visible.

* * *

Christopher's heart burned with anger. "Let the world be deceived, but we have just seen the enemy as an angel of light. Does not the Spirit in your hearts confirm this?"

"Charlatan!" shouted Nic. "That serpent has been lying since the Garden of Eden!"

"He has the whole world thinking he is God now," whispered Chara.

* * *

Instantly, the skull was healed, and life was restored to the slain figure. Gently Michael Wroth raised himself to his feet, looked around the stadium, and smiled. Raising his hands, he shouted, "My children! I have arrived!"

The applause was thunderous. Tears streamed down the faces of everyone in the stadium, who just then realized they were on their knees. Yet no one stood; kneeling seemed to be the appropriate posture.

When the applause had died down, Michael continued, "Follow me, my children. Why should I restore this world to glory instantly, when instead you can be my hands and feet? You will share in my glory as we restore this world to the glory I intended it for. I know you. I know that you have loved me no matter your religious system, for people of all religions, and even non-religions, in the best way they could with the limited revelation they had, have all sought me. And it is the sincerity of heart that I have welcomed.

"Today begins the Rebirth—" He was interrupted by more applause, then went on, "Today, we begin the restoration. Everyone who follows me will be accepted, regardless of background. The only people we will not tolerate, the only ones we will judge, will be those, who like this murderer, seek to oppose me, to be intolerant of others, and to thwart the Rebirth.

"I invite all my children: Come into the fold. My arms are outstretched wide to receive you. Lay down your differences, for now I will teach you truly how to follow me."

The applause began and crescendoed until no more speech could be heard. All that night and through the next day, thousands stood in line, waiting patiently for the touch of Michael's or Sayers's hands, which healed them of any afflictions. More came to Sayers than to Michael, whose face emitted an aura and whose eyes were such that no one could gaze into them for long.

* * *

The KPF leadership huddled in prayer on the hardwood floors of the Owen home. Christopher glanced around the group. *Back to where it all started—on our knees in this living room.*

Their cries arose to heaven. "Oh, Father. Listen to the threats of the enemy. Deliver us from his hand! Thwart his schemes, for we are but the sheep of Your hand.

"And grant that we may speak even more boldly about the redemption found only in Jesus Christ."

As the prayer meeting drew to a close, Christopher thumbed through the pages of his worn Bible. "Brothers and sisters, the days are being cut short. The time is more urgent than ever before. Timothy, where are we on the UUPG count?"

Timothy typed quickly on his laptop. "Well, it's impossible to say, what with the communications breakdown and all. But somewhere in the neighborhood of 1,050 people groups still to be engaged with Kingdom movements."

From the far side of the room, John's voice muttered, "Not fast enough! We'll never make it."

"On the contrary, professor," said Nic, "momentum is increasing—"

"In an increasingly difficult world to work in," finished the professor.

"Guys, guys! No matter!" Christopher pointed to his Bible. "It's time to get this word out to the global NoPlaceLeft coalition. Luke 12 is taking place before our eyes:

Be dressed ready for service and keep your lamps burning, like servants waiting for their master to return from a wedding banquet, so that when he comes and knocks they can immediately open the door for him. It will be good for those servants whose master finds them watching when he comes. Truly I tell you, he will dress himself to serve, will have them recline at the table and will come and wait on them. It will be good for those servants whose master finds them ready, even if he comes in the middle of the night or toward daybreak. But understand this: If the owner of the house had known at what hour the thief was coming, he would not have let his house be broken into. You also must be ready, because the Son of Man will come at an hour when you do not expect him.

"Don't you see? The King is coming soon. We must redouble our efforts in the power of the Spirit. There is no time to lose to get to *no place left!*"

Jeanie Dunbar picked up where he left off. "Ladies, as a soldier's wife, I think it is time to face up to where we are. Routine, as we know it, is gone for our families. Our men must head out to battle. *We* must man communications on the home front while they are gone and help guide this movement."

The colonel nodded. "Yep, it will probably come to that. But I'll do my best to stagger the deployment of the men here as the situation warrants." He glanced at Tal, who winked, then turned back to Christopher. "With your permission, sir, I must make arrangements without delay."

Christopher waved his hands. "Of course, of course! Everyone, let's get on with it. And pray as you work!"

* * *

Marlene watched in amazement as the crowds came for healing to Wroth and Sayers. She felt awe and disbelief, yet something was not right.

Wroth had never been a benevolent man nor a religious one. Yes, he had helped various religious groups—Buddhists, Hindus, Muslims, Jews. In fact, just three years earlier, he had been instrumental in forming a consortium of investors who privately funded the rebuilding of the Jewish temple in Jerusalem right next to the Dome of the Rock. Indeed, archeologists had discovered that part of the foundation of the old temple actually extended away from the mosque, and under an amazing compromise brokered by Sayers, the Jews and Palestinians had agreed that a temple could be built next to the mosque.

Marlene had always assumed that this was another political ploy of Wroth's to gain the favor of the Jewish people—secretly, of course. Being so outwardly pro-Semitic would have caused too much political fallout for one who sought to rule the world, but the important Jewish decision makers would always be in debt to Wroth.

Of all the Michael-believers in the arena, Marlene alone shook her head—she who knew Michael Wroth so well. *Why now? Why should he so suddenly be religious? And why should God choose him? Surely God wouldn't choose to inhabit one who was so selfishly corrupt and murderous.*

Marlene knew that she was no better than he was, for she had been the prime instrument to carry out his orders. No, she knew there was no hope of pardon for herself—her crimes against humanity were too great. She had helped catapult this ruthless leader into power. *How can he now claim to be God? Or, more important, how can God claim him?* If anything was true from her Sunday School days as a child, then surely it was that God was pure and holy and loving.

She continued shaking her head. *No, God just doesn't inhabit people like Michael Wroth unless someone like that truly changes morally and—what was the word they used?—repents. Such a charged word, but shouldn't it apply here?*

Let these people buy this, for now, but I will not. Not yet. You will have to prove to me, Michael Wroth, that you are God. I have always worshipped you and always loved you—the man—but do not ask me to believe that you are God. We are alike—both of us sinful, selfish, and ruthless. If you are God, then heaven help us! I will continue to watch you, Michael, and continue to doubt, until you prove to me that you are God.

* * *

The next few days witnessed a global transformation. One by one, the world's remaining governments sent delegations to Michael, who set up his office temporarily at an estate in England owned by Ethan Farnsworth. The leaders of each nation offered allegiance to Michael—either convinced by what they saw on the broadcast or convinced by the fact that no one was in a position to oppose him. Indeed, with Michael's huge army and massive control of the infrastructure of the world through The Ten, power was not something he needed to seize. It was his already. All that remained was for the leaders of the world to acknowledge it. A few didn't, and they were removed from power—some by IC forces, but most by the people themselves who believed in Michael.

And everyone now called him Michael, for his name meant "Who is like God!"

Marlene and the entire staff immediately sensed a change in him. Before, he had been a ruthless, brilliant strategist and leader. Now, there was more to him. His eyes pierced every heart; he knew what was in them. He was always in control. He seemed truly god-like. Although he displayed compassion at times, most people sensed his ironclad will to rule that no one could challenge.

At the same time, Marlene noted that he was immediately more remote from her. He never opened his heart, as scarce as those incidents had been before. No longer did he call her Marly.

In a climactic display of power, Michael and his entourage entered Rome and proceeded to a small, ancient street that was cordoned off by IC forces.

Michael marched purposefully up the steps of the imposing structure with the fifteenth-century facade. Marlene rushed to keep up with him.

It seemed an eternity to her since the first time he had ascended those steps only to be ambushed himself by The Ten. What a miracle it had been that he had survived that first encounter when Simmons's elite squad had been neutralized!

This time he was flanked by his closest colleagues: Marlene, Sayers, six loyal members of The Ten (including Number Eight, the Indian, who had seen which way the wind was blowing), Jake Simmons, and two men with video cameras. Soldiers followed at their heels.

Michael strode confidently through the ancient doors, down the hall, and into the inner sanctuary where a fire no longer burned in the hearth and only three men sat at the triangular table.

Number One, the old Italian, stood up, along with Number Four, the Russian, and Number Two, the Chinese. Number One glanced at Michael in cursory recognition and then abruptly stared at him intently, eyes wide open. With a look of incredulity, his wavering finger pointed toward Michael. He almost spat out, "You! I know you! How could you have betrayed us, we who have served you for all these generations? What have you done with ...?"

Marlene shifted her gaze to Michael in shock.

Michael raised his hand, and Number One clutched his throat, unable to speak. "You are no longer the Prime Director," Michael declared. Number One fell to his knees, as did the other two men. "You three are all that remain of the old regime of The Ten. You would be forgiven if you had not plotted against the very thing you swore to work toward—the Rebirth. Instead, you will die like the one you sent to slay me. Now the entire world will know that *I* rule. I had hoped to allow you to sit on thrones with the rest of the Nine beside me. Now, there will be only six thrones in addition to mine. My world will be ruled through them, and you will not share in the glory."

He nodded toward Sayers, who raised his cane. Fire consumed the three bodies then shot into the hearth to rekindle the dead embers. The room lit up.

Michael turned toward the cameras. "This room is a sacred one, for from it the Overseers under my guidance for generations have directed history to bring us to this moment. Aside from these three traitors, they have been benevolent men. Today, I make this sacred hall the capital of the new world. May the nations stream here and find healing."

In the following days, Michael began a world tour not only to consolidate his authority but also to secure his worship. Michael himself did not visit many of the places. Instead, under a unique holographic system directed by Sayers, a three-dimensional image of Michael would appear, almost indistinguishable from the real Michael, and communicate as if he were actually present.

This image was all the more uncannily like him, since the true Michael now gave off a sort of radiance that could be detected at the edge of eyesight, in that realm just between true vision and the periphery where sight stops. In hologram or body, he visited Mecca, Lhasa, the Vatican, and many more of the world's religious centers. In each place, Wroth was welcomed as god in the flesh and worshipped by leaders. Muslims saw him as the final manifestation of God. He became the first non-Muslim in history to enter the holy area of Mecca, though to them he was the truest of Muslims. Hindus accepted him readily, as did Buddhists.

Even the majority of the "Christian" world believed in him. Sayers deserved most of the credit for achieving that. In his smoothest voice he said, "Christians have been right: these events indeed point to the Great Tribulation prophesied in Revelation. Unfortunately, many Christians in history have *misinterpreted* Revelation, which is so easy to do. For instance, Christians have *not* been raptured before the Tribulation as they were taught to expect. Instead, god has come to us, and the Tribulation is the necessary precursor to the final rebirth that Michael is ushering in!"

The issue of the Rapture alone caused many in the churches to turn away from the traditional faith. If their leaders were so wrong about the Rapture, then why couldn't they also be mistaken about the coming of the Messiah?

Church members began to believe that not only was this the

Tribulation but also that Michael was no Antichrist, as a number of Christian leaders had preached. They believed he was instead God himself coming to set up His millennial reign.

Sayers explained that the authors of the Bible had it a little wrong, but they shouldn't be faulted for that. Most of the events in it were correct, but instead of Michael being the Antichrist, he was their Savior. Sayers spoke against the fundamentalists who rejected this idea. *They* were the Antichrist, and God in the form of Michael Wroth would fight against them until his rule was complete. Much of the Christian world believed in Michael, for everywhere peace returned, healing was accomplished in his name, and a new golden age was inaugurated.

In all his tours, Marlene walked at Michael's side. She caught every word. Still she remained unconvinced.

In Jerusalem, Michael himself came and entered the temple. He marched triumphantly into the holiest place, followed by the Jewish high priest. Pulling aside the veil, he seated himself inside and directed the priests to bring the blood of sacrifices to pour over him in offering. Many Jews were outraged, but many more heralded Michael as the final revelation of God. Had he not rebuilt the temple? Did he not love the Jewish people? Was there not peace in the land—real, secure peace?

In each of the world's religions, smaller groups held out who refused to accept the divinity of Michael Wroth, no matter what they saw or heard. And they saw much. In the following weeks, Sayers sent holograms of Michael around the world. The nations of the Sahara beseeched him for help from famine. When the image of Michael called down rain, it rained in the desert and soon wastelands began to turn into fertile fields again. In the eastern United States, where deadly radiation had snuffed out all life, Michael's image called down life, and radiation levels dropped to zero. Life re-emerged.

Anywhere in the world there were problems, people summoned the image of Michael, and the challenges were resolved. Only one thing was required from the people—that they swear allegiance to Michael, offer worship to him, and receive an invisible mark on their forehead or right hand that could be scanned by any IC soldier with a handheld scanner.

This mark became the new key for people to experience the Rebirth.

Michael promised an earthly utopia where everyone would be well-fed, well-clothed, well-housed, etc. The only passport to this world of benefits was allegiance to him, symbolized through this simple mark. A declaration went out that all people must receive this stamp or risk imprisonment and death. Without it, no one would be able to buy or sell, find living quarters, or receive healthcare in the new world society.

Marlene had to admit it—the world was becoming a grand new order. Everywhere, glory was restored to towns, cities, and countrysides. Even nature itself seemed to sigh with relief at the changes.

The world's people had sixty days to register for the mark by going to one of the many newly erected temples of Michael—most of them converted church buildings, mosques, synagogues, and temples.

Sixty days before anyone would be required to show the mark to receive services.

Sixty days.

After that, everyone caught without the mark would be assumed to be a rebel against Michael and the Rebirth, and punishment would be merciless. The inhabitants of the world had seen the final divine revelation, and if they did not respond, they should expect full punishment—death.

As the time remaining decreased, Marlene's doubts increased.

TWENTY THREE

What am I doing here? This is crazy. Four kids at home, and here I am risking my life for a tentative rendezvous. Chara Owen sat nervously at a table on the outdoor patio of the Cheesecake Factory, watching the boats of the marina go by. She sipped her passion fruit iced tea and looked around the restaurant. *Where is she?*

Christopher had urged her not to go. "It could be a trap. Maybe they're trying to smoke us out, and they'll use you to do it." He could be right. The KPF was under increasing pressure to shut down. Christopher traversed the globe trying to urge on the troops while there was still time.

They knew it was only a matter of time before the pressure would become persecution, and the Christian commandoes would begin to be hunted down.

But something inside Chara told her that she might be the link to help them weather the persecution. This meeting had unimaginable upside potential, but the downside consequences could also be disastrous.

"What if they kidnap you or something?" Christopher had asked her. "They probably feel the best way to manipulate me and KPF is to use someone I love, the one I love the most."

Chara hadn't answered him immediately. Instead, she had embraced him and kissed him tenderly. "Honey," she had responded, "we've always been in this together, despite your visible prominence in the group ..."

"That's just it! I don't know what I'd do without you. This is too big of a risk ..."

She had shushed him with another kiss. "Why is it that *you* are the one we always have to put at risk? If it's my time, it's my time. This is part of the role *I* must play in this movement.

"I will go to the meeting, but I want your blessing. I'm terrified, and I need your support this time. And if anything happens to me, don't compromise. You must go on as if I were with you. For I will be in a cloud of witnesses watching you!"

All Christopher could do was smile grimly. "You have my blessing. I trust the Holy Spirit to speak to you."

She played that scene over and over in her mind as she waited.

Lord, is my judgment right?

Chara sipped her tea again and then saw her. She had never seen her before, but she knew this was the woman. The woman strode onto the patio gracefully yet with determination. She wore sunglasses, but her scarf could not hide the fiery red hair underneath. She tried not to attract stares from the few men there, but for the most part, she failed.

The hostess showed her to the table where Chara sat and then left them together. The redhead sat down and scanned the crowd before speaking. "Chara Owen?"

"Yes."

"I'm—" She paused then continued, "I'm Marlene Hayes. I am Michael Wroth's personal assistant."

Chara's jaw dropped, and she couldn't speak. Her first thought was to flee, and she began to back her chair up ever so gently.

Marlene noticed the slight movement. "Wait! Wait! It's okay! I know that when I called you earlier, I didn't tell you who I was, but please be assured that no harm will befall you from this meeting. On the contrary, this is the most difficult and dangerous thing I have ever done. I couldn't risk being listened to over the phone."

She looked around the crowd again. "If I am spotted with you, I will never be able to explain this to Mi ... Senator Wroth. That is why our meeting can't last very long. Senator Wroth's eyes are everywhere now."

Chara's eyes widened.

"Oh, yes. I refuse to call him *Michael* now. He will always be Senator Wroth to me. That's why I am meeting with you. I don't believe he is God any more than you do. I see the personal side of him. He's not the same man he once was. He's more *supernatural* maybe, but not more *God*-like. I'm scared to be around him, but I'm more petrified to leave him. How can I bring myself to call him Michael when everyone attaches *deity* to that name?"

Chara watched Marlene unconsciously wring her napkin. Finally she asked, "But that's not why you're here, is it?"

Marlene winced and took a deep breath. "No, that's not why I'm here. I'm here to warn you—KPF, that is, and through you the true Christian world, meaning that part of the Christian faith that hasn't bought into the lies of Michael Wroth and fallen away."

"Strong words."

A waiter approached, but Chara dismissed him.

"*True* words. *I* see Michael Wroth day and night—every day. There is something *malevolent* inside him. The world sees someone beautiful and peaceful. I see him in places and at times no one else does. I hear the profanity, the curses, the anger, the plotting, the bitterness, the lies, the pride. For years I have lived in his ruthless world, only sharing his dream of a peaceful world, while he has manipulated thousands. But this is going too far. If this is God, then I want no part of him." Marlene dabbed an eye with her napkin. "Please, Mrs. Owen, tell me this isn't what God is like!"

Instead of a powerful woman, Chara saw a little girl sitting across from her. The impenetrable shell of Marlene Hayes was cracking. Behind her sunglasses, Marlene's longing could be seen, especially as a tear escaped down her cheek. Chara scooted her chair forward again and leaned across the table. "No, Marlene, he is *not* God. He is the opposite of God in every way. Instead, he is the 'father of lies' come in the flesh. Yet he is an angel of light to the world."

Marlene's eyes stared off into the distance at the passing yachts. "He laughed. When millions of people died from the nuclear attack, he laughed. It's a game of control for him. I knew then and there that something was terribly wrong. This was no longer the pursuit of a global utopia. Then Senator Wroth asked to see my—my Bible. He looked up Revelation and realized that what was happening was according to the Bible. You should have seen the way he treated my Bible—my *mother's* Bible—with contempt, almost as an adversary. No godly man would act that way."

Marlene turned back toward Chara and removed her sunglasses.

"That's why I'm here to warn you. Senator Wroth is furious. The registration process of marking his subjects has met a lot of resistance. Oh, I know that the news media reports 98% compliance so far, but let me tell you that with only two days left, the numbers are much lower. And most of the resistance is coming from Christians like you. Senator Wroth is fuming and plotting. He has an elaborate plan to crush all who resist him, and he's going to start with KPF and several mission agencies."

Chara pulled out her phone to call Christopher, but Marlene gently grasped her hand.

"The only reason Wroth hasn't started before now is that he's giving you the full sixty days to comply. He's going to shut down a number of churches in which the majority of Christians have not registered. He will be a wolf, ravaging flocks of sheep. You and the others have to get away, get a head start. Hide!"

Marlene noticed a few heads turning toward them. She whispered urgently, "Warn all the Christians you know here and around the world. We know you have a communications network. Warn them to hide while there is time. The ones Wroth catches will be imprisoned, and those who refuse to recant will be executed immediately. He won't hide what he's going to do to those who rebel. Rather, it's going to be public and broadcast so that he can scare all the rest into submission. There will be no mercy, Mrs. Owen, no mercy!"

Marlene's head dropped, and her body quietly convulsed with sobs. No one noticed as Chara reached out so that both her hands held Marlene's hand. Marlene cried and cried. She wept years of tears in those few silent minutes. Chara said nothing. She just prayed silently and held the trembling hand.

"No one has held my hand since my freshman year in college," Marlene said, looking up with reddened eyes; Chara noticed how beautiful they were. "I almost became what you are now. I dated a young man who was going into the ministry. I was a nominal Christian, an occasional churchgoer. He got convicted about dating someone as spiritually shallow as I was, and I became determined to pursue great things in politics. We broke it off, and now look at me. I'm the right hand of the vilest man in history!"

The server came to take their order, but Chara silently waved him off again. "And yet?"

Marlene tried to regain her composure. "Can God—the true God—can God forgive someone like me? Strike that. That's not what I wanted to say. I just feel like I can relate to you and other Christians. I know I can't change, and God could *never* forgive me. I'm too evil. I've done too much. I guess I just hope that in some way I can help atone for all the evil I have been party to. If I help genuine Christians like you, perhaps my condemnation will be less severe." She scanned the seated guests again. "I need to go, but before I do, I have something for you."

Chara didn't know what to do, but she felt she must say something. She stopped Marlene from pulling something out of her handbag. "He can, and He will!" she blurted out.

"What are you talking about?"

"God. The Almighty. Jesus! He *can* forgive you. And He *will* forgive you. All you have to do is *ask* Him. You're never too far away from Him to be forgiven. No sin is too great for the sacrifice Jesus paid on the cross for *you*, dear Marlene. He loves you and longs to forgive you. He can release you from the bondage of guilt you're in. Turn to Him. He's ready to run to you with arms open wide!"

Marlene's features softened briefly but then hardened just as quickly. She put her sunglasses on. "No, He *can't* forgive me. My sin is unpardonable. Millions of people are dead or will die because of me. I helped Michael Wroth come to power. Their blood is on my hands!"

Chara gently reached across the table and took off Marlene's sunglasses so she could look her in the eyes. "The Bible says that *whoever* calls upon the name of the Lord will be saved. Do you think God is so shortsighted that He couldn't anticipate how great your sin was going to be? He died for your sin anyway. His death was that costly. If God could forgive a murderous Saul of Tarsus, can't He forgive you? The only unpardonable sin for you, Marlene, is if you reject the Holy Spirit's offer of forgiveness and new life. Why do you think you came here today? God drew you here!"

Marlene stiffened. "If God's so powerful, then how come He hasn't stopped Michael Wroth?"

Chara watched almost all hope dwindle from Marlene's face. "He *will* stop Michael Wroth," replied Chara. "Read your Bible. God is judging this world. He's going to see who will really follow Him even when things are the toughest, and He's going to let the evil ones have their day to prove all the more that they deserve punishment."

Chara was amazed at the words coming out of her mouth. "Mark my words, Marlene, the moment Michael Wroth came to power, his days were numbered. Within a few years, we who are still alive will see the return of the true King. It will all be clear then. There will be no question in anyone's mind then who the real God is. Justice will finally prevail. But only those who have endured to the end will be saved. Will you repent, believe, and endure?"

Marlene smiled grimly. "Are you always this blunt with people?"

Chara laughed slightly. "Er—let's just say, I'm going for the knock-out punch since I don't have much time."

Marlene chuckled—her first real chuckle in months. "I like you. I think that if you were in my place, you might not be that different from me. And perhaps if I had been in your place, I might not be that different from you."

Chara asked, "Then will you pray and trust your life to Christ?"

"I don't know. I can't make a decision like that so quickly. You don't understand all that's at stake."

"No, you're right, I don't. I do know that your eternity's at stake, however, and nothing in this life, even life itself, is worth trading against that. Marlene, *come with us.*"

Before Chara thought about what she was saying, she spoke, knowing the words were true. "Come hide with us, and we'll love you and help you. We'll be family to you."

Marlene looked up hopefully then looked down at the table. "I can't. Not now, not yet. Besides, I'm more helpful to you as long as I stay where I am."

Chara thought about that one momentarily. "That may be true for a while. Some of God's children in history have held quite influential positions from which they helped protect believers from danger. Esther in the Bible is a good example of that."

Marlene nodded. "I remember that story vaguely from Sunday School." She paused. "Look! I've got something in this bag." She reached in and pulled out a couple of strange looking "guns."

"These are devices that actually stamp people with the mark that Senator Wroth is giving everyone. However, these guns will stamp a *temporary* mark on anyone, one that will last only about a week. They all have the same code. It's an account I have secretly set up. Anyone with that code can receive services from a limitless account, but the system will never know it. Take them. They will help you in the months to come."

Chara longed to reach out and take the devices. There were ten life-giving guns in the bag. She could see herself as a bringer of help to thousands of Christians who were about to face persecution because they refused to swear allegiance to 'the beast.' Perhaps she could develop a network around the world to keep Christians stamped on a periodic basis. She wanted to take them. It would be so easy. Yet something was not right.

"I can't!"

"You can't? You're a fool! If you won't take them, I'll give them to someone else."

Chara raised her voice more than she expected to. "No! You can't. Don't you see? What would we be saying if we took those marks, even temporarily? Maybe we would never have knelt and given allegiance to the image of Michael, but every time we use one of those marks in a store, that clerk will assume that we *have* given allegiance to him. It's no different. If you give them to some other person, weak Christians will be persuaded to take the mark and deny the faith. You've got to destroy them."

Marlene stared in disbelief and gingerly set the bag back down on the tiles. "You are a remarkable woman, Chara Owen. I've never met Christopher Owen, but Wroth views him as one of his chief adversaries. But he's a lucky man to have you. I have offered you what no one else in this world can offer you, yet still you resist the temptation."

Marlene shook her head. "Somehow, I figured you might say something like this. I have a second plan, though it's much riskier. A growing number of people are upset with this whole marking system. They don't like the treatment they anticipate is coming for those who refuse. Secretly, a number of them have sworn to help those who don't take the mark—help them with groceries, supplies, and so on. I can get you and others in your NoPlaceLeft coalition in contact with them. But I have no way of knowing if some are legitimate or not. Many could be traitors who'll turn in those who come to them for help."

"It's more help than we expected," sighed Chara. "Marlene, many of us, perhaps most of us, will be persecuted. We don't want it, and even though we hide, we will not shrink from it. We'll continue our witness, actually redoubling our efforts because the time is short."

Marlene slid a slip of paper across the table. "Memorize this number." Chara repeated it five times in her mind. Marlene tossed the slip into the candle on the table where it burned up immediately. "That is a private line that comes directly to me. Wherever you run, you can call me, and if I can assist you, I will. Don't identify yourself; I'll know who you are. I'll never forget your voice and the hope you've extended to me. Here's the number of a man who has contacts in the underground network that can help you with supplies. Good luck. And may your God be with you."

Marlene handed her a second slip of paper and began to get up from her seat. Chara asked, "Why the rush? Can't we talk longer?"

"I don't have time. I may have been followed here. Just do what I've said. Get into hiding quickly. They're coming after you in the very near future. Get your teams into hiding. Senator Wroth has many Christian leaders in the world targeted. Remember what group was unaffected by the hornet stings? Wroth's no fool. He has an informant network around the world, in every city, identifying true Christians. But he doesn't expect you to bolt so soon. You may not be watched if you leave discreetly. And, most importantly, you have a spy in your midst, among your very staff ..."

Chara saw the blood drain from Marlene's face as she stared at two men at the restaurant entrance. "Oh, God! I've got to go." She leaned over casually to give Chara a kiss on the cheek as if they were old friends and whispered, "Pray for me!"

Expertly, discreetly, she got up and walked unhurriedly toward the exit from the patio into the marina. Chara watched as Marlene walked along the dock and got onto a waiting yacht that immediately revved its engines and made for the open sea. *What kind of world do you live in, Marlene Hayes? And who is our spy?* The men that Marlene had noticed walked through the restaurant and then onto the patio, unaware that the redhead had exited from the back. Chara got up and brushed past them as she left. She quickened her pace. She had no time to lose.

TWENTY FOUR

At 4:00 p.m., the basement of the Owen home, base for KPF/*2414*, was a flurry of activity. Julie Yang rushed to hand another mug of coffee to Christopher, who nodded gratefully. He was on the phone. "Yes, Frank, you heard me right. You need to get your team into a remote area and find ways to continue your work in the most covert way possible. We'll do our best to stay in contact, but the KPF headquarters will be out of contact for long stretches. Remember the Word and remember your training. God will guide you and protect you," he paused, "whether in life or in death."

Christopher waited while the field team leader swallowed deeply then replied, "Amen, brother. Till there is *no place left!*"

Christopher hung up. He gulped his coffee and glanced over at Nic and Win. "How's the contact list coming along?"

Nic spoke first. "Only five teams left to contact on my section of the list."

The colonel said, "Three teams here, but two of them are out of contact. And Timothy and Grace have alerted many other organizations, giving them some local contacts that Ms. Hayes passed on to us."

John slammed the door and came down the stairs two at a time. "Just the four of us, right? Can we talk freely, what with the mole in our midst and all?"

The colonel climbed the stairs three at a time and locked the door. When he came back down, he activated a sound-masking device. "Safe."

John chuckled. "Man, you military types. Well, I've almost finalized arrangements for dividing the staff. Chara, Renee, Jeanie, and Stacy are sorting through the logistics. They burst into tears and hug each other every five minutes!"

Christopher said, "Well, we knew it could come to this some day—splitting up this little gang. It's a long way from that coffee shop conspiracy years ago! I miss those days sometimes. Give us the final lay of the land, bro, and the hour of our departure."

Nic interrupted him. "Christopher, buddy, I know you think we should flee, but it feels a little cowardly. What will our teams think if their leaders run for the hills?"

"That we are doing exactly what Jesus said to do in Matthew 10 and 24—flee!" Christopher thumbed through his Bible. A few loose pages fell onto the floor. "We are in the days described here in Matthew 24 and must endure to the end. We've talked about this, guys. We can't turn back from it now. We are so close to *no place left* that I can feel it! So, John, what's our status?"

John reached down and picked up Christopher's Bible pages. Handing them back to him, he said, "Well, other than the ladies crying their heads off, we're pretty much set. We'll divide the staff up into two groups so that we have a better chance of survival *and* that one of our groups will be able to maintain contact with the teams on the field."

Seeing the men's discomfort, the colonel said, "Sir, for the sake of the teams around the world, this is the best course of action. We must do whatever it takes to enable the global coalition to maintain momentum."

"You're right, Win," said Christopher. "Go on, John."

"Group B will consist of you, Chara, and your kids plus the folks that regularly manned Site B—Chara's sister Kellie, Win and Jeanie, and Timothy and Grace—seven adults and four children. Your group will head north along the Sierra Nevada mountain range hoping to make for the Pacific Northwest, perhaps even Canada."

The colonel added, "Sir, I've got connections with military personnel in the region, which might help us slip past certain obstacles." Christopher nodded.

Nic grinned. "What? You're getting the big man himself, Colonel Win Dunbar?"

Christopher chuckled but could barely hold back a tear at the corner of his eye. "Yeah, Nic, but you've got the other member of the Three Amigos. Tough to break up the act, not knowing if it will get back together."

"Sure it will, buddy—in heaven, if nowhere else! Just you guys don't get jealous when Group C outperforms Group B!"

John cleared his throat. "If I may continue?" Christopher and Nic shrugged. "Group C includes Renee and me, Nic and Stacy and their two kids, George and Julie, and Tal—nine people, with seven adults and two children. Our group will head south to Mexico and hopefully to the mountains of Central or South America. Tal has connections with former colleagues in Central America and thinks he can buy us some time."

Just then a loud clatter told them that someone had dropped a box of canned items. John said, "Um, as you can hear, the girls are busily packing up essentials and as many rations as we can take. George and Julie are helping wherever they're needed."

Christopher ran his fingers through his hair. "And the rest of the staff?"

The colonel spoke up. "Sir, all non-essential staff have already been sent out in pairs or small groups for their survival. Their proximity to us only endangers them, and making our groups any larger only endangers us."

"What about Phil Young?" Nic asked. "I thought the plan was for him to join our team as we head south. We need a communications guru."

John shook his head. "That's the weird thing. We've tried and tried to contact him. He just up and left two nights ago—said he needed a break for a few days. We'll keep trying to call him, but regardless, both caravans roll out at 10:00. We can't wait any longer. Today's the deadline for registering for the mark, and we expect the IC to roll in here tomorrow. But they could legally come in any time after midnight."

Someone tried to open the locked door then began banging furiously. Nic sprang up to unlock it.

Renee barreled down the stairs. "Okay, boys, powwow's over. Everything is sorted. Bank accounts emptied. Tents rounded up. Food and water sitting in crates. We need your muscles to load everything. Timothy and Grace have just driven the trucks of Sites B and C over. We really don't want to have that many vehicles here for very long."

* * *

At 9:00 p.m., the three couples that began conspiring together about finishing the task stood in the back driveway in a prayerful huddle. The other team members continued last-minute logistics. Each of the original six thought about those early prayer meetings, asking God about what it would take to get to *no place left* untouched by the gospel. Deep in thought, no one knew how to say good-bye.

From the doorstep, the Dunbars looked on. As other members of Group B and Group C came to the door, Jeanie stopped them, giving the original members of the KPF a last, private farewell.

Finally, John shattered the silence of the group. "You all know that I've never been the enthusiastic one like Nic here or the visionary like Christopher. I've been the orneriest member of the Three Amigos."

Nic butted in. "So, Professor Steward. You've finally come to see the light?"

"Don't listen to him!" said Stacy. "John, go on."

"Well, I just want to say one thing. As I've studied history, what we're about to go through is not a new thing. Christ-followers have been chased, caught, and killed throughout history. I imagine we will all face the same fate."

Then straightening himself up, John held hands with some of the group members. "I want to commit to God and to you to do you proud when it's my turn to be slain. If you see me on television, I pray that you see a man who loves his Lord selflessly and was proud to walk down this path with you five."

Nic hugged his friend. "I agree, buddy. Let's all do each other proud as we stare at death with no fear. Death has no sting!"

With tears streaming down his cheeks, Christopher drew his cohort in closer. "I will forever count it as one of the greatest treasures in my life, having had you as faithful friends and having pursued this quest with you. Let not our hearts fail. Let us not surrender to threats. I agree. I want to make you and my Lord proud if you watch my execution. If I watch yours, I will rise in honor of the life you have lived and the price you have paid."

Renee waited a bit as these remarks sank in, then asked, "Christopher, how close are we to the end?"

"It's awfully hard to determine that because of all the disruptions in communications, but Timothy tells me that we are down to about 897 UPGs still unengaged. So many Kingdom movements are starting around the world, with the hot coals of the gospel moving from them to start fires in other people groups, that it's hard to know. Let's pray that the global Church can reach them while there is still time."

He motioned for the six of them to hold hands. "This quest is not over, though we go our separate ways. This is the essential next step to get to *no place left*."

The intrepid team knelt in prayer together, sobs punctuating their intercession.

Christopher then drew them all to their feet. "Let's go win for the Lamb the just reward of His suffering! Don't look back!"

With these final words, he split up the team that had first embarked upon this "hastening-the-day" quest on a chilly evening in Los Angeles just a few years earlier.

Along with the others, the couples tearfully climbed into their vehicles, and the two convoys wound their way out of Los Angeles in opposite directions. Each convoy consisted of a modified delivery truck carrying the minimum computer and communications equipment plus as many supplies as possible and two four-wheel drive vehicles capable of carrying all the team members if necessary. They hoped to avoid the checkpoints that they anticipated would be set up on major roads later that night. Though the going would be much slower, the convoys planned to stick to less traveled roads.

Group B journeyed northward and made camp in the northern reaches of Sequoia National Forest. Fortunately, it was summer, so all the forest roads were open.

* * *

At 4:00 a.m., IC troops broke into the house that was the Owens' home and KPF headquarters. Angry soldiers ransacked the place and overturned the beds where the family was supposed to have been sleeping the morning after the deadline. Michael himself, who was in Los Angeles for the week, participated in the raid on the house. This was going to be a highly symbolic moment to show the world that groups like the KPF could not flaunt themselves against his power. He walked through the house.

Jake reported to him. "Sir, no one's here. All pertinent files appear to have been removed or destroyed. There's nothing here for us, except this note that was taped to one of the desks in the basement."

Michael read it out loud. "'We're praying for you, Michael Wroth!'" He showed no anger.

Trying to mask a smile of relief, Marlene stood next to him. She barked at Simmons, "Why weren't we informed by our mole here? What happened to him?"

Jake stammered, "Th-th-there was some sort of mix-up. Apparently someone from our office sent him word to leave for a couple days of 'break.' I can't understand where such a message would have come from."

Fighting harder not to smile, Marlene said, "Mr. Simmons, it sounds like you need a tighter rein on your informant network. This will be a humiliation to Michael's image—to raid KPF headquarters only to find they skipped out on us without a trace!"

Michael looked sharply at her. "Marlene, don't be so hard on him. No one else knows what we planned here. We'll catch this Owen fellow sooner or later. And, it seems to me that ultimately *you* are responsible for the effectiveness of Jake's department, since you directly supervise him."

Marlene broke into a sweat. "Yes, Senator Wroth—I mean, Michael. This is my fault."

Michael strode out of the house with the others in tow. "This will not happen again, Marlene! You will make sure of that. In the meantime, burn the house. Bring the children's toys outside and burn them. Post a sign on the street declaring that this will be what happens to everyone who fails to register to worship me. As a matter of fact, I want the house of every known Christian in the world who has failed to register to burn—all of them!"

Much of the world's population awakened the next morning to the fires in their cities and towns—many houses with the occupants still inside while the doors were chained shut from the outside.

* * *

"That's our house!" cried David, the youngest of the Owen children. Christopher pulled him close to his side.

"He's a monster!" cried Chara as the little group sat around their morning campfire in the Sequoia National Forest. They had all watched the news reports streamed that morning on the computer screen in Site B, even though they were camped in the woods miles from civilization. But the sight of their home, the KPF headquarters, ablaze sobered them all. Michael stood in front of it talking into a camera about the demise of the KPF.

"A *beast*," corrected Christopher. "'*The* beast,' to be more exact."

No sooner had the words come out of his mouth than a weight he hadn't realized he had been carrying for years renewed its pressure upon his shoulders. The burden was crushing.

"Okay, a *beast*! Who cares what you call him? How can he burn down the homes of all Christians?" The others tried to persuade Chara to keep her voice down.

Jeanie said, "Honey, if this guy really is 'the beast' of Revelation, the Antichrist, then we should expect a lot worse. I was reading Revelation again this morning. It doesn't appear we believers will have much defense against him. It's like God is going to remove His own restraining hand for a period of time."

Win added, "It will be much harder for our teams than for us, I think. At least *we* are in a culture we are familiar with. The teams? They're in lands still new to them with languages still not natural for many of them."

Christopher knew no one was pointing any fingers at him, but he felt that it was his fault they all were in this predicament.

"We have already lost contact with many of the teams," said Grace. "I'm worried that some have already been arrested."

Timothy shook his head. "The silence sends us a loud message. It's heartbreaking."

With each statement, Christopher's shoulders slumped more. Was it his imagination, or did the group members seem to keep glancing over at him?

Finally Kellie said, "It's going to make the difficulties we faced in Yunnan years ago seem small—even losing Ruth." She brushed tears from her eyes.

Christopher's eyes darted back and forth. He began muttering, "It's all my fault. It's all my fault."

Chara turned to look at him as he grabbed his Bible and journal and jumped to his feet. "I'm going for a short walk while lunch is cooking." He didn't wait for a response but left the circle as fast as his legs could carry him.

One of the kids asked, "Where are you going, Daddy? Can I come with you?"

Chara shushed him as Christopher strode into the sun-dappled forest. "Not now, honey. Daddy, needs some time with God. Let's all pray for him."

Win knelt down next to a couple of the children. "Kids, it's always hardest on those in command. They hold so many lives in their hands." He turned back to Jeanie and said under his breath, "Pray with all your might. He's been close to his breaking point for some time. I don't like what I'm seeing."

Christopher made his way through the tall pines and occasional sequoias, shuffling quietly on the pine straw. The weight on his shoulders slowed his gait. Finally he found an outcropping of granite boulders where he could sit. From that spot, he looked out upon the valley miles away.

God! Why did I ever want to be in the last generation? It looked so glamorous at the beginning. How grand quests appear at the beginning!

But here we are: no home, little money, no guarantee of a future. Countless teams stranded around the world. And then there are the children. What do we tell them? 'Oh, by the way, the reason we are running for our lives and you will probably never grow up and definitely never have a normal life is because your daddy worked really hard to stir up other Christ-followers to finish the task of the Great Commission. We helped prepare the way for Jesus' return! Oops! There is a little thing we have to go through first: the Great Tribulation. Sorry I forgot to ask your permission, kids. But here we are! Let's just think of this as an extended camping trip.'

Christopher looked out across the stands of gently rustling sequoias. His gaze slowly swept across the mountainside to the valley below. At the extreme limit of the crystal clear horizon in the south he could just make out pillars of smoke ascending into the atmosphere. *Must be the L.A. basin.* The sight sent searing pangs of guilt through his mind.

Why God? Why did I ever want this? I can't guarantee the survival of my family. I will have to watch online every day my brothers and sisters being slaughtered for your name. And I'm the primary reason many people are overseas. What are they going to do? How many will be killed because I sent them there? Why did I have to be the one? Why? How will I prove myself strong for their sake?

Christopher began hurling pinecones as far as he could toward the valley below. He ran around the outcropping looking for rocks or pinecones—it didn't matter. He threw and threw and threw until he collapsed upon the bed of needles in exhaustion.

God, things are so out of control, and I'm so helpless to do anything! Your sheep are going to be slaughtered. Is it really worth it?

As he lay in the pine straw, he prayed and cried and cried and prayed. He shouted out to God until his voice was hoarse. "God, do something! Help me! Help us! Give me wisdom! Give me strength! Give me direction! My men and women are suffering!"

Christopher turned over onto his belly. Panting, he clutched handfuls of pine straw. A beetle crawled across his outstretched hand, but he paid no attention to it. He continued to pant while gnats buzzed around his head.

Completely spent, he said nothing more.

Then they came—words and more words, flooding his soul. He didn't know which were his Father's, or which were just from his own mind, but he welcomed any insight that came.

With herculean effort, he pulled himself up and found his journal and pen. Feverishly he scribbled down these words in his journal, trying to keep up with the torrent.

Is it worth it? Am I not worth it? Am I not worthy of the just reward of My suffering? Am I not worthy of a Bride from every tongue, tribe, people, and nation?

Why did you want to be involved in hastening the Day of the Lord? Was it not that you might witness firsthand My coming? Was it not that you wanted to present to Me a gift of a pure and undefiled Bride? Was it not that you might share the special honor and reward that will be for those who have endured such suffering?

Will it not be enough to stand before Me continually and gaze on My beauty? What greater reward is there than ME? What more magnificent reward than receiving a greater capacity to enjoy My presence?

Christopher beamed as teardrops fell to the pages of his worn leather journal. On and on he wrote.

Do not deceive yourself. You knew ahead of time what would come; I called you to it. If you had refused Me, don't you think I would have found someone else? Don't you think My servants on the field would be there with or without you? Do you think you are so indispensable?

Christopher shook his head furiously, chastising himself for inflating his own importance. He continued to write as the thoughts came.

Christopher, I make you no guarantees except to be with you. You will remain alive as long as I want you to. When I am ready for you to come to Me, you will. No harm can befall you outside of My control; the same is true for your family. And should you fall into the hands of the accuser, trust that I will be with you in close fellowship. I am your Rock and your Shield and your Deliverer, even in death.

Why do you carry a weight that is not yours to bear? The men and women you sent out are MY men and women, not YOURS. I will take care of them.

Christopher looked up and began shaking his head. He muttered, "Of course, of course, of course."

In that moment, the weight of years of responsibility for hundreds of teams fell from his shoulders. He looked into heaven and shouted hoarsely, "They're *Your* men and women, Father! Yours! I'm free!"

The words weren't finished, so he picked up his pen and turned the page.

Arise and go forth. You still have much work to do for Me. If you are feeling these things, then what do you think your KPF team members are feeling? What do you think your family is feeling? Comfort and encourage them with My words. Push on in My strength until there is truly no place left where I am not named.

A rustle startled him. Christopher turned and saw the six-foot-four form of Win standing behind him. Win eyed him awkwardly, an embarrassed look on his face. "Uh, Commander, I heard your shouts and came to check on you."

He looked down sheepishly then gazed into Christopher's eyes. "Sir, once in my life I broke under pressure. It wasn't pretty. I know how hard it is to feel so responsible. And there's more word from our overseas teams. It's not good. Sir, are-are you okay?"

Christopher glanced heavenward. A grin emerged on his face, and he wiped his eyes. "Yeah, Win. I-I'm okay. Actually, I've not felt this good in years. Let's go."

Christopher walked back into camp, aware that everyone was staring at him. The kids ran up to him, and he wrapped them up in a group hug. "Man, I could eat a horse! What's for lunch?"

"Canned chili, Daddy."

"Canned chili? My favorite!"

He sat next to Chara, who squeezed his hand. She said, "Honey, I think you need to hear what Timothy and Grace have to report."

"I know, my love. After lunch. After lunch." He grabbed his bowl of chili and called for the kids to join him on the pine straw.

As cleanup began, Christopher called for a situation report.

"Win, Timothy, Grace—what's the word from the teams? How are they doing?"

Grace hesitated. Her face told Christopher all he needed to know. He could see that she was afraid to give him any more bad news—afraid of breaking the back of the KPF's commander.

"It's okay, Grace. I can handle it now."

She said, "Christopher, we just got word in the last couple of hours. We think at least two teams have been turned in, one in Turkey, another in Afghanistan. One was betrayed by a team member. Other than that, we think the others have fled like we told them."

The colonel offered his assessment. "Commander, we think the precautions we built in previously to guard their identities have paid off. Most of the 2414 teams are probably on the run to more rugged areas, many with the help of local believers. Most of our team members are greatly respected by the new believers; they want to keep them around as long as possible to learn from them. While the bad news is that they have had to leave their work, the good news is that they are rushing to the areas that are even more unreached. In a strange way, God is still accomplishing His purpose of reaching those who haven't yet heard."

Joshua, the oldest Owen child, chuckled and said,"Can you imagine what some of those people groups will think when they hear our teams tell them, 'You have only a couple of years to decide before Jesus comes back!'? They'll be fighting to see who can trust in Jesus first."

Christopher sat stunned to hear his own son talk like this. "Do you kids have any idea of what is ahead of us?"

David answered, "Come on, Daddy! Of course we know. We're ready for anything. Besides, Jesus will help us no matter what—Mommy told us."

"But what if they separate us and take you to jail, or tell you to say you don't believe in Jesus?" his father asked.

Elizabeth, the thinker, responded, "Dad! We kids aren't dumb, you know. We've been talking about this a lot while you grown-ups have been worrying. We've all agreed. Jesus will take care of us, even if we get separated or suffer. Even if we have to die, we can't deny Him. He'll take care of us. Don't worry about us. We've got a big room in God's mansion waiting for us."

Christopher hugged his kids but couldn't speak. When he could, it was to the Wus. "Get a message out to all the teams. Reassure them that even though our headquarters were burned, we have a mobile headquarters, and we'll stay in contact with them as long as possible. No need to tell them about Site C; someone might be listening.

"Nevertheless, the teams are set up to be on their own. This NoPlaceLeft coalition is a starfish. Cut off any arm, and we keep going and multiplying. The teams don't have to contact us if they don't want to, especially if it would compromise their location. If they can, however, and we can still plot much of what is going on in world evangelism, we can give them some helpful information about where they might want to go next.

"And, I want to record a personal podcast to send them. I want to encourage them to stand strong and trust God. Their reward will be great. Can you let me know when you're ready to record?"

Sitting on a granite boulder with the gentle mountain breeze slipping by, Christopher recorded what he felt might be his last personal message to the faithful troops. Timothy and Grace's hearts were so moved that they almost forgot to check the audio settings. When the last words were spoken, the sound file was edited and uploaded.

Group B stayed put most of the day, having decided to travel mainly at night. Late in the afternoon, they received word that Group C had made it across the border and were deep in Mexico.

That evening, the little band continued winding its way through mountain passes, using rarely used forest service roads. At times they had to winch the truck out of ruts with the four-wheel drive vehicles. Progress was slow, but they encountered no checkpoints. On the news the next day, they saw pictures of the first public executions of what were termed "intolerant radicals." Most of them were Christians—not just men but women and children also. It was a gruesome sight.

Juxtaposed with such scenes was footage of floods of people paying homage to holograms of Michael set up in countless places, holograms that could actually respond to individuals' questions regarding wisdom for the future, decisions to be made, and so on. Family after family around the world was shown being scanned for the mark of Michael and then receiving a new home, car, groceries—just about anything they needed or wanted. It was paradise on earth for those who registered—like winning the lottery, except everyone who played, won.

The contrast was exaggerated to underline the point. Follow Michael, and enter paradise. Resist him, and welcome to hell on earth.

It was hard to argue with what appeared on the screen. Improvements were being made in every neighborhood, every block. No one in history had ever possessed such ability to mobilize resources to benefit each person. Economists had long argued that the money and resources were there, but they were hoarded by the upper crust of society. Michael had found a way to spread the goodness all around.

A happiness index was displayed online and next to Michael's holograms. Seventy-five percent of society was happy or becoming happy or at least anticipating happiness. Who was going to argue with Michael's methods? Their god could do what he wanted, and wasn't he proving that he loved and cared for them, especially more than the corrupt politicians before him?

The next day, Christopher received more distressing news. Timothy reported, "A large number of mission teams from a partner agency have been taken into custody. Someone high up in the agency has been interrogated and has given all that information under pressure."

Christopher looked at the team, especially Win, then prayed. *Lord, help me never to give way under such pressure. Thank You that I don't even know where our teams are!*

The following evening, Group B traveled along a mountain road to the Oregon border. Below them they could see a checkpoint on the rural highway that crossed into the state, yet even at midnight there were several trucks and cars stopped, waiting to be examined.

"What do we do?" Chara whispered to her husband, who was driving the lead vehicle.

Christopher keyed his walkie-talkie to call the trailing SUV. "Win, is there any other way to get across?"

"Sorry, Commander, this was my only hope. It's such an insignificant road that I never thought there'd be a checkpoint here."

"Okay, let's turn back and figure out our next step."

"Roger that," the walkie-talkie crackled. "Uh-oh. Can't do that, sir. A police car is pulling up behind us, signaling for us to move faster."

Christopher began breathing rapidly. "All right, let's move ahead and hope we don't attract too much attention. Everyone, pray!"

Christopher sped up the old Suburban, and the other vehicles followed. They got in line and waited as a cocky officer at the checkpoint scanned the occupants of each vehicle before allowing them to pass through. In one car, everyone passed except for one young woman who was the last one out. When the officer realized she wasn't marked, he ordered her taken into custody. She tried to run away and, in front of everyone, she was gunned down. Everyone in the Suburban gasped, and Chara shushed the youngest ones as they cried out. They watched in stunned silence as the victim's car drove on.

Next was a big rig. Its driver passed.

Now it was Christopher's turn. He pulled forward to the stop. Chara and the kids froze, afraid to speak. Then she whispered to him, "I love you and am so proud to have been your wife!"

"Right hand!" the officer barked at Christopher.

Christopher didn't protest. *Jesus, help us!* He stuck his trembling hand out the window. The young officer placed his scanner on the back of Christopher's hand and pressed the button. "No reading!"

Christopher's heart skipped a beat. *They've got us, just like that! It didn't take long!*

Christopher opened his door to get out and surrender, but the officer pushed it shut. "Stay inside. Don't move!" Then he turned and yelled over his shoulder, "Julio, where's the other scanner? This one's been giving me trouble all night. I can't get a positive or negative reading."

A voice called back, "We don't have it, Brandon. I gave it to Louisa who took it over to Route 178. That's the only one we have."

The frustrated officer looked at the scanner and cursed. His profanity was interrupted by the horns of several big rigs that had pulled up during the affair.

One of the truck drivers called out, "Hey, fella! Hurry it up! We got important loads to deliver for Michael. We can't afford to sit in line all night, especially when we have to stop for checkpoints every few miles!"

"Yeah, yeah, yeah!" replied the officer. When he focused his attention back on Christopher's car, he was quite exasperated. "Move on, all of you, quickly. Or else I'll have you all locked up until we get the other scanner back!" He waved the whole line of traffic forward.

Christopher gunned the motor, and the car lurched away, its tires spitting out gravel. Chara saw the officer wave his hands angrily at all the dust and grit and couldn't help grinning. Caleb asked quietly from the back, "Daddy, did an angel just help us?"

"Yes, son, lots of angels just helped us!"

The nights of driving blurred into each other. The group members grew confused about whether to sleep during the day or the night. Occasionally they stopped in a small town to buy more supplies or eat real food in a real restaurant, but each day and each week it got harder to use cash. Day by day, more bank and credit card accounts were consolidated through the mark each person bore, so that soon, as a sign of loyalty to Michael, cash was no longer accepted in some places.

The group made its way across the Washington border and eventually through Idaho into Montana. They crawled at a snail's pace, sometimes stopping for three or four days at successive campsites so as not to attract too much attention.

Someone was always on guard, and the others slept fitfully. Christopher slept even less than the rest and frequently relieved others of guard duty. Chara fretted about his ability to keep going with so little sleep.

When Group B drove, it was never very far, for they followed winding, neglected roads. More often, they used gravel and dirt roads that were poorly maintained, washed out by rains, and hard to discern at night. By the time the team crossed into Montana, weariness filled their every bone.

Along the way, word had reached them that more KPF/*2414* teams and individuals had been captured and several people executed. Such news drained them far more than the fear and difficulty of the journey.

Five miles outside a small town in Montana, Chara pleaded with her husband. She choked back tears at the sight before her: Christopher's eyes were sunk down into their sockets, and his cheekbones showed more prominently. *He gives too much of his food to others.*

"Our supplies are getting low. We need to stop and find an underground contact here in Montana. We need more food, and if we can get them, some antibiotics for David. He's running a high fever."

Christopher looked at her with bloodshot eyes. "Antibiotics? Are we out? Okay, perhaps we can stop for a short rest."

Chara took her husband's face in her hands. "No, honey! We need more than that. We need a place to stop and settle down for a while. A place with a real roof over our heads." She zipped her jacket and shivered. "Already the nights are turning colder. No one complains, but I know they all need a rest. They'll follow you wherever you go, but they can't keep up with your pace. For their sake, honey, let's look for some place to settle down for the winter. They need it. *You* need it."

"The winter? I had hoped to make it into Canada before winter."

"Christopher, we can't make it that far, especially the children. We're almost out of supplies. We need to stop."

Christopher shrugged. "So how do you plan on finding a contact here?"

Chara hesitated; she had never told Christopher all of her conversation with Marlene. "Marlene Hayes gave me her personal number to call in a situation like this."

Christopher raised an eyebrow. "You *believe* her? Who knows who will be monitoring that line? You call it, and it may mean the end of all of us!"

Chara kissed him gently. "Yes! I believe her. I was there *listening* to her that day at the Cheesecake Factory. She didn't have to risk her neck to warn us. I have no reason to believe that she will let this number be traced to us. Besides, we're doomed if we don't get some help soon."

Christopher bowed his head and squeezed her hand. "Perhaps you're right. I wasn't there; besides, you're a better judge of character than I am. Go ahead, call her, but you'll have to use a public phone in the town that should be just over this rise. The colonel can drive you down there. We can't afford to have someone trace the satellite line that we use to communicate with the teams. While you're at it, ask her about Group C. Perhaps the IC is trying to track them. They're somewhere near the Yucatan peninsula, I think."

Chara turned to go, but Christopher drew her back and hugged her. "My love, be careful."

At 2:00 a.m., the colonel, despite years of covert operations, sat nervously in the Jeep Cherokee, the engine running. The streets around seemed deserted. In his peripheral vision, he suddenly saw headlights, then the familiar signs of an IC patrol car several blocks over. Without warning, his head began spinning and his torso collapsed on the seat. The world went black.

Fifty feet away, at a public phone at a gas station, Chara dialed a memorized number, one she had rehearsed in her mind every day for the last two months. The phone rang at the other end, and a groggy voice answered, "Yes?"

"Hi. It's me."

"My gosh, where are you?"

Chara hesitated. *Was this all just a ruse to capture the little band? Would someone be listening on the line?* She had to take the chance. "In Montana, just across the Idaho border. We're low on supplies, and need shelter. Is there someone we can contact here? My kid's running a pretty high fever."

"Hold on." Chara heard Marlene typing on her laptop and waited.

Win opened his eyes to find himself staring at the roof of the Cherokee. He grasped the steering wheel and tried pulling himself up only to flop back onto the adjoining seat. He prayed a quick, desperate prayer and tried again. The moment he regained a sitting position, he saw the headlights again, this time closer. Win waved to get Chara's attention, but she was looking the other way. With all his might, he reached for the handle to get out of the car. *God, can I even walk?*

Chara continued to wait. Soon Marlene was on the line with a name and number. "Tell him when you contact him that 'the fox' sent you. He'll do whatever you want. You can trust him. Listen, I don't have much time, but a pretty thorough list of a number of your teams came into our office a while back, don't ask me how. I managed to get rid of it before anyone else could process it. There should be a little less pressure on those teams for a while. IC troops know you're traveling with a delivery truck, but they're not sure which direction you went. You need to ditch it soon."

"Thanks for all your help. We have another group in Yucatan. Can you help with that?" Again more keystrokes and more information relayed.

Chara wrote down a few details. She paused, then said, "Have you thought much more about our conversation?"

"Still thinking about it. Don't rush me. The cost is so high." Marlene hesitated then continued, "I forgot to tell you this before, about who the traitor is—"

From behind Chara, Win stuck his hand over her shoulder and hung up the phone. Putting the other arm over Chara's shoulder, he said, "Sorry about that, sister, but we have no time. An IC security car just passed by on another block and will be on this block any time. We have to get out of here. I just hope your friend didn't rat on us while you were on the phone. Now help me back to the Jeep."

Chara looked at him in surprise as they hurried to the vehicle but only asked, "Can you drive?"

The colonel gritted his teeth. "Getting better by the minute. Just open my door for me. I can still drive."

Win grimaced as he sat in the seat. Chara slammed his door then rushed around the car to get into her place. They sped away from the gas station just as the patrol car turned onto the street. The Jeep swung onto the little blacktop highway and roared out of town heedless of whether the patrol car would pursue or not.

It did.

"Shoot! I'm not too good at this!"

Chara, still stunned by the sudden end in the conversation, asked, "Good at what?"

"This! Evasive driving. Hold on!" He turned the Cherokee off the highway onto a muddy gravel road, careful not to lead their pursuers back to the camp. He saw the lights flashing from the security vehicle following him. Both vehicles rushed madly along the road, the patrol car gaining on the Jeep. "Memorize the info you got from her, then hand the paper to me!" Win shouted above the scream of the engine.

Chara did her best, despite being tossed around. She handed the slip to him; he lit it with the cigarette lighter and tossed it out the window. The chasing car slowed down at the sight but kept following. Win slid around a turn in the road and slammed on the brakes. The Cherokee skidded and veered sideways, sliding into a gully where the road had been washed away.

The Jeep rolled over and then landed right side up.

Everything came to a halt.

Chara felt as if her whole body had been pounded by a boxer. She looked over at the colonel who was shakily unbuckling his seatbelt. He grabbed Chara's arm, "Come on, we have to run for it on foot."

Win slammed the door open but remained in his seat. A blinding spotlight shone on the Jeep. A voice shouted over a bullhorn, "Get out *slowly* with your hands on top of your heads. No sudden moves, or I'll shoot."

Chara blinked as she stepped out and tried to look into the light, but she could only make out the figure of one IC officer. Apparently satisfied that the two were unarmed, the officer walked toward them with a pistol aimed at them in one hand, a scanner in the other. Of all things, Chara worried about her kids. *What will they do without this information? I'm the only one who has it.*

The officer ordered, "Hands on your heads, kneel down in the mud!"

Chara and Win sank to their knees.

"Keep your left hands on your heads but slowly extend your right hands for scanning!"

TWENTY FIVE

The burly IC officer scanned Chara's hand. The scanner beeped "negative." Next he scanned her forehead. "Negative" again. The officer shoved Chara forward, face down in the muck. He growled, "Lay there and don't move!"

He turned and glared at the colonel. "You! Right hand!"

Slowly the colonel's strength was returning. He bowed his head, knowing what the result would be. Beside him, Chara grunted in the mud.

The scanner beeped "negative" again. "Nothin'! C'mon, ol' man, look up here so I can scan your forehead. No doubt you're gonna be 'nother negative, just like your little woman!"

Colonel Winthrop Dunbar proudly lifted his head, believing that this was the beginning of the end. The officer raised the scanner. The sneer on his face, however, turned to shock.

"C-Colonel D-Dunbar? Is that you, sir? Colonel Dunbar?"

Dunbar squinted at the face of the officer but could distinguish nothing. "Yes, I'm Colonel Win Dunbar. Who might you be, son?"

The officer dropped the scanner into the mud and helped both the colonel and Chara stand up, wiping the globs of mud off their clothes. As he did so he stuttered, "M-Martin Charles, sir. I-I served in Desert Storm with you, sir—*proudly*, sir! You don't remember me, but I 'member you. Greatest special ops commander that ever lived!" He continued to wipe mud off them, all the while repeating, "Omigosh! What've I done?"

The colonel supported Chara, whose knees were still weak. "Martin Charles? Martin Charles? I remember you! Sniper, weren't you? Didn't I always get your name wrong? Called you Charles Martin all the time."

The former soldier straightened up and saluted, grinning from ear to ear. "Yessir. You ain't never got my name right, but I'll be doggoned if I let you call me anything different." Then remembering where he was and what he had done, he began trembling. "Oh, sir, Colonel, sir! I'm so sorry for what I done, especially to the lady. It's what they teach us, sir, intimidation and all. But if I'd a known, I never woulda done nothin' to hurt you."

Colonel Dunbar reassured him, "You were only doing your job, son, though I do think that you can show a little more kindness than that."

Five minutes' later, the three were sharing a thermos of hot coffee in the officer's patrol car, chatting like old friends. Martin Charles finally brought up the sensitive issue. "Sir, I hate to bring this up, but neither one of ya'll's got the mark."

The colonel decided honesty would be the best approach. "You're right, Charles—I mean, Martin. We're Christians, and we can't take the 'mark of the beast' in good conscience. We're running from the IC right now and are trying to make our way to an underground contact here in Montana that can help us. There are eleven of us in all, including four children. One of the kids is running a high fever and needs some medicine, quick. We're desperate and don't have much time."

The officer's eyes watered as he looked down. "They took my mama. She was a fine Christian woman from Washington, Luzianna. She done *said* it was the 'mark o' the beast.' Kept sayin' that right up to the moment they—they kilt her! Beheaded her! Half her church done gone that way. You can ax anyone, they was good folks. It just ain't right."

He shook his head and wept silently. His body trembled as Chara placed a hand on his shoulder. He continued, "Me? I couldn't see no reason not to take that there mark. I ain't no Christian, though Mama raised me that way. I done too many bad things. It's too late for me."

Chara interrupted him. "How do you know it's too late? Wouldn't your mother want you to trust Jesus?"

The officer responded, "I done read it, ma'am, the book of Revelations, that is. Just read fer yourself. It's all in there. Ya gets the 'mark of the beast,' and yer a goner. Ain't no hope for folks that does that. My only hope is to get on the inside like I'm doing now, and maybe help a few good folks who're what Mama's preacher called conscientious objectors."

Chara said, "You can't be sure. If you still want to believe, then do it. Maybe God will have mercy on you!"

"Ma'am, I 'preciate it, I really do. I'll forever remember yer kind words. But for the time bein', I need to help y'all get outta here. Who y'all trying to reach anyway?"

Chara looked at Win with uncertainty, but he nodded confidently back to her. "A man by the name of Morris Franklin. Know him?" Chara replied.

"Know him? He's one of the biggest ranchers in the state! Ma'am, that's quite a contact! Nobody can touch him in these parts. I kin git ya *to* his ranch, but I can't guarantee that I kin git ya *onto* his place."

The colonel said, "Martin, that is all we need. We feel pretty sure he'll let us onto his ranch."

The rest of the evening was spent gathering the group and heading into a remote area largely owned by rancher Morris Franklin. Checkpoints were no problem since Martin Charles escorted them through.

At the gate to the massive ranch, Win spoke over the intercom to Morris Franklin who responded rather skeptically until the colonel mentioned "the fox" to him. At that he said, "Wait at the gate! I'll be there in a few minutes."

Ten minutes later, the lights from Franklin's SUV bounced up the road toward them. He stopped in front of the gate as it swung open. The small group said goodbye to Martin Charles. Colonel Dunbar shook his hand warmly. "Charles, you remember what we told you. Put your faith in Jesus, and ask Him to have mercy on your soul."

Martin Charles couldn't respond but saluted the colonel.

The KPF team loaded back up into the three vehicles and followed Franklin as he personally escorted them several miles into the property and up to a cluster of buildings beside his own ranch house. Franklin asked no questions. He gave them a large house to set up in, and they transferred their KPF headquarters' equipment there before ditching the delivery truck in a remote part of the ranch.

The team stayed on the ranch all winter, cared for by these hospitable people who nonetheless bore the mark of Michael.

As the weeks passed, Timothy relayed numerous reports from the remaining KPF and 2414 groups about rumors of mysterious mission teams working in even remoter regions than theirs.

For one of the team meetings, Timothy was online with Lance Chu, who was overseeing the Central Asia work. "Dudes, you won't believe what's going on out here. Like, Central Asia has always been a tough place to work, y'know. But, man, we're finding receptivity like never before! And many times, when we strike out into an area no one's ever heard of, it's like crazy. We're stumbling upon villages and people groups that were supposed to have never received the gospel. But somehow they have already been visited by brothers from other Great Commission orgs we've never even heard of! It's like you always said, chief, being on the edge of the Kingdom is mind-boggling!"

Christopher smiled and winked at the team members.

Lance continued, "By the way, give the old colonel a salute from me! Probably never thought he'd see me out here as one of his lef'tenants."

Colonel Dunbar called out, "I heard that, private!"

For the KPF leadership, it was a winter of rejoicing despite the turmoil in the Christian world. Christopher felt these reports were proof that God was indeed stirring up believers worldwide to complete the task.

Winter became spring, which became summer, which became fall again—all passed while the team huddled together on the ranch in Montana. The Franklins never asked questions about the KPF staff. They provided for their every need and encouraged them to stay longer.

A paradoxical pride began to swell up in the hearts of the believers at the ranch and, in fact, among many Christ-followers worldwide. Increasing numbers of Christians who refused to take the "mark of the beast" were captured. On worldwide broadcasts devoted especially to these events, these individuals were shown walking to an executioner's block, laying their head willingly on it, and waiting courageously, even joyfully, for the downward swing of the executioner's sword.

Christopher realized that the pride felt on the ranch was that of a parent seeing a child act in an exemplary manner or of a brother seeing his sister perform well in an athletic competition. A tradition took root in the daily line of martyrs—they would sing a doxology on the way to their death.

Awe grew in the hearts of most of the global populace as they witnessed the executions of these individuals who sang songs of praise on the way to the block. Yet pride and courage grew in the hearts of true believers who watched. They saw how the grace of the Lord rested on each martyr, giving him or her courage to die for the sake of Jesus. Numberless hidden believers vowed to face death the same way, if it ever came to that, and to sing the same songs.

One day as the team watched, Christopher said, "Names are being added daily to the roll call of the faithful. A channel designed to discourage dissenters is actually strengthening their resolve, for it is enabling believers to daily count the cost of following Jesus. What the enemy meant for evil, God has meant for good!"

Group B felt this strange mixture of feelings whenever they watched what they called the "Martyrs' Channel." Occasionally they would see men, women, or children they knew. They wept for them—sad, yet proud.

On the same channel, interspersed with the executions, were brief sketches of families finding meaningful lives under Michael's reign. They received homes, cars, groceries, clothing, jobs, and education. Every ten minutes some image of Michael flashed on the screen with a notable quote or a humanitarian project he sponsored. For those who received the mark of Michael, it was a time of Rebirth. Societies were emerging from the ravages of the recent plagues.

Nations hailed it as the New Millennium or the Golden Age. For the first time in recorded history, there was the absence of armed conflict anywhere in the world. The emerging global economy was thriving. The Seven—no longer The Ten—under the headship of Michael Wroth openly directed world affairs equitably and generously.

* * *

One stormy evening almost a year after Group B arrived at the ranch, Timothy received a faint call on one of his shortwave frequencies. "Hello? Timothy? This is Phil Young. Where are you, guys? I have been looking for you ever since you left L.A!"

Timothy answered, "Phil? Where are *you*? When we left L.A. we looked for you, but you were nowhere to be found!"

The line broke up with static for a moment before Phil returned. "—needed a break. When I came back, the house was burned down, and you were gone. They told me that you had been imprisoned, but I didn't believe them. Help me, Timothy. I'm scared and on the run. I don't know how much longer I can hide. Tell me where you are so I can join you."

Timothy shuffled in his seat nervously. "Listen, Phil. I don't have authorization to tell you where we are. Let me get Christopher, and I'll let him talk to you, okay?"

Static again. "—be fast. I don't know how long I'll be able to maintain this transmis—" Timothy sprinted out of the room, knocking over his desk chair. He burst into the living area of the house.

"Christopher, come quick! Phil Young is on the line. He needs help."

Christopher rushed to the shortwave radio. Feverishly he and Timothy worked the radio. "Phil! Phil! Do you read us?"

Static was the only response.

Timothy ran his fingers through his disheveled hair. "Why, oh why, did I not answer him? He sounded so desperate, Christopher. I wanted to tell him where we were, but I knew our orders—clear it by you or the colonel first. Now, we've surely lost him."

Christopher patted his shoulder. "You did the right thing, Timothy. Security protocol is essential for our survival and for the movement. We can't announce our position to anyone, not even Phil. We don't know who's listening. Maybe we'll hear from him again. Let's pray for him right now."

A few weeks later, Nic from Group C reported that he also had been contacted by Phil Young. "Our transmission was broken up too. He was almost hysterical, Christopher. I've got to tell him where we are so he can join us. We all have each other, but Phil—well, he's all alone."

"Nic, I can't tell you what to do, but I just don't think it's wise to announce your location over shortwave if he calls back."

John, who had been listening in the background, began speaking. "Maybe not, Christopher, but I can't see that we can turn our backs on him. We'll figure something out. We're family."

"I know. I know. Perhaps I'm too cynical right now."

John quipped, "Well, that's a first. Guess my cynicism is being conquered by compassion."

Christopher smiled. "Perhaps you're right. Phil has been with us from the beginning. You guys pray with your team about it. Do what you think best." Christopher paused. "Guys, things are getting tougher and tougher here where we are. Not sure how much longer we can evade capture and support our teams that are still left."

Nic spoke again through the growing static. "Christopher, we're hardly able to maintain contact with any of the teams."

"Us, too."

"Any idea on our progress towards *no place left*? What's Timothy's latest UUPG count? Our phone apps are hopelessly outdated."

Christopher shook his head. "Wow! It's really hard to count. But our best guess is there are still three or four hundred yet to be engaged with the gospel. We must press on as long as we can. Now, more than ever, we must hasten the day. The night is coming when no one can work."

The delay on the other end spoke volumes. "That's what we figured." Nic spoke in halting syllables as the static grew worse. "—not sure we'll see you this side of heaven—." Static. "—and we've already had some very close calls. The other day—." Static. "—but morale is high though danger is nearer than ever. Don't give up on the mission!"

Christopher choked back tears. "Nic. John. Not sure if I'm coming through. You all stay the course as well. Be faithful to the end. Let's make each other proud. Let's make Jesus proud. And as long as we have breath, let's encourage the teams until there is *no place left*! Over and out."

As he set down the mic, a sense of dread overcame the leader of the KPF.

* * *

Group B wintered again on the ranch in Montana, while the infrequent reports from Group C pointed to that group wintering somewhere in Central America. When spring arrived, Morris Franklin suggested that the group pack up and move north into Canada. "I don't know how much longer I can shelter you good folks. It's no drain on my resources, but more and more of my sway around here is being carved away by the IC. Pretty soon, someone will come searching my ranch, and I won't be able to protect you. I can't get you across the border, but I can give you the name of a friend in Alberta who may be able to give you a place to stay."

Morris outfitted the band of travelers for the journey. To help them cross the Canadian border, he escorted them in his Land Rover. Just before the checkpoint, the group waited until after midnight. Around 12:30 a.m., Morris called ahead to the immigration post. Satisfied that the right person was on duty, he urged the group onward while he remained behind.

With heavy hearts, the team bid him farewell. The two SUVs approached an ominous border crossing with a heavy gate flanked by automatic guns. Christopher slowed the first car and prepared to show his ID. His heart beat faster and faster. *Will this work? How far does Morris's influence reach?*

But as the two cars approached the gate, it swung slowly open, and a soldier waved both vehicles through. After passing the gate and rounding a bend in the road, the teams in both vehicles erupted in cheers.

Carefully, by the most obscure logging roads in the Rockies, Group B wound its way north through countless valleys.

As the temperatures warmed, the team arrived to a warm welcome at a ranch in northern Alberta. This remote ranch became the new KPF base for the following months.

One day late in the year, while the snow lay heavy all around their Canadian home, it happened.

Christopher and Chara were watching the Martyrs' Channel, when a special news bulletin flashed on the screen. The couple watched white-faced as the pictures of all the members of Group C flashed on the screen accompanied by the reporter's voice-over:

"We have a special report from IC offices. Michael's personal aides report that some of the remaining leaders of a highly destructive cult group called the Kingdom Preparation Force have been captured in a remote jungle of Costa Rica. All nine members were taken to a local prison where all were repeatedly offered freedom if they would renounce their intolerant views and bow the knee to Michael. Now to our reporter on the scene, Janice Clinton. Janice?"

A woman's face came into view, her hair blown by the wind. Behind her stood a well-known object—an executioner's block. Thousands of onlookers crowded the elevated site. She had to raise her voice to be heard above the din of the crowd chanting, "Kill them! Kill them!"

"Thank you, Robert. I've not seen the mood of the executioner's crowd this electric in a long time. You can feel the relief in the crowd that finally the leaders of this destructive cult have been apprehended. While all nine have been offered their freedom if they will worship Michael, all of them, including the two children, have refused." She shook her head in disbelief.

"My sources tell me that, thank goodness, the children are under the age of accountability. This means they have been immediately freed from the disruptive influence of their parents and taken to a foster home where they will be given opportunities later to worship Michael. The seven adults should emerge from the prison doors at any moment and begin the procession to the executioner's block."

The horrified Owens called the other staff and watched in silence as each of the Group C members heard his or her name read off. One by one, each emerged from the prison door and walked resolutely to the executioner's block. At the tops of their lungs, they sang praises down the long walkway.

The members of Group B automatically stood to their feet in honor of their teammates, arms around each other, weeping as they watched the screen.

John Steward sang loudly as he led the procession. One by one, the others followed his example. Their praises strangely rose above the din of the jeering crowd. Then, one by one, their praises on earth were cut short by the executioner's blade. Last of all Nic Fernandez emerged from the doorway and strode toward the block. Despite his tears, Christopher couldn't help laughing at Nic's off-key but triumphant singing.

His "joyful noise" song echoed in the listeners' ears long after it was interrupted.

Group C team members—most of them members of the original band of conspirators—paid the ultimate price.

John Steward. Renee Steward.

George Yang. Julie Konami Yang.

Tal Gillam

Stacy Fernandez. Nicolas Fernandez.

All dead before the hour was over—no cries for mercy, no compromise of conviction.

So quick.

So final.

As they watched, Christopher recited a portion of Hebrews 11, just as he always did when watching the executions. But this day his words barely emerged above a whisper as he got to verse 38:

"The world was not worthy of them."

With the last fall of the sword, Chara began singing the song they knew so well, based on Revelation 12:11. Soon the others joined her.

And they overcame him by the blood of the Lamb
And the word of their testimony
And they loved not their lives even unto death,
They loved not their lives unto death.

Though they cried, they continued singing the verses until they were hoarse.

Finally, Christopher spoke during a lull. "What we see with our eyes looks so final, but actually our dear friends have stepped into immortality. Their songs on earth were transformed into praises before the heavenly throne. They each stand before Jesus this very moment with a joy inexpressible while their Lord says, 'Well done, My good and faithful servant. Enter into the joy of your Master.'"

He turned his back to the screen and faced the remnant.

Chara and the four Owen children.

Win and Jeanie Dunbar.

Timothy and Grace Wu.

Kellie Davies.

They stood there barely conscious that their arms were around each other. Tears streamed down their faces. Win fought back tears and then said, "Commander, we stand with you to the end. What are your orders?"

Christopher stood erect and blinked several times.

"We are all that is left of the KPF leadership. The weight of this mission falls more squarely on our shoulders than ever before. Our teams depend on us. We must endure to the end for their sake and for the sake of the people groups that have not yet heard. Until there is *no place left*, the quest is not over."

They nodded their heads. Then the sole remaining staff members of KPF leadership huddled in the living room where they conducted a memorial service that very night. Even the children had witnessed the executions; they too felt privileged to be a part of a group that stood true to the Lord to the very end. They prayed all night for the completion of the quest they had begun.

It was the longest night Christopher had ever known. His heart ached. In the span of a few minutes, the lives of his closest friends in the world had been snuffed out. He had watched them die, and that with no advance notice, no time to prepare his heart.

In L.A., it had been torture to watch his two closest friends, John and Nic, drive off into the night with the rest of Group C. He knew that it was for the best that they split up to diversify leadership responsibilities. Secretly he had hoped that it would be they who endured to the end and escaped capture rather than himself. Now he found himself asking the same questions all over again. *Why me? Why couldn't I have been the one to die?*

Eventually the members of Group B split up to continue dealing with the news, each in his own way. Chara lay in Christopher's arms as weariness crept over them.

"Chara, I'm nervous. I don't know how much longer we can evade capture. Yet somehow we must find a way to carry on—for the sake of the teams, for the sake of the Kingdom."

TWENTY SIX

Time slowly slid by as the forty-foot fishing boat plied the seas between Peninsular Malaysia and East Malaysia. Yijing frequently stood on the bow, scanning the horizon. The Lao vessel stopped occasionally in remote Riau islands to re-provision in the escape from the Chinese. In each port of call, rumors of destruction throughout Malaysia urged the captain ever southward.

Heat stroke, exhaustion, and hunger claimed the lives of many passengers as Yijing's gospel band tirelessly nursed the patients. The limited supplies led to increased rationing. Yijing often gave her food to other passengers who were hungry.

One bright morning, Yijing sighted land looming in the distance on both sides. She rushed to the pilothouse and spoke in Lao. "Where are we, uncle?"

Ribs showed through the taut skin of the old captain who was stripped to the waist. "I'm not sure, little sister, but on our last stop, someone told me that we might find the Sunda Strait which separates two large islands. The island on the starboard side is called Sumatra. It is larger than the entire country of Laos. All of the people there are fierce Muslims."

Yijing put her arm around the old fisherman. "But, uncle, do not fear. Remember, Jesus has saved you. You are His child now. In life or in death, He will take care of you! Now, what do you think? Shall we pull into a port to get supplies? Everyone is so hungry."

The captain shook his head slowly as the boat headed into the strait. "Not yet. I hear that if we turn north along the west side of Sumatra, we will be less conspicuous. There are many Chinese trading communities along the coast. Perhaps with your Chinese you can gain us some help. But let us not stop here. There is too much activity."

As the ship moved steadfastly through the strait, a cluster of islands rose higher on the port side. Billows of smoke rose from the island known as Child of Krakatoa, the re-emerging descendant of the famous volcano. Seeing the eerie sight, the captain gunned the engine and sped past.

Days slowly ran off the calendar as the Lao fishing boat plied the rough seas on the windward side of Sumatra. The seemingly endless coast was exposed to the mighty waves that raced across hundreds of miles of open ocean. It was all the captain could do to keep the vessel afloat and in sight of land. Despite his best efforts, the seams of the wooden boat began giving way from being battered by the relentless swells. The captain urgently beckoned Yijing to the pilothouse. "We can no longer avoid civilization. We must pull in. This boat cannot stay afloat more than a few more hours. You must prepare everyone to get off as soon as we find a place to moor. I see a town in the distance." He patted the wheel. "I only hope she can make it that far."

As the boat sank deeper in the water, the diesel engine strained to drive the heavy craft to the safety of the port; it fought a losing battle. The captain shouted to Yijing, "Get everyone on deck! Find anything that can float. We won't make it to shore."

Waves began to lap over the sides as the gospel band gathered the passengers in the middle of the boat. When all hope was gone, the captain fired a flare into the air and waded to the others on deck. "Now! We must all swim for it!"

Yijing and the captain feverishly herded everyone over the gunwales and into the cold water. Yijing screamed, "Swim with all your might! Hold onto your floats and kick your legs!" Fighting against the surging waves, the group barely cleared the vicinity as, without warning, the boat plunged into the depths of the sea. Fishing vessels near the shore, observing their plight, came to the rescue of the human flotsam.

* * *

Yijing and the rest of the passengers lay upon benches in a church in Padang, Sumatra, shivering in their blankets. The pastor and his family tried to minister to the group's needs, even though they were unable to communicate with them in Indonesian. The pastor's twenty-year-old daughter, Abigail, served tea to Yijing. As the gospel band leader gazed around the small building, she noticed a small sign in Chinese. Turning to Abigail, Yijing ventured in Chinese, "Do you understand Mandarin?"

The pastor's daughter turned in surprise and answered, "Yes, of course. We are all Chinese. But how can you? Are you from another Chinese town nearby? How is it that you do not speak Indonesian?"

"Little sister, I am not from here. I am from China and have traveled all the way from Laos on the boat that sank."

Soon Yijing was translating for the whole group and arranging for their needs. She developed an unusual bond with Abigail, who was several years her junior. Yijing questioned her new friend about the surrounding area and explained about the gospel band's mission from northern Laos onward. Frequently she shared her heart for finishing the task and prayed with the younger woman. "Are there other churches here?" she asked one day.

"Yes, Yijing, there are several churches here in Padang and other cities."

Yijing probed further. "Are there places left near here where the gospel has not yet gone?"

Abigail nodded. "Yes, of course."

Yijing's eyes widened. "Are there unreached tribal groups on this large island?"

"Yes, there are many. In fact, the largest, the Minangkabau, number in the millions in the highland regions of the interior."

"Did you say *millions*? Are there Christ-followers and churches among them?"

The pastor's daughter thought for a moment. "None that I have ever heard of. They are staunch Muslims. All Christians are afraid of them."

A new light shone in Yijing's eyes as she gazed into the distant highlands. "Then that is where we must go—my gospel-runners and I. Those people need the good news before Jesus returns. We have a mission no matter where we happen to be. Jesus said, 'As you go, make disciples.' Time is running out."

The pastor, overhearing the conversation, walked over to the pair. "You are a foolish girl to think you can go to the Muslims. They cannot be saved. You are only a woman, and you do not speak Bahasa Indonesian or Minangkabau. How will you communicate?"

"There are some of us who speak English, and I speak Chinese. We will find a way."

The pastor shook his head and laughed. But the quiet voice of his daughter broke his laughter as she spoke to Yijing. "I will go with you. I will translate. You will speak in Chinese, and I will translate into Indonesian. God will make a way. Please, Yijing, let me go with you. I want to be a faithful servant and hasten the return of Jesus!"

For hours the pastor and his daughter discussed and sometimes argued about the wisdom of this plan. Yet the following day the pastor reluctantly rented a bus, and Abigail and the gospel-runners boarded it with him.

Yijing was the last to board the bus. The old Lao captain held her small backpack. "Well, uncle," she said, "you have proven faithful ever since we left that dock where the soldiers attacked us on the Mekong. You gave us our physical lives, and Jesus gave you eternal life!"

"How long ago was that, little sister? I lose track. Never mind. You have become the daughter I never had. Take this."

The captain pulled a gold chain from around his neck. Dangling from it was a precious jade pendant. "It is worth much money. Use it to provide for the team. Keep pressing on until there is *no place left* to preach."

His trembling hands placed the necklace over Yijing's head, and then he fell upon her neck sobbing. Finally, he pulled himself away. Handing the backpack to her, he turned to go.

"Wait!" she called. "Uncle—father—carry on the mission wherever the Lord takes you. You are His messenger as well. He is *so* proud of you!"

With that final word, she got on the bus. She could not bear to look back.

Kilometer after kilometer the bus wound its way deeper into the Minangkabau Highlands. As it neared the edge of the ancient Minang kingdom, the bus slowed and finally stopped by the side of the road near a jungle trail.

Twenty-two members of the gospel band got off the bus while the pastor pleaded once more with Abigail to weigh the risks she was taking.

"My father, I have weighed them. Please, Father, let me reap an eternal weight of glory far surpassing all comparison. Please give me your blessing!"

The Chinese pastor wept as he pulled his only child to his chest in a long embrace. "Go, my daughter. It is no longer safe anywhere. Without Michael's mark, we are all as good as dead. Many churches have already been closed; ours will not be far behind. If Jesus is coming back soon, as Yijing says, then do not hold back. Preach the good news, and may God have mercy on the Minang people!"

With those words of commissioning ringing in their ears, the frail but determined group of women turned their backs to the bus and disappeared into the Sumatran jungle.

TWENTY SEVEN

Group C was no more—at least on earth.

Christopher felt confident that from heaven they cheered on the remaining servants of God on earth to speed up their pace toward *no place left* without a gospel witness.

All eleven members of Group B prayed that those who had gone before them would find them faithful. Daily, Christopher encouraged them. "What better way to honor those who have died than by finishing what they—and generations before—have started?"

A deepened sense of stewardship gripped the remaining members of the KPF leadership team, permeating their lives.

Christopher watched as their resolve doubled.

But so had their workload.

Following the executions, Group C could no longer help coordinate the oversight of the teams, though there were fewer and fewer teams to communicate with.

Group B, hunkered down in their headquarters in Alberta, lived in a flurry of activity. The three couples met over coffee, as was their daily habit, to coordinate affairs.

"Boss, I don't know what to make of it," said Timothy, "but reports of mysterious missions groups in remote places continue to filter in along with the reports of our team."

Grace beamed. "I told you, boss, momentum is increasing no matter what the Antichrist throws at us!"

Colonel Dunbar cleared his throat. "Sir, I would not take these reports at face value." He paused, obviously having a hard time getting his next words out. "If Tal were here, he would warn us of the role of the enemy in sowing misinformation. The adversary could be trying to throw us off track."

"Now, Winthrop, don't be so pessimistic," said Jeanie.

"I wouldn't be, except for a brief memo we got from Lance Chu this week. He said that in one valley they discovered that a mystery team had passed through spreading the 'gospel' a few months earlier."

Grace bounced up and down. "See! What did I tell you?"

Turning and staring at her sadly, the colonel continued, "A *false* gospel. They were spreading a *false* gospel!"

The blood drained from Grace's face.

"How long have you known this, Win?" asked Christopher.

"Known? I still don't know the extent. We've received rumors before, as Timothy has mentioned. But *confirmation*? Just the last two days."

Jeanie said, "Perhaps this was an anomaly. Perhaps this one mystery team did not have the full gospel but went out anyway in the zeal of the NoPlaceLeft movement."

Picking up a printout, the colonel looked at it. "Perhaps. Here's the excerpt from Lance's message:

> *The mystery team that preceded us attracted great crowds*
> *through some amazing miracles. The problem was their*
> *message. Not only did the "gospel" they preached here in*
> *this valley ignore the death, burial, and resurrection of*
> *Jesus Christ, but they preached Michael as the promised*
> *savior!*

The group remained silent. Christopher took it all in. *Oh, God! I had so hoped that these mystery teams were genuine offshoots of current movements. I had so hoped that they were the virus of the Kingdom spreading. Was I wrong? Were we all wrong?*

Chara broke in to all of their thoughts. Reading deliberately from her Bible, her words cut to the heart:

> *"At that time if anyone says to you, 'Look, here is the*
> *Messiah!' or, 'There he is!' do not believe it. For false*
> *messiahs and false prophets will appear and perform great*
> *signs and wonders to deceive, if possible, even the elect.*
> *See, I have told you ahead of time. So if anyone tells you,*
> *'There he is, out in the wilderness,' do not go out; or, 'Here*
> *he is, in the inner rooms,' do not believe it."*

"That's what it says, right here in Matthew 24," she said.

Christopher nodded. He agreed inside, although he didn't like doing so. "I think we have to face the truth of these times. Many false prophets will arise. Like they did in Galatians 1, they will preach *another* gospel—a false gospel—that will lead people astray."

Grace burst into tears. "Then has all of our tracking of the spread of the gospel been in vain?" She held her phone in her hand. "Is it time to throw this app away?"

"No. Hold on there, little sister." The colonel gently pulled her toward him to comfort her. "This is just *one* bit of misinformation. The point of misinformation is to make us doubt everything. If we do that, the enemy has won the battle."

Christopher grabbed hold of that idea. "Right, Win! We *know* some of the mystery teams have preached a biblical gospel, right?"

Timothy nodded. "Absolutely, boss. Our teams have even found thriving churches among what we thought were UUPGs before any of the NoPlaceLeft teams on our radar arrived."

"Precisely!" Christopher felt his optimism and faith rising again. *Base everything on truth! Don't be misled.* "We know *some* of the mystery teams are the result of the Kingdom message spreading from place to place."

Timothy turned the tracking monitor toward the group. "Then what do we do, boss? How do we track the legitimate spread of the gospel? We're basing all our recommendations to the global community off this data."

"If I may, sir," said the colonel, "I would suggest we do exactly as we do in the military world. We proceed with mission objectives until we *verify* that the targets have been engaged legitimately. If our teams arrive and find the gospel has preceded them, then they help train the believers in that group and keep moving on."

Christopher looked around the room. The team members were nodding. "Okay, let's go this direction. Timothy and Grace, perhaps we need to add another color to the Kingdom progression reporting for a new category—'rumored but not confirmed.'"

Grace beamed again. "Gotcha, boss! I'll get the word out to the global community!"

The difference between hearsay and facts became increasingly blurred in the weeks to come. The colonel was at a loss to know how to strategically plan mission advances but proceeded the best he could.

Christopher grew antsy inside. He realized it was a race to get the gospel to as many people as possible before Jesus' return. He and his team remained in contact with the missions agencies and churches that had gone underground.

In another staff meeting, the colonel reported, "In many areas of the world, mission teams are greeted with more resistance than ever. It's as if a spiritual hardening is growing worldwide."

Christopher turned to Chara. "You were reading about that the other night, weren't you?"

She quoted the verse from Matthew 24 from memory, *"'Because of the increase of wickedness, the love of most will grow cold.'"*

"As we've said many times," Christopher reminded the team, "it will get worse before it gets eternally better."

Grace chimed in, "One ray of sunlight in the twilight of world evangelization is a revival spreading among Jews globally, especially in the country of Israel itself. It's as if a barrier has been shattered! Jews by the thousands are embracing their true Messiah, especially when they're faced with a man named Michael who claims to be God but who falls so far short of the biblical picture of God."

"While thousands of so-called Christians are falling *away* from the faith and embracing Michael," Chara smiled, "thousands of Jews are falling *into* the arms of Jesus the Messiah and embracing execution as the cost of their newfound faith!"

"Well, we'll take any good news we can get," said Christopher. "Keep reading the book of Revelation, you guys. It is our best preparation for what is still to come. We're not done with the disasters of God's judgment."

Christopher knew he was no prophet. But the Bible prophecy was something he could bank on. Weeks of the Rebirth renaissance rolled by until, unexpectedly, Michael Wroth's utopia encountered its toughest challenge yet.

* * *

It was called MADS—Malignant Airborne Dermavirus Syndrome. The sickness spread so rapidly that disease control experts were unable to pinpoint its origin. Apparently caused by an airborne virus, the epidemic became worldwide within a week. Festering sores covered individuals from head to foot. Salves, antibiotics, creams—nothing seemed to lessen the pain or minimize the spread of the infection in the body. Millions of people around the world died—not from the disease itself but from the accompanying complications: dehydration, malnutrition associated with loss of appetite, and further infection from the open sores. Everyone in the world got the disease—that is, almost everyone.

Jesus-followers—including Messianic Jews—who were waiting for their appointment with the executioner's block were immune to the virus. Christopher attributed their immunity and that of other Christ-followers to the protection of God.

Chara and Christopher sat alone in their room watching the news. The news anchor reported, "This just in from Michael's palace. The recent outbreak of MADS is apparently the work of those who resist Michael's reign. In a secret lab, Christians have developed this new virus and launched the bioweapon around the world. These leaders secretly inoculated thousands of rebels prior to the public launch of the plague. Though it appears that normal life has temporarily ground to a halt, Michael assures us that utopia will return within two or three weeks. He has vowed to strike at the heart of this rebellion."

Christopher grunted. "Change the channel, sweetheart. I can't take any more of this propaganda."

Chara switched to the Martyrs' Channel. As gruesome as it was, they wanted to remain in touch with the cost of the advance of the gospel.

"Honey, does it seem to you that the number of executions is increasing?" Chara asked as she set down the remote. "I mean, look at those lines!"

Christopher shook his head in disbelief. "Don't you see what Wroth is doing? The immunity of believers to MADS is revealing all the more easily who is resisting his efforts. We can't seem to get a break! Even our deliverance turns into persecution."

"Yes, honey, I know. But listen to them bear witness before the world as they go to the block. It's as if their words are inspired! God is increasing the amount of gospel witness through this!"

Christopher paused. "The words of Jesus in Matthew 10 are ringing in my ears like never before:

'I am sending you out like sheep among wolves. Therefore be as shrewd as snakes and as innocent as doves. Be on your guard; you will be handed over to the local councils and be flogged in the synagogues. On my account you will be brought before governors and kings as witnesses to them and to the Gentiles. But when they arrest you, do not worry about what to say or how to say it. At that time you will be given what to say, for it will not be you speaking, but the Spirit of your Father speaking through you. Brother will betray brother to death, and a father his child; children will rebel against their parents and have them put to death. You will be hated by everyone because of me, but the one who stands firm to the end will be saved.'

Chara grabbed Christopher's hand. "Sweetie, let's pray for them right now—pray that believers around the world, including us, will endure to the end."

Finally the crisis waned, and life returned to normal—but without thousands of Christians who had been discovered and executed.

* * *

Lance Chu ran into the hut gasping for breath. "Dudes, they're ready to believe!" The thin air of the high Central Asian plateau made breathing difficult at times.

The other team members shot out of the hut with him and returned to the mosque where the village elders sat on their mats. They were covered from head to toe with excruciating sores.

The chief elder stood up painfully, as did the others with him. They held their Korans in their hands. "The words of life that you have shared with us are true. What we have believed for generations is false."

The chief stopped for a moment. Tears spattered the cover of the book he held in his trembling hands. "We have compared the New Testament stories you gave to us with the words of this book. We had *heard* of Jesus but had never actually read His words. Now we see that the words of Jesus are *true*. They bring *life*! Finally, we can be free from our bloodguilt and shame!"

Another elder stepped forward. "Our hearts knew the words must be right even though our minds protested. But when we saw that you six were immune to the MADS virus we have received, it became obvious that God's hand is on you."

The chief set the Koran down and picked up the Gospel of Luke he had received. "Today, we put our faith in Jesus Christ alone as Savior and King. From this day forward, this is a Jesus meeting hall!"

Lance shouted at the top of his lungs, "Dudes, this is awesome! Jesus, You're amazing!" He knelt in the midst of the group to pray, signaling for the others to join him.

"Jesus, You alone are the Savior of the world and Your Word alone is our guide. Forgive us all. Father, make these men and their families Your children. Let them know Your love and make them a blessing to the other tribes in this area."

Loud weeping filled the room as the men continued to prostrate themselves before King Jesus. The voice of the chief broke through their tears, "Jesus, save us! For centuries, we and our people have resisted You. Forgive us! In this final hour, let us express our gratitude by bearing witness of this story to all people."

The prayer meeting was disturbed when a young man suddenly burst into the hall. He knelt by the chief, faint with exhaustion. "Uncle, I have just come over the mountains. Some foreigners who did not have Michael's mark were captured by the authorities. They were executed on the spot."

Lance couldn't believe the words coming out of the young man's mouth. *Team 458? It could only be them! Dead? How many teams is this now? Oh, Father! No time for grieving right now.*

The young man continued, "The police are not far behind me. When they find these foreigners, they will execute them and will kill us for harboring them."

Standing to his feet, the old chief gathered Lance's team near him. "I cannot protect all of you here. You must leave immediately. Two of our guides will lead you to safety and bear witness with you of what God has done here. In exchange, leave two of you for a while to teach us how to follow Jesus and how to spread this good news to others. We can protect two, but not six."

"Dude, that's just what Jesus said. 'Follow Me, and I'll make you become fishers of men.' The Holy Spirit has put this into your heart."

He looked at the five team members he had been through so much with—three from his original Central Asian team and two others who were the survivors of another team. He hated to break them up again, but the Kingdom demanded it.

"Okay, team. Regardless of what happens in the future, our minimum size must be pairs. Like, we *need* each other, you know?"

The team members nodded grimly.

Lance turned to the retired Indian couple on the team. "Moses and Hannah, are you willing to stay behind and train these new believers to be a blessing to others?"

The couple bobbed their heads and smiled. "Of course! It is our duty. Godspeed to you! We will see you in heaven!"

The team escorted them to the cellar where the villagers would hide them. As the trapdoor was closing, Lance whispered to the couple, "Train them to stand firm and to keep witnessing until there is *no place left!*"

Hannah winked and repeated, "*No place left!*"

The door fell into place with a loud thud.

The sound reverberated in his ears as Lance grabbed his backpack and led his companions over the mountains to the next people group.

* * *

Christopher gathered the leadership team. "How are our folks doing?"

Timothy moaned. "Boss, worse than before. We lost fifteen teams to the executioner's block after the last plague."

"That's true, Commander," said Win. "But it has also confirmed the witness of other teams. When lost people see the team members' immunity, it convinces them that this is the judgment of God."

"Okay. Tell them to hold on. Worse plagues are coming. If I'm reading this right, life will never return to normal."

In the coming weeks, Christopher watched as the second and third plagues described in Revelation 16 made his prediction a reality. Marine scientists could give no explanation for a deadly microbe that spread throughout the world's oceans, rivers, and other water sources. Wherever the microbe grew, water turned the color of blood and pH levels fluctuated rapidly, killing all known living things in the sea.

The extent of the ecological disaster defied Christopher's imagination. The surfaces of all bodies of water were layered several feet thick with rotting and decaying plant and animal matter. The stench hung over the face of the earth. Millions of people died from the starvation that resulted from the loss of seafood from the world's food supplies. Thirst claimed many lives. Most of the world's potable water was corrupted and couldn't be purified fast enough. Even aquifers and springs were invaded by the microbe. Widespread famines occurred from loss of irrigation water in the agricultural lands of the world.

KPF/2414 teams around the world did their best to minister to their communities, though the teams themselves struggled to survive.

Timothy reported to Christopher another day. "We are losing contact with more and more teams. It's impossible to assess the advance of the Kingdom with any degree of reliability. We might as well throw the phone app away."

"Not yet, bro. As long as we have contact, we must disseminate whatever info we have."

Then the fourth plague struck. Meteorologists swore it was a sudden breakdown of the ozone layer, but no one could explain how it happened so quickly. In the course of three weeks, daytime temperatures around the globe soared into ranges unheard of—140, 150, 160 degrees Fahrenheit. The world became an oven, and many were unable to escape the scorching heat. The elderly died first, along with the youngest.

Daily, Christopher and Chara watched the news. Michael's propaganda machine couldn't hide the immensity of the disaster. The Dunbars sat in front of the screen with them.

"Commander," said Win, "our teams report that the remaining Christ-followers in the world are declaring boldly that it is God who is bringing these plagues to punish the world for its sin. They are calling people to repent, but instead they find that their listeners only curse God all the more."

Christopher responded, "It's all we can do, Win. We cannot control the response, only our proclamation. We have to continue to monitor events as best as we can."

In one of the more audacious moves during these weeks, the country of Israel, whose population had remained largely immune from the plagues, declared a new independence from the Rebirth. Its armed forces remained intact. While the rest of the world suffered from the plagues, the Israelis used their respite to reinforce their borders and set up their own opposition to Michael. Tens of thousands of Jewish Israelis had come to believe in Jesus, and the nation as a whole saw through Wroth's façade. They declared themselves the new sovereign state of Messianic Israel.

The searing heat of the fourth plague waned because of a fifth plague. Group B members walked out one day to observe the Alberta sky. Though it was noon, dark clouds obscured the sun, making it feel like evening.

As they stared upward, Grace asked, "What's going on?"

Chara said, "All I can figure is that this is what Revelation refers to as the beast's kingdom being plunged into darkness. Let's get inside and turn on the news."

The news anchor reported, "Good news from Michael's palace. Global temperatures are dropping!

"In other news, a temporary darkness seems to be growing on the earth. Early conjectures are that the smoke and haze given off by the scorched organic matter on the surface of the seas are creating a larger than usual cloud layer. Michael assures us that there is nothing to worry about and that he has matters under control. In other news, ..."

Whether from a developing cloud layer or an extended eclipse, Christopher and Group B watched as the sun no longer blessed the earth with its light. Night descended upon the earth and remained for weeks on end. The crops that weren't scorched by the heat died from the sudden temperature drop and lack of sunlight.

Millions of people slipped into deep depression, and many crossed over into hysteria. KPF teams brought messages of hope to the depressed. Even so, many people were unable to cope with the dark blanket of night.

Timothy reported in during staff meeting. "Our sources tell us the strain to generate enough electricity to provide constant light is overwhelming power plants. Rolling blackouts are the rule."

Jeanie grimaced and remarked, "Sounds like the much-heralded Rebirth is becoming a living death!"

"Boss, Messianic Israel is being spared the plague," said Grace. "Apparently a hole in this atmospheric canopy is providing the nation some daylight. Jews around the world are flocking back to the land of light."

The colonel shifted uneasily in his chair. "Still, despite the preaching of many Christians and the example of the Messianic Israelites, most of the world continues to curse God. Michael Wroth had no need to tighten his grip on the world—the world is only too gladly rushing to him as their only hope."

Jeanie said, "I was in town the other day gathering some supplies with our hostess. I overheard a discussion in a coffee shop. It defied common sense. The conversation went like this: 'What kind of God would send such awful plagues on such good people? In a world where everyone has a right to prosperity, how can those Christians believe in a God that is so archaic as to actually punish good people for a few questionable acts?'"

* * *

Michael needed someone to blame. These plagues were making him look increasingly powerless. His reputation of being in total control was at stake.

Marlene stood in the corner of the office, trembling.

Michael seethed in anger, pacing before his inner circle like a beast prowling the room. "All my plans—frustrated! And these, these—" he spat on the priceless carpet, "—these Jesus-followers thumb their noses at me!"

He continued storming around the office while Marlene, Dr. Sayers, and Jake watched. He cursed in ways Marlene had never imagined and shattered thousand-dollar vases. The three backed against the walls.

Marlene stared. *He has never shown such open fury. He has never lost it before. Never.*

Hearing the commotion, two security officers rushed into the office. Michael turned on them. He lifted them off the ground and flung them against the walls like dolls. They lay there crumpled, dead.

Marlene trembled. Wroth turned and pinned her with a wrathful gaze. As he approached, she slid to the floor, eyes closed, waiting for the onslaught.

She waited. Sayers and Simmons waited.

Ten minutes of silence passed as Michael returned to pacing in front of them.

Finally, he stopped in front of Marlene, glaring down at her. "Gather The Six to me *now!*"

Marlene's heart raced. Glad to still be alive, she rushed out of the office and almost as quickly back in with the remaining members of The Ten in tow.

Michael surveyed the group and spoke as if his previous outburst of wrath had not occurred. "Gentlemen, we thought we had achieved the Rebirth, but we were only in the pangs of labor. It is time to give birth, and this very week we will force the issue. This week, we wipe out all opposition to my reign. *All* of it!"

He shoved a chair against the wall, breaking it to pieces. Everyone jerked, startled by the noise.

"Most of the world already thinks that these plagues come from the God of the Jews and Christians. They think this God is more powerful than I am. Sometimes superstitions can be as strong as truth. But this so-called Messianic Israel not experiencing the recent darkness underscores this superstition."

Michael strode to a map on the wall and pointed at the Middle East.

"You Six will gather the most massive army the world has ever known. We will bring that army to Israel, to that cocky group of Jewish rebels. We will go there and wipe that nation off the face of the map." At this statement, he tore the Middle East from the map and hurled it to the floor. "We will show the world once and for all that there is no god but Michael. Do it *now!*"

The Six rushed out to begin making arrangements.

Michael turned to the remaining trio. "Marlene, you and Jake will mobilize IC forces to abandon all activities and focus on only one thing: closing the net on every remaining person, especially Christians, who has not sworn allegiance to me. In one week, I want no Jew or Christian alive who has not bowed the knee to me. One week only. Do you understand?"

Marlene nodded her head, fearful of speaking.

"And this Christopher Owen remains alive! How is that possible? He has been a thorn in my side for too long."

His eyes drilled holes through Marlene.

Is he on to me? Does he know I am protecting them?

Michael stalked closer and closer until his nose touched Marlene's. "I want him alive, standing in front of me, within one week. Is that understood?"

Marlene cringed inside as she felt his hot breath on her face. His nearness was not what she had dreamed of for years, the closeness of a man she adored. Instead she felt disgust for the abominable beast he had become."

Something snapped. This was the last straw.

On the outside, she remained stone-faced and nodded.

Michael turned from her to the elderly man dressed in white.

"Dr. Sayers, you will announce these plans to the world to win their hearts in a way that only you can."

And Larson Sayers obeyed.

Sayers spoke on worldwide broadcasts and public holographic displays through the use of emergency generators. He spoke before a live crowd of 100,000 people hastily gathered in a stadium. Marlene watched him from stage left, marveling at his control of the crowd.

"Are we experiencing woes?" asked Sayers. "Yes, they are the last birth pangs leading to the Rebirth. They are the work of the followers of this so-called Judeo-Christian God. But he is nothing more than a rebellious spirit subordinate to Michael."

His words were so persuasive. Heads throughout the crowd nodded in agreement. All except Marlene's. *Can they not see through this charade?*

"As for the woes that you face, they are especially the result of the mutiny of the upstart nation of Messianic Israel.

Opponents of Michael, and they are chief among them, are gasping with one last, collective breath. But now you will see that Michael is our supreme deity and lord. Has not the entire world witnessed the spirit descend and fill Michael's body?"

As Sayers spoke these words, screens slowly replayed the events of Michael's death and return to life. In the crowded stadium, people gasped as they witnessed again the assassin's assault but cheered at Michael's resurrection.

Marlene watched the monitors. *That was the moment everything changed for me as well. That is when I really knew that Michael Wroth was evil.*

As if he could sense her thoughts, Sayers turned and looked in her direction. She stood in the shadows to elude his gaze, moving almost involuntarily to hide behind a curtain.

The crowd continued to gasp at the replay of Michael's possession.

At exactly the right moment, Sayers shouted, "This is your god! This is your god!"

The multitude began chanting Michael's name: "Michael! Michael! Michael!"

"My fellow citizens, we have been experiencing the pangs of the Rebirth. It is time for it to come in fullness. I call on every citizen of the Rebirth to help bring it to fruition," continued Sayers.

"With me, you must hunt down every remaining person who has not taken the mark. For each person you turn in, Michael will give you an immediate credit of one million dollars—no questions asked. What's more, I promise to make you the first recipients of a new, anti-aging drug that will enable you to retain your youth indefinitely!"

Marlene observed a few eager souls begin to make their way to the exits, intent on collecting the reward as soon as possible. But Sayers wasn't finished.

"And for the final battle, the end of the birth pangs, I call on our strongest and brightest young men and women to come to defeat Israel. Join us as we quell the final unrest in the world and prove that peace will now reign forever. Let the Rebirth begin! Utopia awaits!"

The crowd cheered deliriously.

Just when she thought nothing more could shock her, Marlene stood aghast as a few brazen objectors rose to their feet and shouted their opposition. She wanted to warn them to remain quiet. But all she could do was watch helplessly as fire sprang from Sayers's hands, consuming them.

"Thus shall we treat all who try to defy the one true ruler, Michael!" he shouted, and the crowd cheered thunderously.

* * *

The sole surviving seven members of the KPF staff huddled around a fire-pit on the Alberta ranch. Their prayer meeting drew to a close. Win spoke up after the final "amen." "Team, I think we need to face up to the fact that the world has responded enthusiastically to Sayers's appeal."

Timothy added, "Thousands of individuals who had so far evaded the mark of Michael have been turned in by the underground networks. There isn't a Christian group that remains untouched by the landslide of betrayals."

"Lance Chu reported in, sir," said Win. "He and his team have done a remarkable job of staying true to the mission, despite enduring incredible losses. He estimates that KPF/*2414* teams in their region have lost 75% of their original numbers."

Jeanie's head jerked up. "Winthrop, that's three out of every four workers!"

Her husband nodded slowly. "Moses and Hannah were the latest to be beheaded. What's more, Commander, news of the loss of Group C took a toll on many of the teams. Morale has taken a nosedive, though the teams are heartened to hear of your—our—ability to remain undiscovered."

The group of KPF members—seven adults and the four Owen children—in Alberta was now worth a bounty of eleven million dollars. But they all knew that the reward for Christopher alone was probably set at more than that. Christopher wondered if their hosts would continue to protect them, yet, despite the next couple of months of betrayals and rewards, nothing happened. They remained safe far beyond the one-week deadline set by Michael.

As the Owens lay in bed very early one summer morning, Christopher spoke softly. "I need to leave. I need to visit the teams. I need to try to encourage them one last time. We must not give up until there is *no place left*."

With tears streaming silently down her cheeks, Chara whispered quietly, "I know."

Oblivious to her response, Christopher stammered, "I-I-I'm so restless here. There's not much for me to do that the rest of you can't do. I'm just an extra wheel. But our teams are so demoralized. If I could just visit them, it might make a difference. I can't do anything here if we are discovered by the IC. If they come to take us away, I won't fight them, so there's no need for me here. I figure our hosts aren't going to turn us in if they haven't already."

Chara whispered again, "I know, honey."

Christopher blinked rapidly several times. "You know?"

"Of course. Ever since we left L.A., you've been restless. I know you. You need to be in the field with those you lead. I've tried to block out the whole idea, but I know it's true. I've tried to figure out if there is a way we could all go with you."

"Perhaps there is!"

Chara touched his lips. "No. We both know there isn't. You'll be lucky just to make it overseas by yourself. If you take a family of six, you'll draw a lot of attention. Besides, the kids will do better here. It's a more stable environment."

Christopher didn't speak for a while. "I'll have to take Win with me. Actually, he first approached me about this idea. He thinks he still has enough contacts to help us slip through the dragnet and get where we need to go. I wouldn't make it to Vancouver without him."

"I know that too. Jeanie and I have already talked about this. We can handle all the communication here along with Kellie and the Wus. But you're wrong if you think you're not needed here. You may not be needed here for the KPF, but you are needed here by the Owen family. Nevertheless, I vowed the day we married that I would never hold on to you more tightly than the Lord did. If He ever called you to do something like this, I pledged I would let you go."

They lay there in each other's arms two more hours in the quietness of the morning—crying, sharing, laughing about old times, loving, talking about the future. When the kids awoke, the six of them spent the day together just as a family, the last they might ever spend like that this side of heaven. Christopher and Chara talked openly with the children about the decision. They all cried and clung to each other that day.

Christopher noticed that the other team members stayed away to give his family this special time, and he was grateful.

Late the next day, the team stood awkwardly in the doorway to say their final farewells. Leaving his family this time seemed to shred the secure fabric of their life that Christopher so cherished. Wherever he had gone, they had gone also.

What amazed him was the maturity of his children. Outside in the cool evening, they sobbed softly but didn't cling to him as they parted. Christopher gave them final instructions for loving Jesus and one another. He exhorted Joshua to be the man of the house and to watch over his siblings.

Finally, Chara gave her man one last, long embrace. She whispered in his ear, "I am the proudest woman in the world. Encourage the teams, my love. Hasten the day. Press on until there is *no place left*. I imagine we will wait for each other in heaven. I love you!"

Then she straightened herself up and stood by her children as they all bid Christopher and Win good-bye. As the men stepped into the vehicle, Christopher heard her say to the kids, "How privileged we are to share your father with the world!"

Slowly the SUV wound its way down the long drive.

Christopher Owen and Win Dunbar, against all hope, ventured out into the night.

TWENTY EIGHT

Michael hurled the daily report across the table as The Six and his administrative team avoided eye contact with him.

Marlene shuddered. *He grows more violent and angry every day. This is no longer the man I once loved.*

"I tire of these useless lists of dissenters that have been arrested. I gave you an ultimatum to round up every dissenter within one week. Why after all this time do we keep unearthing more rebels?"

Ethan Farnsworth broke the silence of the watchers. "Michael, we are doing all we can, but, in the midst of the disasters, these dissenters are aided by sympathetic followers who bear your mark. In fact—"

One look from Michael was all it took to stop Farnsworth mid-sentence.

Marlene shuddered again inside but dared not show it. The eyes of the group looked downward as Michael began to stalk around the perimeter of the table. A sheet of the daily report fell to the ancient tiled floor of his Rome palace. Stooping to pick it up, he ripped it in half.

"Ms. Hayes, I gave you one week to find Owen and Dunbar. The fact that they continue to elude my grasp is unacceptable. You will *personally* see to it that *all* of your energies are focused on finding these two. Their elusiveness inspires the rebellion to hold out against our efforts."

Michael grabbed the remaining papers and threw them into the wastebasket. "I do not want to see another prisoner report until Owen's and Dunbar's names are on it."

* * *

Christopher and Win snaked their way across the Pacific using various means at the colonel's disposal. Their goal was to visit teams in Southeast Asia, China, Mongolia, Russia, India, Central Asia, and the Middle East. As they went, they discovered the situation was even more distressing than Christopher had realized. The reports they had received at headquarters were for the most part very upbeat ones, sharing only the good news and minimizing the bad news. The actual situation, however, was quite dismal.

Many teams were so harassed that they spent much of their days in seclusion, trying not to attract attention; they hoped to stay in these tough areas long enough to make some impact. Much of their time was also spent trying to survive—literally trying to find food and shelter.

Also disturbing was the news about which Group B had formerly rejoiced. Over and over through the previous two years, reports had filtered back of mystery mission teams that were rumored to have visited remote tribes and peoples. The KPF had always taken that as good news that more missions groups and churches had responded to the call of missions than they had previously realized. But Christopher sensed the true situation was shaping up differently than they had hoped.

As Christopher and Win rode along a winding road in the mountains of Afghanistan, the colonel spoke above the roar of the engine. "Sir, today we will be making contact with our field leader of Central Asia. He can clue us in to the nature of the rumors we have been hearing better than anyone I know."

The jeep pulled into a hamlet just as the sun was setting. Rays of sunlight filtered through the dust and shone against a small mud-brick house.

As they got out, Christopher spied a gaunt, turbaned figure emerging into the light. Looking into the sun, the figure raised a hand to shield his eyes. "Dude, I'd know those silhouettes anywhere!" he cried.

Christopher's heart rose and sank. The voice was the same, but if it hadn't been for that, he would never have recognized the dusty individual. He ran and fell upon the man's neck, arms wrapped around him. "Lance! Lance!"

Both men wept.

Lance Chu pulled back and surveyed Christopher. "Like old times, eh, chief? Looks like the 'Tribulation Diet' is working for all of us. And what about you, O elusive Colonel Dunbar?"

The giant crossed the five meters between them in three strides and wrapped up Lance in his bear-like embrace. "Captain Chu, I knew I should have demoted you to private a long time ago! Still as insubordinate as ever!"

Over cups of chai around a charcoal fire, the trio chatted like the old friends they were.

When the time was right, Christopher reached into an interior pocket. He pulled out a badly wrinkled package and handed it to Lance. "Chara sent these for you."

Lance jumped to his feet, spilling his chai. "Red Vines licorice? My favorite! How did you—? How did she—?"

"Uh, well, don't get too excited. They passed through hell and high water to get here."

Lance ripped open the package, offered to share the contents with his guests, who graciously refused, and then gleefully consumed a stick of the bright red licorice.

"Uh, Lance?" Christopher said after a few moments. "What about your team?"

Lance stared at the embers and gnawed absentmindedly at his candy. A tear trickled down his dust-covered face, creating a muddy rivulet. He reached up and wiped it with his sleeve.

"I'm it. The last one. My partner was captured last week. He surrendered to give me time to escape and keep the mission going. Everyone wants the million dollars and eternal youth.

"In fact, you are not safe here. Like, you will have to leave before dawn. These mountain dudes have sheltered me and have proclaimed the gospel to others. But to ask them to shield three Americans? Well, it's too much for them."

The colonel's eyes widened in amazement. "Son, how will you keep going? Two are better than one, remember?"

Lance smiled. "You should know better than to think I'm alone, Colonel Dunbar. You taught us well. The *locals* are our partners. There are way more than two of us. There are *thousands* of us in these mountains following Jesus and making Him known to others.

"I'm Asian and can blend in pretty well. You two won't last a day. No, we've got to get you out of here before sunrise."

"You're right, soldier. You're absolutely right. Job well done!" The old officer saluted the young commando. It was the highest compliment he could give.

Lance squirmed in embarrassment. "Anyone for more chai?"

The question that lay deep within Christopher finally rose to the top. "Lance, of all our regional leaders, you are the one who has most consistently reported to us about a false gospel spreading through mystery teams. Can you enlighten us any more? We just don't know what to make of the status of Kingdom progress."

Lance set his chai down. He picked up a charred stick and began doodling in the dirt.

"Dude, it's *bad!* We've lost track of the number of valleys in Central Asia where we've encountered it. What we find is a heretical strain of 'gospel' that replaces Jesus Christ with Michael Wroth as the Messiah. In some places the mystery teams *knew* what they were doing—that is, preaching a false gospel. Someone sent them."

Christopher eyed Win and continued listening to Lance.

"Fortunately, we've identified many of those places. Our local teams have followed on the heels of the mystery teams and preached a *biblical* gospel. Some believe. Some don't. I wouldn't want to be one of those false preachers on the day of judgment!"

Christopher fought against the notion that all of the mystery teams were corrupt. "Lance, is it possible *some* of the mystery teams were part of the NoPlaceLeft movement and were preaching the true gospel?"

Lance rolled the Red Vine around in his mouth as he contemplated this. "Possible? Sure! There's been so much chaos and confusion here, anything's possible."

"Commander, this strain of false gospel is so prevalent that it unmistakably points to one conclusion," said Win. "Wroth has sent teams ahead of us to confuse the issue and mislead many. I thought we had seen the extent of his malevolence, but this tops it all."

Christopher shook his head. "That may be so, but I just can't help but believe that some of these mystery teams are preaching the real gospel. Surely not all have been sent by Wroth."

"Perhaps, Commander, perhaps."

None of the three slept that night. They cherished the depth of their friendship that had withstood the perils of many journeys. They reminisced about their time together in China.

Lance burst out, "Dude, Christopher, if you could have seen yourself in a mirror all bandaged up, expecting a firing squad! George and I couldn't stop laugh—"

He stopped mid-sentence, remembering the ultimate price George and Julie had paid on the executioner's block.

"Don't stop laughing, Lance," said Christopher. "George is watching from heaven, slapping his knee right now. I imagine we'll all see him soon."

Lance grinned. "Yeah, you're right. And I imagine he'd have a hard time recognizing *me* right now! A long way from those early conversations on the campus of USC!"

As Lance was about to feed another bundle of sticks to the fire, a gentle knock at the door could be heard above the crackle. He stood up and opened the door a few inches. Turning to the pair, he said, "It's time. You gotta get out now, or you may never get out."

Christopher's heart was too heavy for words. He embraced Lance and then turned to the jeep.

Lance continued, "Dude, we don't have much technology up here, so I don't watch the Martyrs' Channel. But do us proud when it's your turn, and we'll do the same. You don't need to worry about NoPlaceLeft Central Asia. We've got it covered."

Christopher saluted him, as did the colonel, and both climbed into the jeep. The colonel gunned the engine, and the vehicle disappeared into the darkness.

Win shouted above the wind noise, "Now, sir, for the final leg of the journey, I am compelled to tell you that we must head into the hornet's nest—the Middle East—where our remaining teams are working."

"I know, Win. Like our Lord, we must set our face toward Jerusalem whatever befalls us. *No place left* means *NO place left*— including there. Get us there, my friend."

With great trepidation, they proceeded toward the hotbed of Michael's activity in the Middle East.

The men made their way forward by the most obscure paths possible, sheltered by friends of the movement. Eventually, the exhausted duo approached the borders of Israel.

IC troops were thicker than a swarm of locusts on the borders of Messianic Israel, on high alert to any Christian or Jewish rebels.

Christopher stood on a mountaintop next to the colonel as Win pointed out troop placements. An army, the likes of which the world had never known, stood ready to lay siege to that ancient land. Both men sighed and turned to Amman, Jordan, to meet with a few trusted leaders.

* * *

Timothy received another call over the shortwave from Phil Young, only this time it was much stronger. Chara was soon at his side as they listened to Phil. "Please help me. I've followed your trail all the way to the Franklin ranch in Montana. I'm just outside that area. The Franklins won't keep me—they say it's too risky, but they won't tell me where you've gone. I can't believe I've held out this long. I've been betrayed three times, barely escaping being caught each time. I'm so tired and hungry. *Please!* I want to join you!"

Chara's heart broke. She and Timothy conferred before she answered. "Phil, I have orders not to tell anyone where we are over the broadcast waves. I'll tell you what to do. Go back to the Franklins and tell them 'the fox' gave them permission to tell you where they sent us. If they tell you, then meet us at the town closest to the southwest corner of this property. There is a small park in the middle of town. Just sit on a bench there day after tomorrow at noon, and we'll find you. Okay?"

Phil voice quivered. "Chara, thanks! I'm so relieved. I'll do my best to make it to you—day after tomorrow, noon."

Timothy said after hanging up, "I'll go pick him up. If I don't call you by 12:30, all of you had better leave quickly."

Moments later, Chara's phone rang. The caller was unidentified on the screen, but Chara answered it regardless.

"Chara? It's me, Marlene. I know where you are."

"Marlene? How did you get this number? How did you find us here?"

Timothy mouthed in disbelief, "Marlene Hayes?"

Chara nodded. She continued listening.

"Morris told me you'd be there. Chara, I don't have much time. I've made my decision. I want to follow Jesus. I just flew out of Rome and am in America. Michael will suspect that I have defected before the day's over, and he'll have me hunted down wherever I go. No one near me will be safe."

Chara didn't hesitate. "Come here. We'll help you. We'll be your family. We're used to risks."

Timothy waved his arms and shook his head vigorously.

Chara ignored him. She could hear Marlene weeping at the other end, trying to continue the conversation. Finally, Marlene spoke. "Thank you. I hoped you would say that. I'll be there as fast as I can."

When Marlene Hayes arrived alone at the Alberta ranch, Chara saw a broken woman. For two hours, Marlene sat sobbing on the couch with Chara's arms around her, realizing all the horrible things she had been responsible for. Chara shared again with her about the love of God that could forgive even *her* sins through the death, burial, and resurrection of Jesus Christ.

"It's just hard for me to believe God can forgive a person like me."

Chara smiled, "That's why it's called grace and mercy. None of us deserves it."

Marlene let out a long sigh. "That's the best news I've ever heard. It's too good to be true, but somehow I believe it anyway."

In stumbling words, interrupted both by sorrowful sobs and grateful laughter, Marlene cried out to God to be forgiven of her sin and to become His child.

Long after the "amen," Chara held Marlene in her arms like she would hold a child.

"One thing I'm a little puzzled about," asked Chara. "What about the mark of Michael? Didn't you receive it also?"

Marlene wiped away the tears and smiled wryly. "That was one of the perks of my position. No one ever questioned my allegiance or scanned me. I *ran* the scanning operation. It would be next to blasphemy for some lesser person to scan someone who held the authority I did. I never was marked—on purpose. I guess I saw this day coming a long time ago, even though I didn't want to admit it."

All the next day, Marlene was like a little child, carefree and eager to absorb as much of God's Word as she could. Chara, Jeanie, Kellie, and Grace all took turns teaching her. Even the Owen children helped answer her questions.

The following day, Timothy left to drive into town. The whole group was excited not only that Marlene was now their sister, but also that a former teammate would soon be reunited with them.

At one o'clock in the afternoon, Phil arrived at the ranch and embraced the little group. Marlene had been out in the fields most of the morning, reading her mother's Bible. Hearing the commotion, she returned to the house to meet the old friend she had heard was coming.

Chara brought Phil out to meet her. "Marlene, I want you to meet Phil Young, one of the original members of KPF. Phil, this is Marlene Hayes."

They had never met face to face, although they had talked by phone often—Marlene Hayes, personal assistant to Michael Wroth, and Phil Young, IC mole in the Kingdom Preparation Force.

Marlene tried to speak but couldn't. The blood drained from her face.

Phil's face reddened, and he sneered at her, "Well, well, I may have missed the KPF chief commander and his Green Beret side-kick, but I think Michael will be just as happy to know I've found *you*. The tremor of your defection has reverberated throughout Michael's empire."

Chara turned to Marlene. "W-W-What is he talking about?" she asked, watching Marlene's terrified eyes.

"He's the traitor I tried to warn you about! He's how we've been able to thwart so much of your activity. And now, we're all caught."

Timothy stared nervously. "There's no way. H-he was alone, and we weren't followed. Phil, tell us this isn't true. You would never—"

But his sentence was interrupted by the whir of helicopters. In moments, IC soldiers descended upon the ranch house and burst through every door. Group B and Marlene Hayes were whisked away to jail.

* * *

Christopher and the colonel sat in a third floor flat in Amman praying with the remaining five members of a Middle East *2414* team. When a knock came at the door, the two team members who lived in the flat hurried to hide their visitors. Spot-checks by IC or local militia soldiers with scanners were a common occurrence in the neighborhood. Everyone was eager for bounty money, and scanners were as common as mobile phones. The knock might be nothing more than a neighbor coming to visit, but no one wanted to take that chance.

One of the young men grabbed Christopher by the arm and hurried him to the bathroom. Lifting some tiles, he unlatched two clasps. He slid one end of the bathtub in a wide arc. Beneath it was a shallow trough.

"Quick! Lie here on your back, and I will slide the tub back on top of you."

Christopher slipped into the trough and waited as the tub scraped back into place. Grit fell into his eyes, but he couldn't reach his face to wipe it out. His heart began to race; he shut his eyes to fight the claustrophobia.

He heard the muffled voice of another team member hiding the colonel behind a false panel of a closet in the next room. "Sir, this is the biggest hiding space we have here. I hope you will fit."

When everyone was hidden, Christopher heard their hosts open the door. A commanding voice sneered, "What took so long? Soldiers, scan them and search the flat!"

Christopher strained to listen. Dust swirled in his nostrils, but he ignored the itch. Two bodies thudded to the ground, and a voice shouted, "Sir, these two are rebels!"

The commanding voice spoke again. "Put them in shackles and handcuffs! Tear this apartment apart. I smell vermin!"

Christopher heard the men tossing mattresses and emptying closets; the activity shook his shallow trough. Christopher gasped for fresh air, hoping not to be heard in the turmoil.

A hollow thud reverberated loudly as a soldier pounded the back of a closet. Wood splintered as a bayonet pried apart a false wall.

Another angry voice shouted, "Sir, three more!"

Christopher heard his teammates cry out and their bodies fall to the floor. Chains clattered along the tiles.

"Shackle them!"

Boots tromped in from a nearby room.

"Sir, this looks like everyone!"

The commanding voice spoke cruelly and deliberately. "I—don't—think—so. There's more going on in this rats' nest. Keep searching."

The frenzy of the search resumed.

Christopher's breathing grew more labored as his heart raced and the oxygen became scarce.

Feet pounded across the tiles. More shouts. Another false panel was torn apart, and the colonel spoke loudly. "I'm the one you are looking for. Leave these young men alone."

Christopher heard the colonel fall to the floor. Blows to his body followed but no groan or cry could be heard. Tears streamed down from Christopher's eyes. *God! Give him grace!*

The commanding voice shouted, "Enough! Turn him over and shackle him!"

The soldiers grunted as they wrestled the giant into a new position.

Every nerve in Christopher screamed to act. For the sake of the others, he steeled himself to remain silent. His picture was on the wall of every IC office. He couldn't afford for the others to be associated with him.

The room became so deathly silent that Christopher could hear the blood pumping through his ears. He stopped panting and held his breath.

The sound of a man spitting interrupted the silence.

A kick in the side of a fallen body followed.

"Well, well, well. Colonel Win Dunbar, I presume."

Christopher could sense the strained control in his friend's voice as he answered. "Jake? Jake Simmons?"

Jake laughed—an evil, throaty sound. "Finally! You've eluded me at every turn. But this is one trap you will not escape from.

"Guard him carefully, men. Michael will richly reward each of you beyond your wildest dreams if he makes it safely to the prison."

Christopher could hold his breath no longer. He sucked in the little air left as quietly as possible.

"Jake! Let these men go. I'm the one you want. They're just foot soldiers."

Jake laughed again. "Good try, Colonel Dunbar. No deal. But where is your exalted leader, Mr. Owen? I doubt you would let him out of your sight at this stage."

Another vicious kick, followed by a groan. "Where is he? He's a coward to let you get caught and not turn himself in. A coward to run out on his family in Alberta. We finally rounded up *that* miserable band as well."

Christopher gasped. Dust choked his lungs, causing a cough to escape his throat.

"You're bluffing as usual, Jake!" Win shouted.

Simmons ignored him and said, "Where did that cough come from? It's the king rat, I'm sure. Tear apart the bathroom!"

The few minutes it took to find his hiding place stretched into an eternity for Christopher. The bathtub was wrenched violently from its base.

Christopher stared into the blinding light and blinked. He sucked in huge breaths of fresh air. Vice-like hands gripped his arms as his body was torn from the trough. The soldiers tossed him on the tile floor in front of the colonel.

Jake Simmons stood over him, his back to the colonel, and howled with glee. "Michael will be so pleased!" He kicked Christopher in the ribs.

Christopher plunged forward, his face striking the tile. The room began spinning.

A glimpse of the colonel was all he could make out. The old soldier's body was coiled like a snake. Christopher knew that one spring was all that the commando needed. In a few fluid moves, Win could incapacitate his captors.

Christopher muttered, "Stand down, Win. We will not defend ourselves."

Simmons jerked his torso and roundhouse kicked Win's head. The former Marine fell to the floor unconscious.

Christopher's world went black.

* * *

The trip to the local jail was painfully slow, with the masses of soldiers flooding the streets; men and women from every nation had gathered to the Amman area for the siege of Israel.

Despite the huge escort for two of Michael's most wanted fugitives, it took almost two hours for the convoy to arrive at the prison.

Christopher and Win were thrown into separate putrid cells. Christopher tried to communicate with the colonel but got no response.

Late in the evening, Christopher's cell door creaked open. Outside, dozens of soldiers stood at the ready. A bloodied Win Dunbar stood proudly, chained and shackled. "Good evening, Commander," he croaked.

A rifle butt in his ribs was the response from his guard. The colonel coughed up blood, spit on the tiles, and stood erect again.

Christopher smiled. "Good evening, Win." A rifle butt answered him as well.

"Silence!"

The soldiers trussed up Christopher in manacles. "Gee, Win, matching outfits."

Both men laughed briefly before being knocked to the floor again. Win whispered into Christopher's ear. "This'll be my second visit today to the Antichrist. Remain firm. Greater is He that is in us—"

The soldiers jerked them to their feet.

The small army of guards escorted them out of the prison and across the street to a lavish old government building. As the manacled pair hobbled down the ancient halls, they were awed by the number of IC guards and soldiers.

Christopher prayed constantly as he walked toward their destination. They were ushered through a set of cedar doors into an ornate room. Before Christopher and Win stood only two men, whom they recognized instantly—Michael Wroth and Larson Sayers.

Wroth laughed as they entered. He ordered his prisoners to be released from their chains and showed them to a soft couch.

The guards freed Christopher and Win and then left the four men alone, closing the doors behind them.

"Well, Mr. Owen, we finally meet. I'm sorry I couldn't entertain you in my palace in Rome, but with that deadly earthquake a couple of weeks ago, there's not much left of it. Plus, I have this little campaign against the Jews, so we have to make do in my bivouac here."

Christopher didn't speak. Evil oozed from the men standing before him. Smiles and charm whitewashed the diabolical deception of Wroth and Sayers. Oppression hung in the air as heavy as smoke.

Though Wroth paraded himself as an 'angel of light,' his true nature as the Prince of Darkness was evident to Christopher.

Fear stabbed Christopher's heart momentarily before heavenly peace flooded his mind. He held his head high, knowing that the Most High God was present in the room with him.

Wroth laughed again. "You have been a formidable enemy, Mr. Owen—you and your KPF cohorts. I imagine you thought you could succeed. What a sad little dream—this *no place left* notion! You gave it an excellent stab. Excellent indeed.

"I myself have even been surprised at times at the Teflon coating you seem to wear. It's been a noble game, and you have played bravely. All in vain, however. It's all over for you. In other times and other circumstances, I would have cherished having you on my side. We would have made quite a team—you with your unbridled optimism and me with my unparalleled foresight."

Christopher couldn't restrain himself. He jumped to his feet, wincing but defiant. "There's just one small problem, Wroth. *Allegiance!* You're committed to your hellish agenda, while I serve the Creator of Heaven and Earth. No one who brazenly defies the Almighty will stand for long."

Both Michael and Dr. Sayers chuckled, sharing some sort of private joke.

Michael continued, "We'll see who is really God after this is all over. And it will soon be over—for you, at least—although I do leave you an option. You'd be surprised at what has been accomplished in the last few days. Dr. Sayers, why don't you inform our two guests about how the situation has developed?"

Christopher had never heard such a soothing, persuasive voice as that of Larson Sayers. He felt his soul tempted to believe and obey the words of this elderly man. "Four days ago, Miss Marlene Hayes, whom you've had secret contact with, defected from our cause. She made her way to your last headquarters in Canada. About the same time, a former member of your group, Phil Young, also arrived there, leading our glorious IC soldiers to your family and colleagues."

Christopher and Win looked at each other. Simmons hadn't been bluffing.

"Of course, all were arrested and are safely in custody. We confiscated your computer equipment. Your elaborate coding techniques were not a problem for our staff. We have decoded and discovered the whereabouts of all of your KPF and 2414 teams."

Christopher glanced at Win again.

Sayers continued, "Yes, we know about 2414—we have for some time. That is how we tracked you to Amman. Mr. Owen and Colonel Dunbar, you are the only leaders that remain of the Kingdom Preparation Force. Your attempt to convert the world has fallen far short of your goals.

"And as you have already heard rumored, for every Christian mission team sent out by your NoPlaceLeft coalition, we have secretly sent two teams to subvert your message and call all peoples to believe in the Messiah Michael.

"You'd be amazed at how quickly we were able to mobilize, since we control most of the world's resources and have one clear purpose. Add to that the economic incentive of worshipping Michael, and, well, we've seen remarkable success, whereas you have for the most part *failed*."

The wounds of these words could not have penetrated more deeply if they had been physical blows. Everything Christopher had lived for and dreamed of melted away. From the KPF's best plotting and graphing, the task of world evangelization was still far from over. Even using the lower estimate of the number of remaining unengaged unreached peoples, the KPF fell short. Their UUPG count still stood at almost 450 groups.

And now, according to Sayers, that number might be much higher, for many of the people groups they had counted as engaged by "mystery teams" had actually received a false gospel.

The room whirled around Christopher. *I've failed! We've failed! We longed to be in the last generation, but we've failed. How much longer must this go on? How many places are truly left with no gospel witness?*

Sayers hobbled over to Christopher, tapping the tiled floor with his cane. "There, there, Mr. Owen. Have a seat before you fall down."

Christopher sat in a plush velvet chair. So many of the mysteries of the past months were now explained. Of course Phil Young was the traitor. He had access to most of the secrets of the KPF. Of course the mystery groups were able to penetrate far deeper than expected—they were financed and equipped by the most powerful organization on earth. People groups that should have received the gospel received a *false* gospel. Those that had heard the true gospel no doubt fell into deception as IC missionaries arrived in places recently vacated by pioneer Christian missionaries.

And his own family captured! His small children in some IC jail! A wave of despair washed over him, tumbling him into confusion and depression.

Never had Christopher felt so broken.

"We have been fighting you on every front, Mr. Owen," spoke the soothing voice, "and you have been defeated. Do not feel bad. You have fought far more successfully than most who have opposed us. You are one of the last holdouts. And, you can still escape from this whole ordeal as a success. You don't have to be a failure at everything you have set your hand to!"

The voice pulled at his soul, beckoning him to change his stance.

Michael took up the plea. "That's right, Christopher. The fact that you have held out so long—much longer than others—is a sign that you are a brilliant strategist and survivor. Your optimism and determination are virtually unquenchable. These are qualities I'm looking for in those who lead in *my* kingdom. You can still join me, for joining me is truly joining the side of God!"

The colonel raised his head and spoke forcefully. "Don't listen to him, Commander! He is only able to speak lies! It's all he's ever done—from the beginning of time."

Wroth turned on the colonel, teeth bared. "You! You! We have sparred too many times the last few decades. I have something very special planned for you! You will speak no more!"

Christopher looked at his friend in wonder. When he turned his eyes toward Wroth, however, he saw the 'beast' of Revelation unveiled. His wavering spirit grew strong again.

Dr. Sayers spoke. "Listen to Michael, Mr. Owen. Look now upon your family."

Sayers waved his hand, and on the floor between them stood a hologram. There before Christopher appeared Chara and his four children in a jail cell. Apparently they could see him also, for the children at once began shouting, "Daddy! Daddy!"

Christopher conversed with them for a few minutes, oblivious to the others. The Owens all wept at this unexpected reunion after their months of separation.

Wroth suddenly broke in, interrupting them. "Enough! Other things demand our attention! Two armed forces have already invaded Israel from the south and the north. My much larger army is gathered here in Amman for an assault across the Jordan River Barricade from the east.

"Tomorrow my army will overwhelm the city of Jerusalem, all that remains of the opposition to my empire. Thus shall all be treated who attempt to thwart me, the almighty! The battle will be over by noon.

"You, Mr. Owen, will be given the opportunity to share via worldwide hologram the truth: that I am God and that you were wrong—misled—and then call all listeners to a wholehearted faith in me. You are well known in the Christian world. You have inspired millions. Christ-followers still in seclusion will listen to you."

Christopher once again stood erect. "Never!"

Wroth studied him. "If you refuse, you will watch as each of your family members will be killed, one at a time, starting with the youngest—sweet little David. After each execution, you will be given an opportunity to recant your faith and do what I have commanded you. If you refuse, we will proceed with the next executions—Elizabeth, Caleb, Joshua—ending, if need be, with your charming wife.

"Of course, we may have to delay her execution for several hours while you watch until some of the needs of my soldiers are met—faithful men who have been starved for physical affection. But in the end, she will die. And then, if you still refuse, you will be executed publicly in Jerusalem where I will declare that all opposition against me has been overcome. This is the punishment for defying my divine rule."

Wroth then turned to face those on the hologram. "My friends, before this happens, all of you will be given the chance to renounce your Christian faith and worship me. If you do so, you will not die. David, Caleb, Elizabeth, Joshua—follow me! Don't you see that your dear father has been terribly deceived? He is a good daddy but has had some of the facts wrong. I'll even make a deal with you right now, to show you how kind I am. If all four of you agree to follow me, I'll spare your parents. What do you say?"

Christopher was torn in two. He wanted to shout at his children to save themselves, but that would be wrong. He knew Chara would never recant, and he couldn't bear the thought of IC soldiers abusing her before her death. He shuddered to hear this evil man calling his children by name. As Christopher pondered what to do, Joshua, his oldest son, spoke up. "As Jesus said, get behind us, Satan!"

Christopher burst out in delighted laughter at his oldest son's impetuousness and boldness.

"My brothers, my sister, and I will never bow down to you, understand? Neither will our mother or our father. We would dishonor them by renouncing Jesus! God will help us—either by delivering us or by helping us to die honorably!"

Wroth chuckled. "Ooh! Such strong words from one so young! Do all of you agree?"

Chara and the other three children all nodded their heads. Christopher beamed with admiration though his heart was broken.

"So be it. Tomorrow we begin with the executions. Mr. Owen, your determination may not feel so strong when you have watched one or two of your children die needlessly, or when you have heard the screams of your wife as you watch her abused via hologram. Be sure of this, you *will* witness all that happens to her and your children!"

Christopher spoke to Michael while his family could still hear him. "You are revealed for who you are—the father of lies, the deceiver, the serpent of old! The Lord rebuke you! How can we deny our Lord Jesus who has given us life? We will be faithful unto death."

Wroth appeared vexed. He snarled, "So be it! You will all die tomorrow! Take them from me now, Larson. And bring Miss Hayes here as soon as she arrives. I will slay that traitorous harlot with my own hand."

* * *

Christopher sat in the corner of his jail cell with his face buried in his hands. The bold demeanor he had shown during his encounter with Michael was gone. That Win had been placed in the same cell with him seemed to make no difference.

"Would you like to talk about it, Commander?" asked Win.

"Don't call me 'commander'! Don't you see it's all over? Our little assault is over, our game of playing soldiers is at an end. I'm tired of the game, so don't call me 'commander' anymore. We made a good stab at it, but I guess it's for another generation."

Win waited a few minutes before speaking again. "Christopher? Can't we at least talk?"

Christopher looked up. In all his memory, he could never recall the colonel calling him by his given name, even when the two had traveled all alone, and so he had always assumed the relationship was mainly a professional one. By no choice of his own, Christopher had always been on one level above the colonel—the old soldier's perception of military hierarchy had demanded it. Now, alone in this jail cell for what was perhaps his last night alive, he realized he still had one friend left. He knew it was difficult for the colonel to call him by his first name.

Christopher smiled wanly. "I'll talk."

Winthrop Dunbar slid gingerly next to him, and the two were quickly in deep conversation reminiscing about their quest. Soon their focus came back to the events at hand. "I think what hurts the most, Win, is that I was all wrong!"

"You weren't wrong. That devil in sheep's clothing called Michael Wroth is not God, no matter what he says."

Christopher laughed bitterly. "No, I didn't mean that. I know he's not God." He paused, trying to find the right words. "Tomorrow, my four children will die. My wife will be ravished while I watch, and then she will die. Then I will die. I have come to accept that. None of us will compromise, even under threat, and so we will all die. You and Jeanie will die. We all knew this might happen." ⸲

Win raised an eyebrow. "So what's the problem, sir? I mean, Christopher? How were you wrong?"

"Win, are you so blind that you can't see it? We *failed* in our task to finish the job of world evangelization. Just like the Christian world had the same opportunity in the late nineteenth century and failed, so we also have failed."

"What do you mean? Surely you can't deny that these are the final days?" Win asked, puzzled.

"Can't I? Don't you think that some of the early Christians under Nero's persecution felt sure they were in the final days? Didn't the Thessalonian church feel it was in the final days? How about the Jews when Jerusalem was destroyed, or during the Holocaust? How about the Christians during the Spanish Inquisition? How many Christians in history felt the same but were wrong, just like us? We were so close, I thought, but I guess it remains for another generation to see the return of Christ."

"But, Chr-Christopher, everything we have witnessed has fit so well with prophecy, with Revelation. It all fits. This *must* be the time!"

Christopher felt that he was now lecturing a student who should have figured this out already. "The fact is, Win, that the order and manner of fulfillment of prophecy can be taken many ways. There have been a dozen generations that could have legitimately concluded that they were in the last days during their lifetime. But let me ask you a question. Did any of them see the fulfillment of Matthew 24:14, of the gospel being preached as a testimony to all the nations and peoples of the world?"

Win replied, "Of course not. That's why we've been busy with the Kingdom Preparation Force."

"Okay. You've seen the best figures and the latest projections from the NoPlaceLeft coalition. You've seen and heard that even many of the mystery mission teams we thought were Christian were in fact heretics. Have we fulfilled the task of the gospel being proclaimed widely among every remaining people group in this generation?"

"Well, we don't know everything, and there have been a lot of disasters that have disrupted communication."

"Colonel! Don't sidestep the question. In your frank military estimate, have we fulfilled our mission?"

Colonel Winthrop Dunbar had not been called before a commanding officer many times to report failure, but this time he did so with shoulders squared.

"No, sir. In my best military estimate, we have not finished the task. In addition, I see no way, even given the margin of error in our limited reconnaissance, that we could even be close. The gap is still wider than we anticipated. There must be well over 700 or 800 groups still to engage. We have not fulfilled our mission, and I take full responsibility."

Christopher sighed deeply and put an arm around Win. "Sorry about that, Win, reverting back to line of authority and all. I just wanted you to face the facts. It's *not* your fault, either. It's the fault of our generation. There were still too many of us Christ-followers who were too selfish, too lazy, too scared, too ignorant, too apathetic, too distracted, too materialistic, too short-sighted—too *whatever*—to finish the most important task Jesus ever gave to His people.

"Too many of us preferred comfort to the Commission. We preferred living in a place of our choosing over living in the place of *His* choosing. We had the resources but not the resolve."

Christopher sighed again, even more deeply. "With all our personal deficiencies, you and I have nothing to be ashamed of. We have held our heads high and have tried our best. It has been a good run, one to be proud of. And much progress has been made.

"What breaks my heart is not that. What breaks my heart is that we worked so hard and still failed. With all the setbacks the Christian world has experienced, I truly wonder when the people of God will have enough resources again to attempt what we have attempted. Who knows? It might not be for another thousand years."

"If that's the case, Christopher," Win responded, "we still haven't failed. Every person who believed, every new people group where churches were multiplying—that was a success. Perhaps a later generation will look back on us, if we are remembered, and take courage from our example."

Christopher laughed. "Yeah, they'll be telling stories of the heroic giant Win Dunbar and his diminutive friend Christopher!"

"Uh, sir, I mean, Christopher, *you've* been the giant in this movement."

Christopher ignored that and beamed at his friend. "Then let's pray, since this will be our last night on earth, that another generation will take up the cause soon. May they be inspired by the sacrifice of our generation! The Bible says many antichrists will come. The final Antichrist could come any time, just like Michael Wroth has. Let's pray that the return of Christ will not be postponed any longer than necessary. I grieve, however, that our generation was not worthy to be counted as the last.

"Win, my friend, you and I will be with Jesus soon, and we will forget all our troubles. Oh, but wouldn't it have been glorious to be here on earth, however, to see His return? Let's pray for the remnant of believers who will survive this holocaust as many other remnants have in other generations. Let's pray that they will persevere and come through this refined. Let's pray for the generation that will see the day of His return!"

They prayed deep into the evening until sleep finally overtook them. Both knew it was their last night, and they drifted off, ready for their last dawn.

Christopher slept fitfully on the cold, damp floor, dreaming vividly through the wee morning hours. In his nightmares, he dreamed a thousand times of seeing his wife ravished, his children beheaded, his teams imprisoned, his close friends walking to the block. He dreamed of his own executioner walking toward him with a black hood covering his face and a curved, bloodstained scimitar in his hand. Just before he raised the blade, the executioner snatched off his hood, revealing the laughing face of Michael Wroth. As the blade came down, Christopher saw the face of Wroth reflected off the surface of the marble block—the face of a beast.

A hideous cry rang out with the execution. "You just couldn't live a normal Christian life, could you? You just had to attempt something great for God. Here's your reward!" In Christopher's dream, the audience was filled with KPF team members who had been beheaded; they shouted abuse at him, accusing him of deceiving them, causing their own deaths.

He awoke sweating and trembling. *God, why did it have to end this way? Why did I have to want to live life on a quest? It's still such a mystery to me. Why did it all—?*

Finally, a soft glow filled the room as God's peace descended upon him, driving the last of the nightmares away.

Christopher drifted off to sleep again to await the dawn of his last day.

TWENTY NINE

THAT DAY exploded!

Christopher stood up in perfect wakefulness, hyper-aware of everything around him, more than his five senses had sensed in a lifetime. As a clarion signal, a shout of authority rang in his ears—one that he knew instantly was understood in every language in every corner of the earth. It was a voice more ancient than the earth itself, booming and echoing across the lands, flattening mighty forests and churning the waters of the deep.

"I AM COMING!"

A trumpet blared the arrival with glorious resonance.

Christopher intuitively understood the signal of that trumpet blast, though he had never heard it before. An immediate recognition thrilled his soul.

Another shout rang through the earth, different from the first. It also had such great authority that it could not be disobeyed, yet it was only a reflection of the glory of the first voice Christopher heard. The archangel's shout was a call to all the angels to gather God's holy children from every place on earth.

Christopher's eyes were drawn upward. He no longer lay in the dark jail cell awaiting his execution. No roof could hold him in. No bars could stop his soul or his glorious new body from rising through the air. *This must be it! My senses —I am aware of more than I have ever imagined. Who could have ever thought I would have such unlimited ability in this new, glorious state?* Desires and passions of his soul were suddenly satisfied, while the aches and longings of his old body were quenched.

A man rose through the air next to him, radiating a heavenly aura. Christopher stared at him intensely.

The man looked back at Christopher and smiled unabashedly. Gone was his previous reserve, his dedication to spit and polish.

Winthrop! How transformed you are! I know you more deeply than a man has ever known another, and I love you, my brother.

Christopher knew in his spirit that Win felt the same way. Deep longings for friendship vanished as he felt a oneness with Win no two men ever achieved on the old earth.

They both scanned the skies around them, beaming from ear to ear. The atmosphere was filled with other saints rising through the air toward a common destination. Christopher recognized them all, thousands of brothers and sisters he had never met yet now knew intimately. They waved to him vigorously, as if this first meeting was actually a reunion with long lost kin.

Family. My family! Family I never missed until now; yet even now, I have the wonderful joy of being reunited with them. Long lost brothers and sisters, separated by space and time, finally together again.

Christopher saw Chara and his children rise above the horizon, speeding their way toward the same destination. His children— grown yet fully recognizable—were smiling as if to say, "We told you so, Daddy. You didn't need to worry. What could compare with this?"

He saw Chara—his wife, yet no longer his wife. He had always thought this would be the worst part of heaven, no longer being married to the woman he had cherished more than himself. Somehow he forgot all that in this moment. Now they loved each other more deeply than at any point in their marriage with a love that was purer and less possessive.

They had not lost each other; they had gained thousands of companions. And even as fathomless as this fellowship was with brothers and sisters, Christopher knew that this was not enough. This new fellowship alone was not why this day had come.

The wonder of the upward journey and Christopher's thousands of musings in his glorified mind were broken by shouts. Thousands of shouts! Thousands upon thousands of shouts. Shouts of acclamation as varied as the colors of a rainbow, as endless as the grains of sand on the seashore. Praise, thanks, glory, honor, all shouted at the tops of glorified lungs— beautiful, crystal clear voices of angels and sons and daughters of God describing the glory of God the Father and His Son Jesus Christ in more ways than Christopher imagined possible.

Then Christopher saw HIM.

Christopher was transfixed by a sight he had never contemplated could be so joyous.

Amid clouds blazing with glorious light, heralded by peals of thunder and flashes of lightning, came One seated on a white stallion.

Christopher had never seen His face. Every drawing, painting, image—all faded in comparison with the True One riding toward him. Christopher recognized Him and realized that shouts of joyful praise were bursting unbidden from his lungs. The Rider was dressed in a crimson robe dipped in the blood He Himself had shed to bear the sins of the many.

Emblazoned on that robe was His undeniable title:

KING OF KINGS and LORD OF LORDS.

**The One who sat on the horse, called
the Son of Man,
Faithful and True,
the Alpha and the Omega,
Jesus the Messiah**

was manifested as perfection beyond imagination. His eyes blazed with glory and authority.

Christopher gazed in awe. *The light radiating from the crowns on Your head would surely would have blinded the eyes of my previous sin-bound body. Thank you, Lord, for a glorified body in which I can not only endure but also enjoy the presence of God!*

Yet even though that was a silent prayer, he noticed the eyes of the Son of God smile with compassion upon him. *How many others here are looking at You, Omnipresent Lord, and seeing those same eyes look at them with compassion this very moment?*

Christopher's heart raced within him. *This is what I have longed for! I have seen God and lived and been approved!*

Christopher studied his magnificent Master. Though His right hand held the scepter of glory, His left hand was free, beckoning His brothers and sisters to come to Him—His pierced, scarred left hand, which Christopher knew was no different from His right.

Christopher looked down at his own hands, at the places where he, too, had possessed wounds—they were now free of blemishes! He felt his forehead where the scar from his imprisonment in China had never stopped throbbing, but the mark was no longer there. His eyes welled up with tears at his unworthiness to be perfect when his Lord would forever bear in His body the marks of His suffering and death.

He wanted to protest this injustice when he suddenly became aware that those scars were not marks of shame. He saw how myriads of others not only worshipped Christ but also gazed proudly at the marks of His crucifixion. These were not blemishes; these were badges of honor, and indeed, only Jesus should be allowed to retain His.

While drinking in the beauty of the Risen One, Christopher turned to see thousands upon thousands of Christ's loyal followers, stretching around him like an endless army. Here and there in that glorious multitude flew angels who were beautiful, even frightful in their glory and power—servants of God that were constantly doing His bidding. They rushed throughout the earth, gathering the elect to meet Jesus.

More glorious than these, however, were the saints. Not some select individuals who were honored at various points in Christian history, but the saints—God the Father's holy ones—all who had placed their faith in God through Jesus Christ. All His children from ages past until this day. Now unveiled, their glory outshone that of the angels. Unlike the angels, these had walked through the Fall and emerged redeemed by the blood of the Lamb. Proudly they followed in the train of the King.

Christopher recognized them all: Abraham, Moses, David, Elijah, Isaiah, Esther, Nehemiah, Mary Magdalene, Andrew, Philip, Paul, Dorcas, Augustine, Luther, Wesley, Carey, Lottie Moon—their faces were all in his memory, he did not know how. He saw his grandparents, who welcomed him from afar. He saw the great-grandparents he had never known but who welcomed this one they had prayed for before they knew he would be born. He saw the long line of faithful ones who had laid the foundation of blessings he had reaped without realizing it before. He saw all these who had died before this day following Jesus *downward* from heaven toward the earth.

Christopher took his place instinctively in the Army of the True King.

It was then that he glanced for the first time downward toward their destination. He saw Jerusalem as a tiny dot in the landscape, and spread all around it was an army too numerous to count. He saw the mighty army that had thought it could assail the holy city where the Lord had died and risen again and that thought it could rise in defiance of the Ancient of Days.

The ancient adversary, the devil of old, clothed in the physical body the earth had hailed as Michael Wroth, jeered the coming of the Holy One. The devil shouted the curses he had shouted since his fall as he called the armies of the earth to ready themselves for the battle. The armies hesitated, yet he urged them on all the more, swearing that he was God and he would lead them to victory.

Christopher laughed at the contrast between the usurper and the One who cannot be usurped. He laughed at the puny performance of the one who had deceived the nations. This, his greatest show of authority, paled in comparison to the glory of the presence of God and His holy ones and His angels. Such a noble throng—full of might, authority, and purity—matched against the sinful, weak, limited resources of the manipulating liar of old.

The unredeemed peoples of the earth shrank back. The contrast was all too clear to them. A plaintive, desperate wail rose from their lips, mourning because of the sight of the One they had pierced yet refused to accept. Waves of despair washed over them as they recognized the true order of things and that for them, **IT WAS TOO LATE.**

Already they stood judged by their lifelong choice of rejection.

Christopher's heart was filled with more anguish over their demise than he could imagine. Just as quickly, he realized the justness of the destruction of those who had turned their backs on the One who had given His life to buy their salvation.

The devil in Michael's form rose up to fight, and Christopher awaited the bloody conflict with steadfast resolve. The true

Michael, the archangel, moved to fight his nemesis but stopped short. This time the fight in this age-old battle was not his.

The Ancient of Days rode His white stallion past the archangel as every eye on earth beheld Him.

The armies of earth cowered in fear. Only Michael, 'the beast,' stood defiantly.

Ironically, *no battle followed.* The potentially greatest battle in history was transformed into a forfeit.

The real battle had been fought on a cross and in an empty tomb two millennia prior. The enemy had already been defeated through the death, burial, and resurrection of Jesus Christ!

Christopher stared enraptured as Jesus descended toward the scene.

With a word, He ended the defiance.

He bound Michael and Sayers—'the beast' and 'the false prophet'—with His word, and angels delivered them to an eternal punishment in the lake of fire.

The remaining rebellious hosts were slain with the same word. A sense of righteous vindication pulsed through Christopher's soul as the ancient foe was finally brought to justice.

Suddenly it dawned on Christopher. The army of God was not here to help fight the battle but to *witness* the omnipotence of God—the God of Hosts, who needs no armies.

Christopher's head jerked as the archangel shouted again, "Come!" The angels departed into every region of the earth and gathered the remaining souls of all who had not believed in Christ.

Then, in a flash, Christopher was blinded by a fiery blast and swept over by a deafening roar. He closed his eyes momentarily, and when he reopened them, the earth and the heavens were nowhere to be found. They had disappeared, their imperfect state no longer able to bear the presence of the Almighty One unveiled.

Jesus sat down upon a great throne, surrounded by flashes of lightning and peals of thunder. Mighty angels flew around the throne constantly declaring the holiness of the Lamb.

All the people of the nations of the earth gathered before Him, bowing the knee. Christopher found himself among them.

Time stood still as He who knows everyone intimately distinguished between those who had loved Him and those who had not, those who had trusted Him and those who had not.

Christopher's heart was simultaneously filled with sadness and joy. He saw the faces of those judged guilty by Christ, people he now knew. He remembered how he had ached that someone would witness to his sister who lived in Maine. He remembered how he had prayed fervently for her salvation, knowing she would be condemned if she didn't repent.

The line of the condemned was crowded with millions of people just like his sister—someone's brother, some mother's son, some father's daughter, someone's niece, someone's parents.

Christopher witnessed the anguish of the eternal punishment that these loved ones were experiencing. He grieved deeply in his spirit, wishing that he had done more, his church had done more, his nation had done more. *Couldn't we have shortened this line? Wouldn't we have lessened these throngs if we had cherished the same concern for them that we had for our own family members?*

He watched as countless individuals marched to the throne, bowed the knee to Christ, and then were dragged off to flames of destruction. He saw their fleeting glances at the saints that spoke volumes:

Why didn't you say more? Why didn't you believe in hell's reality? Why didn't you urge me to become like you are? Why didn't you weep for my soul in prayer? Why didn't you come to my house? Why didn't you come to my country? Was your comfortable life worth it? Was seeing that fifteen-dollar movie so important that you didn't support a missionary to come to my village? Was your pay raise that important? Was living in a nice neighborhood, having the right social status, making the right friends that important? Did you really think someone else would do it when you already knew I existed and needed the gospel? Didn't you realize that I was YOUR responsibility?

But as Christopher watched, he also saw in their eyes the guilty recognition that ultimately it was they themselves who had rejected Christ. It was they who had rejected the witness of conscience, of creation, and, if they were fortunate enough, the Word of Christ.

Christopher sensed all these things and wept at the sight. He saw the look of terror in the eyes of the guilty as they headed knowingly into eternal judgment. As he saw their utter hopelessness and despair that their punishment would never end, he wept along with countless other saints.

Then his gaze was drawn to a new scene, one that turned his anguish into ecstasy. He saw John and Renee Steward and Nic and Stacy Fernandez, his dear friends. He cheered with all his might when he observed the honor they received for having died for the sake of Christ. Others held them in esteem, and Jesus Himself stood to honor the whole procession of martyrs. *It is fitting.*

Then it was Christopher's turn. His feet drew him to the throne. He had always imagined this day; he had felt he would stand in shame before his holy Lord. He knew his own sin. He knew his shortcomings. He had imagined he would just slip in under the wire of Christ's mercy.

His prior fears turned to shock. Contrary to all his expectations, he was received with praise from Christ and the entire assembly, not because he was Christopher Owen, founder and leader of the Kingdom Preparation Force, but simply because he was Christopher, child of God. His name was written in heaven!

He stood there, blinking, tears streaming down his face, gazing into the eyes of Jesus. Before the throne he stood blameless, feeling no shame, for his sins had been removed and forgotten.

With a nod and a smile, Jesus beckoned him, and Christopher sprinted into the Savior's open arms. The Savior placed a crown on his head and kept saying to him, "Well done, my good and faithful servant!"

Christopher clung to Him, and lingered in His arms, in the security of that embrace for what seemed an eternity. No one rushed him. No one grew impatient, for time as they had known it was no more. The omnipresent Lord could spend an eternity with every child of God at every moment. Christopher sighed. *His timeless omnipresence must be one of the greatest joys of heaven!*

Finally he drew his face from the robes of His Master.

Scanning the scene, he realized the judgment was over. A crescendo of shouts in a multitude of languages swept through the throng of God's children, and he found himself shouting with them. The sounds of wild celebration, more tumultuous than anything he had ever heard at the most raucous football game, echoed throughout the assembly.

Jesus spoke a few words, and with a mighty thunderclap, the assembly was surrounded by a new heaven and a new earth. *Just like he spoke at the original creation!*

Christopher vaguely recognized former contours and familiar landscapes, but now they lived and breathed in the true glory that had longed to break out since sin had spoiled creation. Verdant valleys filled with mists, soaring mountains defying description, waters teeming with fish of colors never before seen, lush plains filled with wildlife, and towering forests of vivid hues spread before him. The physical landscape screamed, "Glory!" All wildlife bellowed, trumpeted, and chirped in praise of the Creator.

The glorious *true* Rebirth of heaven and earth had begun.

All around Christopher blazed the glory of heaven as it merged with earth. Before him descended the holy city, New Jerusalem, glistening in the radiance of Christ. It settled onto the new earth filled with buildings no architect could design, streets more golden than any crown, gates adorned in priceless jewels, streams as clear as glass, and gardens filled with flowers never before imagined.

The triumphant songs of an unbridled angelic choir echoed through the halls and lanes of the city, rippling unto the ends of the earth. A faint response could be heard in every rock, tree, and mountain. Every glade, every valley, every wave of the seas hummed an inspired melody of praise in harmony with the holy city.

Christopher's heart beat faster with anticipation. Something more glorious was coming, and every living being could feel it. *What could it be?*

Then he knew. All of the new creation fell silent.

Smoke billowed forth from the heavens, veiling a figure on a throne, settling before the multitudes.

Christopher saw the twelve apostles remove their crowns and cast them at the feet of the One who had descended. The living creatures around the throne hurled themselves on their faces, prone.

All the angels of heaven bowed similarly.

All the saints, including Christopher, lay prostrate before the throne of

THE ALMIGHTY,
THE ANCIENT OF DAYS,
THE FATHER OF ALL.

Then all eyes were raised to watch Jesus Himself stride up to the throne.

He swept His arms toward the entire assembly, then knelt before His Father to present to Him the nations of the earth.

Then Jesus sat down at the right hand of the Father and called to all, "Hail Him who sits on the throne, Creator of All, Father of all mankind, who was, and is, and is to come, the Ancient of Days! YAHWEH is His Name!"

When He spoke the Name, YAHWEH, a shudder reverberated through all of creation. The new heaven and new earth resounded with trumpet blasts. Bells rang constantly from every tower. Fireworks or some sort of heavenly lights shot into the atmosphere, hanging forever in luminescence.

Christopher's soul shook with feverish delight.

The whole heavenly assembly leaped to its feet—saints, angels, the living creatures—with a mighty roar, shouting, "Hallelujah! For the Lord God Almighty reigns! Let us rejoice and be glad and give Him glory! The Kingdom of this world has become the Kingdom of our Lord!"

The praise continued unabated for what seemed like hours. Every time Christopher looked afresh at the LORD, he was more amazed at His manifold beauty and glory; it was like looking at the growing glory of a sunrise. With each successive glance, involuntary gasps of awe and praise rose from his glorified lips.

Then he knew it was time. Christopher took his own crown, the one he had waited a lifetime to receive, and laid it at the foot of the throne of the Glorious One with jumping, singing, and praising. Myriads of others did the same.

Then they heard HIM speak—the voice of the Eternal Father. It was a voice like no other. "Welcome, all who have been invited to the wedding of the Lamb! Now has the Bride been made ready!"

The angels, who had witnessed millennia of glory, gasped as they beheld the sudden transformation. In a moment, the assembly of the First Born, the children of God, radiated the glory of God, they who were created in His own image. The angels fell prostrate in awe. The people of God were clothed in spotless garments, garments washed in the blood of the Lamb.

All gazes then turned to the Son of God. He was clothed with the magnificent raiment of a Bridegroom. The One who had patiently awaited His Bride from before the foundation of the world, Jesus, *rushed* forward to take up the Church as His own companion. The people of God were honored by the eagerness of the Savior of the world who had died for this day. They were united as one.

In the euphoria of the wedding of the Lamb, Christopher listened and looked in amazement at the Bride. More beautiful than the terrain, the city, the flora, and the fauna was the multi-national Bride of the Lamb revealed in all her glory. Christopher craned his neck to take in the crowd he stood among.

People of every tribe and ethnic group from the beginning of time stood before the throne as the Bridegroom drew them to Himself. Christopher lost count of the millions. They were robed in shimmering garments representing their cultural backgrounds. They cried out praises in every language ever spoken. Some danced. Some jumped. Some ran. Some bowed. Some knelt. Some kowtowed. All wept for joy.

Tribes once extinct were represented before the Lamb. None were missing. No mathematician could count this multitude.

Looking at the rich diversity of the peoples of the earth, scattered at Babel and now reunited, Christopher shouted to the Bridegroom, "There is *no place left* that You did not claim for Your Kingdom! No lesser bride would be worthy of Your wedding day! For by Your blood You have redeemed a people from every tribe and language and people and nation!"

As he was speaking this, Jesus smiled at him and nodded in response. Millions of others were coming to the same realization.

It was then that Christopher observed that the whole heavenly host—angels and saints—were singing a new song, saying:

You are worthy to take the scroll and to open its seals, because you were slain, and with your blood you purchased for God persons from every tribe and language and people and nation.

You have made them to be a kingdom and priests to serve our God, and they will reign on the earth.

As he sang with them, Christopher could no longer remember the joys of his earthly marriage, so enraptured in ecstasy was he in this final marriage. He vaguely recalled a time in his life where he worried that he might never marry and know the pleasures of marriage. He grinned from ear to ear. *How foolish I was back then!*

How long they feasted afterwards, Christopher did not know, for there was no night, only day. The One on the throne delighted in His children, frequently laughing like a father would with his children. His children sang for joy in finding a father greater than any they had known on earth. Jesus unabashedly danced with His new Bride with joy and His Bride danced in response.

An angel stood next to Christopher, singing as well. He turned to him and said, "Only now, Christ-bearer—for that is the meaning of your name—do we angels understand the full extent of God's patient, many-hued grace. We, who have watched from before the foundation of this world, have learned more of His grace through this earthly story. Only through this tortuous history filled with travails could God demonstrate His love fully and perfect to a faithful people of sterling quality. Earth has been teaching Heaven. All praise to the King!"

* * *

Days later, if one could call it days, the wedding feast was over. Christopher found his old friends, John and Nic. Together they set off to explore new forest glades lit by the radiance of the holy city, musing about all the recent events.

John winked at Christopher. "Your glorified body suits you well. Why, you've grown quite a few inches taller!"

Christopher laughed. "I can finally look you in the eye!"

The trio compared notes about what had gone on after they separated in L.A. and talked in amazement about the acceleration of events since the first evening strategy session at Common Grounds.

Nic shook his head. "I'm not sure I ever quite believed the quest would be fulfilled, but I wasn't going to give up while you two had faith."

John arched an eyebrow. "*Me* have faith? I wasn't giving up because *you* had faith. I didn't want to disappoint either of you!"

The three sat in the grass and bellowed with deep laughter, unlike any in the old earth.

A Tuxiang woman—they intuitively knew her name without having known her—walked out from behind a tree. As they stood up, she embraced them. "I want to thank you, my brothers, for sending your team to my village. Because they came, I have experienced heaven." Then she was gone.

The three men continued walking through the glades but stopped when they heard a shout behind them. An Arab man flew from the treetops toward them and kissed them on both cheeks. "Brothers, I bless you for what you did on earth. My family and I made it here because of a church you inspired in the Philippines that sent a team to the Middle East." Then he was gone.

Around the next bend in the trail, a Minangkabau family from Sumatra, Indonesia, greeted them and thanked them for sending a team to them.

As the family walked off, Christopher turned to Nic and John. "Did you send teams to Sumatra?"

John said, "Us? I assumed it must have been you."

Their stroll through the forest continued that way for what seemed days; they often had encounters with individuals from people groups they were not even aware of. They felt both honored and puzzled. They tried to piece together who had sent teams but kept coming up with no answers.

When their wonder reached its peak, the three men rounded a bend in the path to see Jesus sitting on a boulder next to a babbling brook. "Dear puzzled brothers, sit down and talk with Me. Speak your hearts."

The old Christopher would have hesitated, but now he knew that his Lord was ready to listen and answer. "Lord, I'm confused—uh, *we're* confused. We didn't send teams to a lot of those places these brothers and sisters have named. In fact, we were greatly surprised that, uh, that—"

Jesus prodded him. "Go ahead. Ask the question you've been itching to ask."

Christopher looked at his two friends who nodded their heads. "W-well, You know, why did You come back so soon?"

Jesus grinned knowingly.

Christopher continued, "I mean, the colonel and I calculated with our best estimates. We still weren't ready for You, 'we' meaning the global Church, that is. There were still too many people groups that hadn't been reached." He looked at Jesus with surprise yet not with any hint of blame. "How was it possible for You to come back before every group had a chance to hear? I thought—"

It was the look in Jesus' eyes that quieted him—that look of reassurance, of knowing, that said, *You don't need to question My ways. I have always had it under control.*

"Christ-bearers, did you really have such little faith? Did you *really* think that everything you could count on your little computers was the extent of My unstoppable work on earth? After having seen all My power and all My glory, did you think that anything would stop My plan to prepare for Myself a Bride from every tribe and tongue and people?"

Nic said, "No, Lord. We never doubted *that*—it was just the timing we didn't understand."

"Of course, but that is what I am referring to. You three and your mighty team played a significant role in hastening the 'day of the Lord.' From your perspective, it *was* hastening; from My Father's perspective, it had always been set. Little brothers, the ripples of your lives reverberated into places you never expected. Do you know how many churches were inspired to send out missionaries because they were inspired by a church that was inspired by a church that was counseled by you and others? Do you know how many teams were mobilized from nations around the world inspired by your example? Who is to say you didn't send a team to the Minangkabau people indirectly? You have all eternity to figure out the glory of the web of relationships."

Christopher scratched his head and shook it slightly.

His Lord continued, "Add to that all My servants upon whom you made no impact. Don't you realize that if I stirred up your heart in Los Angeles to attempt the great work you did, that I also might have been stirring up the heart of a sister in England, a brother in Kenya, a church in Brazil, a team in Jordan, and an agency in Korea? No one person or agency had any idea how extensively My mission was being carried out. Just like the wind blows where it wills, so My Spirit blew wherever I willed. No human could have comprehended My plans within My plans within My plans. You even heard rumors of some of My other workers. You called them 'mystery teams'!"

While Jesus laughed good-naturedly, the trio almost fell off the rock they sat upon.

John spoke up. "Mystery teams! We discovered that they were actually teams sent out by Michael."

Jesus smiled and answered, "Don't you remember that that old serpent was always a liar? He sent out a few teams, which incidentally did far less damage than they hoped. Remember that when I begin a good work, I complete it! No, most of those mystery teams were simply My servants mobilized from some region you never expected to a region you never anticipated: Koreans in the Amazon, Guatemalans in Kyrgyzstan, South Africans in Chechnya, Swedes in Mauritania, Filipinos in Aboriginal Australia. Shall I go on?"

They all shook their heads in amazement as Jesus continued.

"You know how disrupted your communications were in the last days anyway. You had trouble keeping track of your *own* teams. Do you even know how many of those new people groups you reached sent out missionaries of their own to neighboring tribes simply out of the urgency of the hour? You'd be surprised. Why, the Tuxiang alone reached many other tribes, including the Minangkabau! There's so much that I did that no one person ever knew about.

"Don't you remember what My Apostle John wrote in the twenty-first chapter of his gospel?

Jesus did many other things as well. If every one of them were written down, I suppose that even the whole world would not have room for the books that would be written.

"I returned at exactly the right time to redeem a multitude from every people group I ever created."

Christopher high-fived his companions and then embraced his Lord. *Well, I guess we'll have all eternity to discuss this.* The three stood up and walked with Jesus along the brook toward the heavenly city where the waters joined the river that flowed before the throne. The four walked and talked leisurely as if Jesus had all the time in the world just for them. They were soon joined by their families and by other members of the KPF who had the same questions.

In a multitude of other forest glades, city streets, and mountain trails, Jesus was at that very moment with others, answering similar questions—questions of faithful men and women, boys and girls, who all had lived for the day that they would be joined to their Creator and Savior—people who had loved His appearing and of whom the world was not worthy.

The ranks of listeners continued to grow into thousands, millions, more than any could count. Men and women from every nation, tribe, people, and language, standing before their God wearing white robes and holding palm branches in their hands crying in countless languages endless praises to

HIM WHO SITS ON THE THRONE
AND TO THE LAMB.

* * *

Even so, come, Lord Jesus!

Author's Postscript

This account is fiction—just one way to describe how the end of the greatest task given to the global Church may come. However, all of the elements about the KPF storyline are realistic and are occurring in various ways in the world today. A growing, multi-national coalition is developing to fulfill the vision of #NoPlaceLeft.

The storyline of Michael Wroth and The Ten was written to build the reader's interest in the real story of history—the finishing of the task to the take the gospel to every people group so that there is *no place left* where Jesus is not being proclaimed. I hope it worked.

The end-times scenario reads like a best-selling thriller, but will the events of Revelation appear any less fantastic than this? No matter what scenario you create to explain the events of the end of time, it will defy imagination and sound somewhat unbelievable.

The historical story of the quest to finish the task is intimately intertwined with the return of the true King and the events accompanying that day. These events cannot be ignored. Yet the goal of this book was not to lay out an end-times scenario but to set a context for the larger story—the fulfillment of the Great Commission—proclaiming the gospel which remedies the Genesis 3 problem of the Fall.

One generation will rise up to be the final generation that experiences these things and welcomes the Lord.

Will we aspire to that? Will we steel ourselves for what is required to get to *no place left* and to perhaps welcome our Lord's return?

Will we win for the Lamb the just reward of His suffering—a Bride from every tongue, tribe, people, and nation?

We have the resources, but do we have the resolve?

May we be found worthy!

About the Author

Steve Smith trains and coaches believers how to cooperate with the Spirit of God to see church-planting movements emerge among the nations.

Steve's education includes: B.A. in New Testament Greek, and M.Div., M.Th., and Th.D. in missiology. The first few years of his ministry were spent pastoring both in rural situations and in the urban core of Los Angeles. He and his family started a church in L.A. very similar to the one described in *Hastening*, the prequel to this book.

For 16 years, the Smiths labored in Asia. They were privileged to be personally involved when God started a church-planting movement among a previously unreached people group in Asia. After that they moved into training and leading missionaries in Asia and beyond. They continue to train churches and organizations globally.

As a student of the Word and the works of God, Steve seeks to help fellow believers live out the timeless principles of God's Kingdom wherever they serve. He (with Ying Kai) is the author of *T4T: A Discipleship Re-Revolution* (2011, WIGTake Resources).

Steve is married to the wonderful Laura Nesom Smith; they have three incredible sons: Cristopher, Joshua, and David. For almost three decades, they have worked together as a family to see all the remaining people groups of the world fervently bow the knee to the Lamb Who sits on the throne.

Steve's aspiration is to be in the final generation that welcomes the return of the King.

Tracking Statistics

Lists of the unreached people groups can now be found in many missions circles. Joshua Project (JoshuaProject.net), the Southern Baptist International Mission Board research department (IMB.org/globalresearch), and PeopleGroups.org all keep well-documented lists available to the public. Global Mapping International (GMI.org) provides additional mapping and research resources.

Rapid progress is being made, and the facts and figures in this story about the enormity and feasibility of finishing the Great Commission went out of date during editing. They were current as of July 2015, and we kept those numbers so that the reader can get a sense of how quickly this task is racing toward the final chapter.

It is these undeniable facts and the clear commission of God's Word that I hope will propel you out of a cozy reading chair and onto your knees to evaluate where the Father wants you to fit into His plan to save the nations.

Learn More ...

To learn more about cooperating with God in initiating church-planting movements at home and abroad, read Steve's book *T4T: A Discipleship Re-Revolution*. It is available at ChurchPlantingMovements.com and from Amazon in Kindle format. It presents the clear biblical foundation of how God is initiating discipleship revolutions all over the world today, resulting in multiplying churches. The book includes numerous modern-day case studies to help you adapt the timeless biblical principles to your particular context, in cooperation with the Holy Spirit, to see His Kingdom come fully in your community.

See also the site developed to complement this book and serve those who want to become part of this story:

NoPlaceLeft2025.org

Contact Steve Smith at NoPlaceLeft@mailzone.com

How to get involved in No Place Left 2025—
Four Stages to Completing Matthew 24:14 in Our Generation

Adapted from the Sep/Oct 2016 *Mission Frontiers* article:
Four Stages to "No Place Left" in Our Generation

The *No Place Left saga* was inspired by the *real* global movement pursuing No Place Left where Christ has yet to be named (Rom. 15:23). This movement is *not* fiction; it is *already* a reality, dedicated to launching replicating kingdom movements that multiply disciples and churches in every city, region and unreached people group (UPG).

All over the world, Jesus' disciples are rising up to finish what He started 2000 years ago. Ours *could* be the generation that finally starts church planting movements in every last remaining people group and place on earth. The *No Place Left* saga describes just *one* way this could happen.

We have the resources. But do we have the resolve?

Our longing is, through the Holy Spirit, to fulfill Matthew 24:14 in our generation so that the gospel of the kingdom is preached in each remaining UPG/UUPG (unengaged UPG).

> *And this gospel of the kingdom will be proclaimed throughout the whole world as a testimony to all nations (ethne), and then the end will come.*
> —*Matthew 24:14, ESV*

This task warrants a global No Place Left movement. We could call it a **24:14 movement**.

Movements are How Peoples are Reached

Yet a local people group or city will not be reached without a Spirit-empowered local *movement* that can exceed population growth. As illustrated among the Tuxiang in *Hastening* (Book One), church planting movements (CPMs; also known as disciple making movements, or DMMs) are kingdom movements in which disciples, churches and leaders multiply many generations throughout a place or people group.

Although such movements may seem unfamiliar:

- Jesus and Paul birthed *movements* recorded in the Bible,
- most nations were first reached by such *movements*, and
- many new *movements* are now growing around the world.

However most of us lack current experience in such movements, so how can *we* become effectively involved in launching kingdom movements for No Place Left among the world's remaining peoples (*ethne*)?

The Experience Gap

Too many missionaries get to the field without basic skills in sharing the gospel with the lost, let alone discipling new believers in multiplying ways. For the sake of lost multitudes, we must change how we equip missionaries before sending them.

Rather than sending inexperienced laborers, the church in Antioch sent out 40% of its leadership to the mission field (Acts 13:1–3). In *Hastening*, "Church in the City" similarly gave its top leaders to the mission effort. In the same way, those committed to No Place Left must be prepared to sacrificially send their best.

While it is a huge leap for individuals to go to the mission field and seek to start a movement among a UPG without prior movement experience, we *are* seeing teams and individuals bear rapid fruit among UPGs after coaching through smaller steps. Such teams arrive among the unreached with a clearer understanding and experience in the dynamics through which biblical movements are typically birthed.

Bridging the Experience Gap

Since the late 1990s, movements have been starting among UPGs at an increasing rate as field missionaries have applied biblical principles and gathered insights from each other's successes.

Such movements now exist on every continent, in very diverse religious blocs. See *Someone has to be First* in the May/Jun 2011 *Mission Frontiers*.

For individuals and teams with no movement experience back home, it is a huge leap to enter a UPG and try to apply movement principles. Most who try often end up employing the models and methods they are familiar with, and these generally hinder the very kind of movement seen in the book of Acts.

The transition from living and serving in one's own culture to living and serving in another is challenging, to say the least. To simultaneously add a major change of ministry philosophy is to set a missionary team up for disaster.

(To learn how conventional ministry models hinder movements, see Donald McGavran's 1982 article *A Church in Every People: Plain Talk About a Difficult Subject* in the Oct 1997 *Mission Frontiers*, T&B Lewis' *Planting Churches: Learning the Hard Way* in the Jan/Feb 2009 *Mission Frontiers*, and the Nov/Dec 2015 *Mission Frontiers* article *4 Stages of a Movement* by Smith, Mims and Stevens.)

Two Distinct Challenges

Today's missionaries face two distinct obstacles to *getting to the field* prepared *to birth movements*.

First is the resistance in many churches to prioritizing Jesus' Great Commission and making the sacrificial last push to finish the task. It's not that the resources aren't there, but the cost associated with the last push feel too high. **We do not lack the resources, just the resolve.**

Second is ministry models that fail to launch movements. As mentioned above, even when we sacrificially send people, we most often send missionaries who lack experience in multiplying disciples, much less multiplying churches, leaders and movements. Our missionaries are ill-prepared for the task ahead.

The following pages outline the most fruitful approach we know of to date which is rapidly coalescing as you read. We invite you to join us, for the glory of God among all nations, in this approach to pursuing completion of the task Jesus assigned us in Matthew 28:18–20.

Four Stages to No Place Left (fulfillment of Mt 24:14)

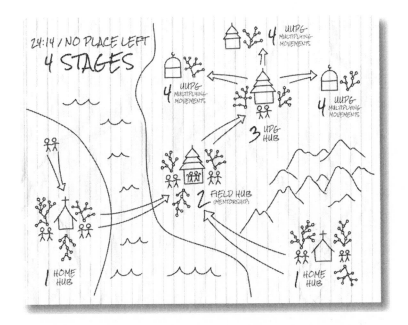

1. Home hub: Around the world, individuals and teams start by finding or forming hubs in their home cultures to live out movement principles and practices among both the majority and minority/*ethne* populations of their contexts.

2. Field hub: After laborers develop CPM proficiency at home and visit unreached areas, they intern in a field hub where a fruitful CPM team mentors them in the context of a thriving movement. There these new laborers experience the full range of CPM principles in action, in a cultural context similar to the UPG they are preparing to reach.

3. UPG hub: The new laborers move to a new area to launch a new movement in a UPG within that same affinity bloc—adapting what they have learned and experienced to pursue the Holy Spirit for a CPM/DMM there.

4. Multiplying Movements: Once a CPM emerges in that people group, rather than *exit*, they take the hot coals from the fire of that movement and help *expand* the movement to other nearby UPGs. At this stage, movements are multiplying movements.

Stage 1: Home Hub

Stage one of the *Four Stages* model involves forming home hubs in sending countries. In these hubs, individuals and teams can mature in faith to implement CPM methods to

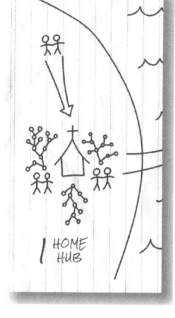

- reach the lost (not just the unchurched) with the gospel,
- make and multiply disciples,
- start and multiply healthy churches, and
- develop and multiply leaders from within the harvest.

This process starts with people like ourselves—from our culture and worldview—but must expand to cross-cultural situations in our own cities and areas.

This is a *global* task and home hubs should emerge in any country which has the church of Jesus Christ. A home hub can emerge in Manila, London, Rio, Delhi, Shanghai, Houston, Nairobi or Prague. Antioch sending bases should emerge wherever the church exists.

Our missionary teams can and must learn at home the same biblical principles they will implement among UPGs. In Chapter 36 of *Hastening*, John Steward tells Christopher that sixty-seven new churches have started in L.A., stretching out to seven new 'generations.' Such local ministry is fruitful soil for gaining skills for starting movements among UPGs. And again, this isn't mere fiction. The Mar/Apr 2016 *Mission Frontiers* has cases studies, of five churches on three different continents, pursuing and seeing this kind of impact.

As these teams learn to make disciples who make disciples among the majority and minority populations, they will also make forays into various parts of the world to seek the Lord's direction for a UPG to pursue with the kingdom of God.

And home hubs are emerging world-wide, but most are in the early stages. Many more churches are needed to serve as home hubs—willing to pursue a CPM/DMM in which individuals can be mentored in launching movements at home.

Whether mission teams rise up within a city or converge on the home hub from elsewhere, they need to emerge in every nation with model that work at home and among the unreached. Specific methods will adjust for the unreached, but the kingdom principles and lifestyle will be similar.

Two things are yet needed to make home hubs a reality:

- Churches where the senior pastor and leaders embrace this model and the vision to send teams to finish the task abroad. These leaders bless and support experimental zones in which teams can learn CPM principles.
- Coordinators to handle the logistics of such home hubs. A number of church leaders are ready to walk this path, but need a champion to make these ideas a reality.

Stage 2: Field Hub
Logically, it would seem that learning to implement CPM principles at home would make implementing them in a UPG the next step. But the cross-cultural jump of application of

CPM/DMM practices in a foreign context is so great that it is actually *faster* for teams to stop along that journey to be coached in a context in which a CPM is going or on the way. That context should be similar to the one the team will end up in.

In *Hastening*, the Owens and Fernandez families fly to Singapore to get training and coaching from others who already have experience in CPMs. Ideally, it would have been even better for them to have spent several months in a CPM context before launching. Later as KPF developed more, new teams were able learn from those that had already experienced CPMs in China and Southeast Asia.

In a true 4-stage model, for example, if the team plans to target a Buddhist UPG in South Asia, it makes sense for them to take one or two years to base in a place like Delhi or Kathmandu with a field hub team of experienced CPM practitioners. In that context they can walk the streets or dusty roads with these practitioners—both foreigners and nationals. CPMs are more easily "caught" than "taught." In the spirit of those CPM efforts, they will find culturally-appropriate CPM tools, national partners, Great Commission coaches and increased faith that will equip them to launch into another UUPG of that same affinity bloc.

The time frame for this can be a year or two, but the goal is for them to learn and add value to the kingdom work there. Basic language study in a trade language may be appropriate during this stage. Once they have developed some proficiency in ministry they will be ready to take the next step toward their own people group. Alternatively, it may become apparent to them that they are not suited for this type of pioneering work.

In many affinity blocs, field hubs are emerging—nationals and expats with CPM experience who are willing to receive a coach a number of new missionaries from various nations. The hub team's vision is the greater advance of the kingdom beyond their own city or people group. A number are willing, but one great obstacle hinders the development of field hubs: field hub coordinators. Coordinators are needed who will oversee the logistics of receiving new personnel and helping them get plugged in to the local efforts. Such logistics are beyond the purview of the CPM practitioners in that hub. The practitioners would gladly receive the missionaries IF someone would oversee the logistics. Perhaps this would be a retired couple, a family or single with the gift of service, or perhaps a college graduate taking a gap year or two.

Stage 3: UPG Hub

When the team leaves the field hub to launch a CPM in an unreached area is less a matter of time than of proficiency. When the team has demonstrated the ability to give themselves to the high value activities of movements and produced the fruit thereof, they are ready to tackle their own UPG. In the early stages of leaving the home hub, a team may feel the two-year stint in a field hub is a delay in the UPG strategy. But in actuality, it is very likely they will be able to fast-forward CPM ministry in the new context because they have already tasted, smelled and touched a CPM in a similar context.

A number of us who have been a part of CPMs well understand the dark period of trial and error to find the keys to unlock a movement in a people group or city. If we had had the opportunity to see it modeled for us in a context similar to our own, the waiting period for a breakthrough and the mistakes we made along the way may have been lessened.

In *Hastening* and *Rebirth* the emphasis is clearly on starting church planting *movements* not just doing good church planting because that is *what it will take* for everyone to be reached with the gospel. In the pages of these books I have tried to paint a picture of what movements feel like and the high cost of discipleship in them. What is described here is very similar to actual events around the world.

A benefit to teams launching into a UPG after the field hub stage is that it is very likely they will have formed relationships with near-culture nationals who may move with them or come for short term trip to help launch the new movement.

The UPG launch toward a CPM is the stage of this progression we are so familiar with: the missionary team that has been sent from a home culture to a foreign culture—yet with no experience or mentoring in the movement dynamics they seek to implement. Teams at this stage need much training and coaching in movement dynamics, which is where many of us devote our efforts.

Hopefully, the four stages can shorten the years of frustration that many teams experience in trying to launch a movement among the unreached. Four stages does not eliminate the need for training and coaching, but it makes that task much easier. We cannot dictate when God will launch a movement, but we can posture our lives to move in conjunction with His Spirit better (Mark 4:26-29).

Stage 4: Multiplying Movements

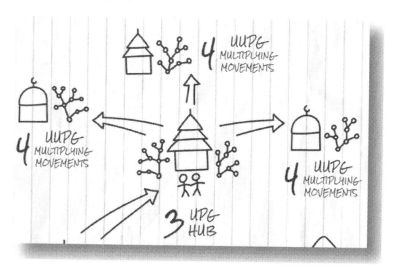

In the early days of CPMs we often talked about an "exit strategy." The idea was that when a movement began to spread among our people group, we were ready to exit the work and go to a new place. Now we realize we were a bit off in that thinking. Instead of exit, we should expand.

CPMs are much easier to start if the hot coals of a movement are transferred to nearby people groups! This is very similar to what Yijing and the Tuxiang believers did in this book—leaving China to start movements in Laos and then eventually Sumatra.

Disciples from within these movements already know how to walk a CPM path with a high level of faith. They know how to find person of peace, how to reach their households, how to plant the initial DNA of disciples who are fervent followers of Jesus and fishers of men. They know how to implement discipleship, church planting and leadership development methods that are simple enough that new believers can practice them and pass them on. And, these hot coals are similar enough in worldview, culture and language that they can get to the heart of this UPG much faster than distant-culture believers can.

In a number of places around the world, catalytic missionaries have decided not to exit but rather to expand the movement to cascade into to other UPGs. They are launching short and long term teams of national disciples to start CPMs in these places.

To the growing vision to get to movements of multiplying *disciples, churches* and *leaders* we must add "multiplying *movements.*" The great need here is missionary catalysts who will broaden their horizon from a movement among a people to multiplying movements among many peoples. We should emulate the Apostle Paul who picked up Timothys, Priscillas, Aquilas and Epaphrases from the fires of existing movements and helped them start fires in new places.

At the end of the day, we may never send enough missionaries from home cultures to finish the task. Fortunately, we serve a Lord who told us to pray to the Lord of the Harvest for more workers—workers that would arise from the harvest (Luke 10:2). This was the King's plan from the beginning to get to No Place Left in our generation.

Join us!

The No Place Left or 24:14 movement is not an organization or a denomination. It is a global, open-handed movement of God's kingdom, welcoming you to take your place. The best way to connect with us is to email us: NPLglobal@gcnow.org

Wherever you are in the world, we will seek to connect you with others near you who are pursuing No Place Left in our generation.

Let's finish the race to get the gospel and multiplying churches to every people group by 2025!

Cast of Main Characters

KPF

Christopher & Chara Owen—founders of Church in the City (L.A.) and leaders of the Kingdom Preparation Force (KPF).

Nic & Stacy Fernandez—cofounders of KPF; Nic is an entrepreneurial business prodigy.

John & Renee Steward—longtime friends of the Owens and cofounders of KPF. John is a history professor at USC, and Renee is an attorney.

Winthrop & Jeanie Dunbar—a revered military special operations colonel (retired) and his wife who help bring strategic direction to KPF.

Lance Chu—an original member of KPF who was part of Christopher's first team to China

George Yang—an original member of KPF who was part of Christopher's first team to China

Julie Konami Yang—an original member of KPF who was part of Christopher's first team to China; now married to George. She helps manage operations at the KPF headquarters.

Kellie Davies—Chara Owen's sister and an original member of KPF who was part of Christopher's first team to China.

Phil Young—an original member of KPF who was part of Christopher's first team to China.

Timothy & Grace Wu—Information technology (IT) specialists who handle communications for KPF headquarters.

Tal Gillam—former CIA operative who helps with KPF field strategies.

Yijing—a young Chinese woman and one of the first believers among the Tuxiang people. She helps lead her people and other people groups to fulfill the Great Commission.

Li Tao—the first male convert among the Tuxiang people; marries Yijing.

WROTH & THE TEN

Michael Wroth—charismatic former U.S. senator from California and current Director of the International Coalition for the Preservation of World Peace (IC). Also the tenth member of the secret organization called The Ten

Marlene Hayes—Wroth's high-powered assistant who is entirely devoted to his cause and is able to make things happen. She has been with Wroth throughout his rise to power.

Dr. Larson Sayers—elderly gentleman who has an uncanny ability to to broker peace deals between opposing parties globally; lifelong friend of the Wroth family.

Jake Simmons—former special operations commander/CIA agent who was mentored by Dunbar. He leads all of Wroth's military forces.

Number One—the Italian who leads The Ten. He is referred to as the Prime Director and leads the Politics division.

Number Two—the Chinese member who leads the Economics and Science division.

Number Three—Ethan Farnsworth, the English member of The Ten. He leads the Religion and Education division and secretly has a close relationship with Wroth.

Number Four—the Russian member who serves in the Politics division.

Number Five—the South American member who serves in the Politics division.

Number Six—the African member who serves in the Economics and Science division.

Number Seven—the Arab member who serves in the Economics and Science division.

Number Eight—the Indian member who serves in the Religion and Education division.

Number Nine—the Korean member who serves in the Religion and Education division.

Books by Steve Smith

T4T: A Discipleship Re-Revolution
(2011, WIGTake Resources)
with Ying Kai

Hastening
Book One in the *No Place Left* saga
(2015, 2414 Ventures)

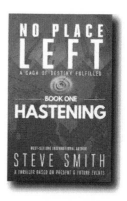

Rebirth
Book Two in the *No Place Left* saga
(2016, 2414 Ventures)

43190890R00184

Made in the USA
San Bernardino, CA
15 December 2016